Stories from the Handbasket

Stories from the Handbasket

Sean Gorman

ISBN-13: 9781542729192
ISBN-10: 154272919X
Library of Congress Control Number: 2017901607
CreateSpace Independent Publishing Platform
North Charleston, South Carolina

This is a work of nonfiction. The events and experiences detailed herein have been faithfully rendered to the best of the author's memory. To protect the privacy of individuals not already known to the public, some dates, names, identities, and circumstances have been changed, or altered into composites.

This one is for Katherine and John

This book is also dedicated
to the loving memory of
Timothy James Gorman

—It's been so long since you've been home—

Even the best of us are at least part-time bastards.

—MARY KARR

Everyone, deep in their hearts, is waiting for the end of the world to come.

—HARUKI MURAKAMI, *IQ84*

The End of the Beginning

MCMXC

One must shed the bad taste of wanting to agree with many.

—Friedrich Nietzsche, *Beyond Good and Evil*

One gets large impressions in boyhood, sometimes, which he has to fight against his whole life.

—Mark Twain, *The Innocents Abroad*

"Fuck you."

The officer looked up. He scanned the busy restaurant. The look on his face said, *Did I just hear that?*

He had.

Because I had just said it.

My friends buried their heads in the cubbies of their arms. Some swallowed their laughter; others peeked with one eye. A few adult patrons looked over at me. They had heard me clearly, and uncomfortably went back to eating.

We were sitting in a booth at Friendly's—an East Coast ice cream shop and summertime tradition in my small hometown,

Medfield, Massachusetts. It was the sort of place where customers paid the check at the register instead of leaving it at the table. On warm summer nights, teenage employees hurriedly served cones and sundaes from a small sliding window to long lines of families waiting outside. Almost every Friendly's looked the same—a freestanding white building with a gabled roof, fake dormers, and a white cupola topped with a weathervane.

It was a new decade at the end of an old century.

I was thirteen years old and about to explode.

Fifth grade had not gone well. Sixth grade had gone even worse. I had no reason to think that seventh grade would be any better. Besides one sweet woman in the third grade, my teachers had all been gray-haired, short-tempered women whose personalities bordered on bipolar and whose old-school teaching methods bordered on sadistic. They yelled and screamed and played favorites. They ostracized and humiliated. Their targets were my friends and me. We were not the jocks. We were not the brains. We were not the rich kids.

We were the troublemakers, the losers, and the geeks. We dressed in outdated clothes that didn't fit right. We came from homes that were either broken or unstable. We watched too much TV.

I was a bully. I had been bullied. I had gotten into fistfights. I was just starting to take an interest in girls, but they had no interest in me. I was skinny. I was weird. I had silver braces and red acne and woke up every morning with my middle finger erect.

I had spent the past two years of my life fighting with my teachers, my parents, or any other authority figure that came into my line of vision. I spent a lot of time with learning specialists and school psychologists. Anxiety ran a constant pace through my veins. I threw up in the bathroom at junior high dances out of sheer panic. My knee bobbed in class like a piston. My fingernails were chewed. I slept without sleep.

My relationship with my mother was like cold war. My relationship with my stepfather was like war itself. My home was not home. My bedroom was home. I could be found anywhere anyone could not. Suppertime at the house was promptly at five-thirty and lights-out was at nine. Beyond the roundtable dinner chats where my parents debriefed their respective days over roast chicken or meatloaf, I spent nearly all of my time alone in my bedroom listening to heavy metal—a new kind of music I had just discovered that was retwisting my DNA.

My solution to not wanting to be at home was to not be there. Sticking around my parent's house meant my stepfather finding some sort of manual labor for me to do and telling me everything that was wrong with me while I did it. My stepfather was not the only source of my rage, but he sat dead center in its fiery core. Much of my teenage frustration came from the fact that I wouldn't—and couldn't—do anything about him. He provided the food and the clothes and the roof. He was bigger and stronger and meaner. My anger toward him gave me a focus, however. Even in the midst of adolescent ire, I knew I had to get away from him and put him aside…for the time being and then hopefully forever.

So I left the house.

Frequently and often.

And as much as I could.

On the weekends, I left at noon and didn't come back until five-thirty…then I left again at six-thirty and came back at nine. After school during the week, I either hung out with my friends in the center of town, or in finished basements in the homes of the latchkey kids, provided their parents hadn't changed the locks after some incident involving our blasting heavy metal, or smashing up their deck furniture, or lighting something on fire. My solution to escaping home life and school life was to live outside in the real world—the world in which I could only see on television—the world in which I wanted to be and in which I intended to grow.

Prior to thirteen, my life had been quiet and unremarkable. Trouble at school had been minimal. Fighting had been minor. I got good grades. I played Little League one year and had done well, but I was really just feigning an interest in baseball. What I really wanted to do was listen to Guns N' Roses. What I really wanted to do was watch movies and ride my bike. What I really wanted to do was bullshit with my friends, then search the woods for empty beer cans to recycle and the *Playboy* magazines the older kids had left behind. I was, by American standards, a normal adolescent male. But by thirteen, something in me had changed. A door in my mind had come unhinged. A branch in my psyche had finally snapped.

I didn't know who the cop at the register was. All I knew was that he was wearing the same uniform as the officers who had been harassing my friends and me for the past year—before any of us had actually become petty, small-town vandals. Before seventh grade, we were really just pissed-off nerds. The only thing I knew about the officer was that he was wearing a gun and a badge and had some sort of authority over me. All I knew was that we were *us* and he was *them*.

"Fuck you," I repeated.

The officer paused from handing the cashier his money. He looked over Friendly's again, this time knowing full well that he had just heard what he had just heard. Still, he couldn't quite make out who it was or where it was coming from. The din of Friendly's on a Saturday night camouflaged me. He looked past the families and the screaming children and then directly at my friends and me. I wasn't the only teenager in the restaurant, but I was the only one staring right at him. I wasn't going to stand up and advertise that it had been me, but I wasn't afraid of him knowing, either. Part of me desperately wanted him to know. I was ready for anything.

But he never locked eyes with me. He glanced at me for a second and then looked away. He focused on an older group of teenagers sitting just a few booths away. It made sense. My body had not yet aligned with my attitude. There was no way a skinny little shit like me had the balls to say "Fuck you" to a cop.

Realizing that he wasn't going to figure it out, the officer turned back to the cashier and gave her his money. He kept his eyes fixed on the restaurant while she dropped change into the palm of his hand. She turned around and poured him a Styrofoam cup of coffee and when she finally handed it to him, he said "Thank you" without looking at her. With his focus still on the older kids behind me, he opened the top of his coffee, blew away the steam, and took a careful sip. Then he walked out the door.

I stared at him the entire time.

I was in a state I had never been in.

My friends released their laughter. They dead-armed me and brought me back to reality, albeit a new one. It was like a curtain had descended between two acts of my life, between boyhood and something else entirely. My friend Eric, who was sitting beside me, said, "What the fuck, Gorman?"

"Fuck him," I said.

He looked back to the empty space where the cop had been standing and said, "No, seriously, what the fuck?"

I didn't answer. I didn't know what I was doing, or why I was doing it. But after that night in Friendly's, I began to destroy everything around me. I threw rocks through school windows, kicked over trash cans, and smashed wooden fences with baseball bats. Reading the reports of my vandalism in the police log of *The Medfield Suburban Press* was nothing more than an enticing reward. Each Thursday, I would take a pair of scissors and carefully clip out reports like: *A caller reported youths throwing fireworks from the railroad bridge on Frairy Street at 7:55 p.m. on Sunday, August 2. The youths were gone when police arrived.* I did this for posterity and also for proof that authority could lie (we weren't gone by the time the police arrived—the officer was just too obese to run and catch us).

My juvenile delinquency was a principled mosaic of anarchy. I stole from school (mostly library books), but I never shoplifted from stores, even though I was accused of it nearly every time I walked through the door of one. And I never burglarized people's homes. I vandalized public property, but never touched anyone's private possessions. The psychologists at school never asked me why my theft and destruction was so keenly focused, but if they had I probably would have told them that I didn't have a problem with some random guy who lived on Phillips Street, but I did have a problem with *this place*. All the shrinks ever asked me about was why I was so angry, and all I ever answered was "I don't know." And when they asked me what the point of smashing things was, I would tell them the God's honest truth: "Because it's fun."

I was becoming what the teachers and cops had already made me out to be.

And I had never been caught.

I felt exhilarated. I felt empowered. For the first time in my life, I felt like I had control over something, maybe even everything. I could shape myself and everything around me. It seemed like my view of the world would always be from the outside, looking in, and that felt just fine. I feared nothing.

I was a punk.

"Fuck him," I said again.

My other friends just shrugged and went back to sipping their Cokes. One of them unscrewed the top of a salt shaker and left it just loose enough so that the next patron would dump a mountain of salt on his French fries. We paid him no mind, as if this was something that someone in a restaurant just *had* to do. He put the shaker down as the waitress came over with our order. She was a pretty high school girl whose two most notable features were memorialized in graffiti on a large rock by the junior high:

Beverly Mancini Has Big Tits. The rock was in a small clearing of woods ominously called "The Path." It was where the bad kids sneaked joints and cigarettes after class. Although we all knew about the graffiti, we weren't sure whether Beverly did. The nametag pinned on Beverly's chest read: *My Name is Beverly and I'm Fast & Friendly.*

When Beverly leaned over the table to set down the plates of cheeseburgers and fries, she might have noticed that each of my friends took a quick and guilty glance down her shirt. Normally, I might have glanced too, but I was still in a bit of a state—too distracted to be distracted. Beverly put down the last plate, stood upright, and flipped her hair to the left. "Are you guys all set?" she asked lazily. My friends looked up and nodded in unison, silently overcome by both young beauty and young hormones. I watched Beverly walk away. It looked like she may have hated her life, at least for the moment. Eric reached across me and grabbed the plastic ketchup bottle. He squirted it on his cheeseburger, which made a fart noise, which made everyone laugh, except me.

"Seriously, Gorman," he said as he covered his food with an enormous glob of ketchup. "What the fuck is wrong with you? Are you crazy or something?"

I looked back to the empty space where the cop had been standing. I thought about it for a second before giving the best answer I could.

"I have no idea."

Eric shook his head and reached back across me to put the ketchup back. For just a moment, he looked like an adult sitting among a group of boys. My saying "Fuck you" to the cop was never mentioned again.

My friends talked briefly about nothing. They finished their burgers and fries. I finished my free glass of water, which was paid for by the money I didn't have. The others gathered their cash, mostly loose change, and paid the bill up at the register. They left a handful of nickels and dimes back at the table for Beverly. We didn't stay long enough to see her reaction.

We walked out into the breezy night air. The sun had been setting when we got there, but now it was dark. The lights on Main Street illuminated downtown Medfield, which was bustling with carfuls of older guys driving aimlessly with girls, their windows down, an arm hung out the side. Loud music was blaring from every vehicle. Bell Biv DeVoe and Technotronic were the unwelcome soundtracks to my life. We stood around for a while, watching traffic go by. None of us spoke, but I was sure we were all wishing to be older so we could be driving with girls. I could have stayed there forever, but it wouldn't be long before a cop, maybe even the same cop from earlier, chased us away for loitering.

I finally broke the silence.

"Where should we go?"

The One You Love the Most

MCMXCII

There are things about growing up in a small town
that you can't necessarily quantify.

—Brandon Routh

"Get me a soda, faggot."

"Get it yourself, faggot."

The summer days were long and they always ended in the same place. There wasn't much hustle and bustle in Medfield, but what little there was, was all around us. Baker's Pond was a small park nestled in the town's heart. Its name, Baker's, was fitting because it was where the stoners got stoned. Older kids wearing Misfits T-shirts puffed on joints and drank cheap vodka from dumped-out Gatorade bottles. Younger kids with skateboards watched their every move. It was where we spit and swore and fought. It was where we listened to "Paradise City" from boom boxes. It was where the girls showed the boys how to French-kiss and where to put their finger.

We were too old to play, but too young to work. We met up in the haze of the late afternoon and went home when the moon was bright or the cops threw us out—whichever came first. It wasn't unusual to get stopped and frisked for just walking down the street, or to be called a faggot through the open window of a police cruiser. Though I was no angel, I was far from a dangerous criminal. But the young, cancerous anger that had been growing in the pit of my stomach for the past year was spreading rapidly.

We had no cash and spent time instead. Hunger was prevalent and poorly satisfied. We scrounged money together for sodas and microwavable hotdogs from Cumberland Farms ("Cumby's"), the nearby convenience store. We were a motley crew of lower-class outcasts. We were the children of the blue-collar townies. Our own collars were black and tattered and our blue jeans were ripped at the knees. We lived in the small houses in the older part of town. As the 1980s came to an end, my friends and I found ourselves outnumbered by the rich kids whose parents had moved into the bigger houses in the newer part of town. We were far from poor, but by the standards of nouveau Medfield, we were practically homeless, and we all probably looked it from the way we dressed and because we spent so much time loitering on sidewalks and hanging around in parks.

My hair was long, and even though I hated my bony, goose-fleshed body, I still dreamed of being a glitzy rock star. My bedroom walls were covered with posters from magazines like *Hit Parader* and *RIP*. I idolized Steven Tyler and Axl Rose. Whenever I posed shirtless in the mirror trying to look like them, I would see myself as the coolest guy on the planet, and at the same time, as something totally grotesque.

My other long-haired friend was Fraser. We didn't drink alcohol or do drugs, but hung around everyone who did. Fraser only smoked cigarettes—a habit he had enjoyed since the age of ten, when he tried one of his dad's Camels out in the garage one day. After years of asphyxiating in my grandmother's nicotined smokehouse, I had never tried a cigarette, or given smoking even the slightest consideration. Fraser and I spent long hours in his living room watching MTV and listening to Iron Maiden until the cassette tapes either broke or spiraled out of his stereo in a wild mess of brown ribbon.

The first time Fraser and I turned on MTV and saw two cartoon metalheads named Beavis and Butt-Head staring back at us, the two of us just looked at each other as if to say, *Is it you? Is it me?* Then we laughed hysterically and watched the show every week. Fraser and I weren't exactly like Beavis and Butt-Head, but there was no denying the similarities. Like the two animated idiots on MTV, the three things Fraser and I loved the most were heavy metal, boobs, and setting things on fire. And anything in our lives could be broken down into two simple categories: something either "sucked," or it was "cool."

Fraser and I had been friends since kindergarten. We never had the same teacher, but always found each other on the playground during recess. As kids, we reenacted scenes from *The Three Stooges*, poking each other's eyeballs or falling down dramatically after walking into the flagpole. From the first day we met, Fraser and I made fun of everyone, and everything became funny. In junior high, the two of us had some classes together, but the first thing the teachers did when they saw how inseparable we were, was separate us.

Because Fraser's parents got home late in the day, his house became the place to be after school. At first it was just a small gathering of guys, but once word got out that we had an empty

house all to ourselves, more and more kids started showing up…
and more and more furniture got broken.

The after-school parties became known as "Fraser Days." We
would get hopped up on soda, blast Judas Priest, and slam dance
around his living room. It was ideal therapy after the long days of
junior high, enduring venomous, domineering teachers and vapid,
entitled classmates. Fraser's dad was an editor for the *Worcester
Telegram and Gazette.* He was also a self-professed Deadhead.
Hung on the wall in Fraser's living room was a framed newspaper illustration of his dad tearing off his suit like Superman,
but instead of the Superman logo, Fraser's dad revealed the skull-
and-roses emblem of the Grateful Dead. Even at fourteen, the
symbolism of Fraser's Deadhead father looming over us while we
violently thrashed around his living room was not lost on me.

We were countering the counterculture.

We were rebels without a cause, or a clue.

Fraser was Buddha-like in both spirit and form. While I
fidgeted and agonized, Fraser sat back and relaxed. He was
calm, funny, and smart. He liked to eat junk food, drink Diet
Coke, and read comic books with his dog, Bandit, curled up by
his side. If something valuable got broken during a Fraser Day,
he'd get angry for a few minutes, but then seemingly forget all
about it. Although he was a metalhead, you could tell Fraser
was raised by past-life flower children. He was the most generous guy I knew—always letting friends borrow his books and
tapes. I would do the same, except whenever Fraser borrowed
one of my books, one of the pages usually came back with a
mustard stain.

Eventually, Fraser's parents shut down Fraser Days, which was an understandable move, but also a move that disappointed and embarrassed the rest of us. Although we were all unhappy that we no longer had a place to crash after school, we were also ashamed, partly because we knew what we were doing was wrong, and partly because Fraser's parents were two of the nicest people in the world. The day Fraser told us that we were no longer allowed at his house when his parents weren't home, we all just nodded our heads solemnly and looked at the ground with mournful understanding.

After literally being padlocked out of Fraser's house, the two of us spent more time at Baker's Pond, which was where we met Johnny Bators and Nicky Harper. They were older than us, and even though Fraser and I had never spoken to them in school, being friends with them seemed totally natural because they both wore metal T-shirts.

Harper lived with his mother at Wilkins Glen—a small cluster of state-mandated apartments for low-income families set far back in the woods near Medfield center. Harper grew up in Medfield, but attended a vocational school in Franklin called Tri-County, which everyone called "Fry High" (referring to all the burnouts typically shipped off there after eighth grade). Harper majored in plumbing—a trade he was oddly passionate about. While most kids aspired to be ballplayers or astronauts when they grew up, Harper had wanted to be a plumber ever since he had even wanted things. He was short and sinewy, exposing his wiry arms by cutting the sleeves off his Metallica shirts. His long, floppy hair was constantly in his eyes and he was always shaking it away like a sheepdog. Whenever he stood around at Baker's, Harper tilted so far backwards that he resembled the Leaning Tower of Pisa. It always seemed like he might topple over, but he never did.

Johnny was the oldest and most charismatic, and his laugh was infectious. He told stories and jokes like a professional comedian and could imitate anyone, especially Harper. Johnny would do Harper's lean and mock the way he said "Fuckin'," which Harper pronounced "Feckin'." Johnny would say, "Hey, guys, is the feckin' Arab who sells butts to minors still workin' at the feckin' gas station?"

One day at Baker's, Harper took out a crumpled piece of notebook paper and read a haiku that he had written in English class. Harper cleared his throat and stretched one of his arms up to the sky as if he were about to say something profound:

Sitting in a cage
All ready for me to eat
A big, juicy bird

Everyone doubled over in wild gales of laughter while Harper stood proud, shaking the hair out of his eyes.

Johnny said, "You're like a retarded Shakespeare, Harper!"

After the laughter died, Harper finally smiled and said, "Feck you, Johnny, you feckin' bitch...cunt...dick...fag...puss...ass..."

"All right, Harper, enough!" Johnny shouted as we all broke up with laughter again.

I liked them all. My buddies meant everything to me. There was an honor among us that I had just never found with any of the other kids in Medfield. If the police were questioning us about something, no one ever ratted on anyone else. We knew we were all guilty of *something* so we had to maintain our code of silence—our metalhead omertá. There was a flowing current of honesty between my delinquent friends and I that could only have germinated from our place of small-town, social exile. Because we were outcasts and at war with the world, our bonds felt stronger than the ones the other kids at school had. Against all of society, they almost had to be.

Others came and went from Baker's as the days and nights wore on. Older guys with cars would come by and hang out with us for a while before calling us losers and going off to the mall to pick up girls. Some were the older brothers of kids we knew, but most were just townies who still lived at home with their parents. A full-on beating from the older guys was rare, but at the very least you could expect to get punched or choked before they left for the night, peeling out in their Monte Carlos or Chevy Impalas.

One night, two guys showed up who were noticeably older than anyone else who usually stopped by. I knew neither, but was familiar with both. Johnny knew them and greeted them as soon as they walked up from the shadows.

"What's up, guys?"

"What's up, Bators?" one of them said.

"Hello, Johnny," the other said in a high-pitched voice.

I knew the shifty-eyed blond as Clete Marshall, the older brother of a kid in our grade. He had a reputation. Although I didn't know why he had been to jail, I knew he had been to jail. I figured it was for drugs or theft, only because it seemed like drugs and theft were the only two things any kid from Medfield ever went to jail for. Clete didn't seem violent, just dumb and untrustworthy.

I knew the shorter man with thick glasses as Dodo, whose real name was Arthur Dodaro. His resemblance to Danny DeVito in *One Flew over the Cuckoo's Nest* was so uncanny that we probably would have made fun of him had we known him better and he wasn't so much older—a bona fide *adult*. There was something undoubtedly wrong with Dodo. He rarely spoke, and most of the time just stood around silently with his eyes half-shut, sporting an odd grin on his face. When he did speak, he said something banal and apropos of nothing—mentioning how much he liked pizza, or worrying about children falling into the pond. Although he and Clete smoked weed right out in the open, I assumed Dodo's nature had less to do with him being stoned and more to do with him being mentally retarded.

People like Dodo hanging around Medfield was neither alarming nor uncommon. The Medfield State Hospital had been a fixture on the secluded north side of town since the late 1800s. Nonviolent inmates could often be seen walking down Main Street, or on supervised errands with nurses. It wasn't unusual to see a van full of people who were rocking back and forth pull into the grocery store, get out, and descend like children toward the candy aisle. The alarm at the State Hospital sounded like an air raid siren and went off several times a day. It meant a patient had escaped, but none of us ever paid any attention to it, except maybe to drop down on the grass at Baker's in a mock duck-and-cover routine.

Medfield was populated with a small cast of characters who had spent time in the State Hospital. No one was afraid of them. Sometimes if we were bored, we would walk up to the hospital just to look around. If an inmate approached us, it was usually to bum a cigarette off Fraser or Johnny. I was never afraid of the patients or looked down on them. If anything, I liked them and related to them because they were weirdos like my friends and me. All the old townies knew the patients and made polite conversation with them whenever they ventured uptown. To me, they always seemed like characters in a movie, except some were probably too unreal for anyone to believe actually existed.

There was a tall, low-browed man who lumbered around Medfield named Ben. Everyone called him "Big Ben." He bought a coffee and a newspaper each morning at Cumby's. Big Ben had menacing Frankenstein features, but was very friendly if you talked to him. Apparently Ben had only a physical condition. I had heard that he was sent off to a state school as a kid because they thought he was mentally challenged. But in reality, Ben's IQ was fine and the only reason he had been sent off to the state school was because he looked so freakishly different. It was hard for me not to feel sorry for Big Ben whenever I saw a mother nervously take her child by the hand and make noticeable space as Ben approached them on the sidewalk.

There was Ellis—a middle-aged man who actually *was* mentally challenged and whose androgynously round body left his specific gender forever unknown. We used to see Ellis at the store buying treats for the cat he called Precious Penny. Ellis spent his days at home on his CB scanner, talking to the police and firemen. He'd start his broadcast each morning at sunrise by saying in his falsetto voice, "You all look good out there today!"

The only person who ever mildly concerned me was Denny. Denny was a sun-beaten older man with a shaved head and a long, lumberjack beard. He rode around town on a pink girl's bicycle, smoking a cigar. Unlike Big Ben's eyes, which were sort of expressionless, or Ellis's eyes, which were actually friendly, Denny's eyes were narrow and unkind. Whenever he rode his bike, he cradled a bundle of flattened cardboard boxes under one arm. Denny spent his days collecting them from random dumpsters around town. No one knew what they were for, until one day Johnny got up the courage to ask him while he was peddling past Baker's.

"Hey, Denny!" Johnny shouted. "What are those boxes for?"

Denny smiled a toothless grin and said, "For burning coons!"

Johnny let out a quick laugh and said, "For burning *what*?"

"Coons!" Denny repeated before riding away.

Johnny just looked at us and said, "All right, then."

By the 1990s, the State Hospital was in the process of being closed by the state. The abandoned brick buildings were being boarded up one barred window at a time. When I was fourteen, the sprawling campus overlooking dead, grassy meadows looked like something from a horror movie. I had heard that Dodo had spent some time up at the State Hospital, but I didn't know why or for how long. I did know that more people like him were being put on meds and being placed in group homes that gave them more freedom and fewer bars on their windows.

Bators had apparently known Dodo his whole life. "As a matter of fact," he told us while Clete and Dodo went to Cumby's to buy butts, "Arthur stayed at my house a few times."

"Really?" I asked.

"Yeah," Johnny laughed. "He used to answer the phone and go, 'This is Arthur Dodaro. This is the Bators residence. I do not live here. I am just answering the telephone.'" Johnny imitated Dodo's high-pitched voice and all of us chuckled.

"Why was he staying at your house?" I asked.

"Friend of the family," Johnny said. "He had nowhere to go."

Clete and Dodo came back from the store and sat down with us. We were all sitting on the grass around the "cock rock"—a two-foot stone sticking half out of the dirt that looked unquestionably like a penis and two balls. Fraser and Harper smoked cigarettes while Clete and Dodo lit another joint.

The two of them started showing up regularly at Baker's Pond. We were not ourselves when Clete and Dodo were around. Their presence brought a quiet social tension. Clete had been in jail, Dodo had been hospitalized, and they both did illegal drugs in public. Though I never said anything out loud, Clete and Dodo made me think of my mother. Sitting in a park at night-time with people like them was a sudden realization that I was definitely hanging out with "the wrong crowd." Johnny was the only conduit between Clete, Dodo, and the rest of us, so he began every conversation with small talk.

"So, what are you guys up to tonight?"

"I dunno," Clete said, rubbing the grass back and forth with his hand. "Maybe we'll go to the Gook if I can get in."

"Yeah," Dodo chimed in. "That a good idea, Clete."

I looked over at the Golden Rice, a Chinese restaurant some townies called the Gook. The bright-yellow sign across the street was illuminated and, as always, drunks were staggering out the door. My mother told me that back in the '70s it was the only place in Medfield that had a bar besides the Legion. She said in the past that there were fights there every night, which wasn't too far off from the present. Fraser loved the Golden Rice because there was a cigarette machine in the lobby and none of the bored Asians at the counter cared whether underage kids bought packs from it.

"You wanna go to the Gook, Clete?" Dodo said. "Go to the Gook and pick up girls?"

Everyone snickered and Clete looked at us with a smile as if to say, *Can you believe I hang out with this idiot?* Clete and Dodo reminded me of some warped version of George and Lennie from *Of Mice and Men*.

Clete said, "I'm not sure if I'm allowed in the Gook anymore, but I can try."

"We can go in," Dodo said. "Get some fuckin' spareribs and go pick up some fuckin' girls."

"You got money, Dodo?" Clete asked.

"I got fuckin' money, Clete."

"Okay, Dodo, you wanna go to the fuckin' Gook? Let's go."

The two of them stood, as did the rest of us. It was like we were at a formal dinner party and rose when the guests of honor left the table. Johnny shook their hands and the rest of us said, "See you later." I watched the two of them walk across Frairy Street, Dodo just a few steps behind Clete.

Dodo stabbed his grandmother to death a few weeks later.

The story never made the TV news, and if it made the local paper, I never saw it. All anyone had to go on was what everyone around town was talking about.

"What the feck?" Harper asked Johnny up at Baker's. It was the first time we had seen each other since the murder. "Why the feck did he do that?"

"He was hearing voices again," Johnny said.

"*Again?*" I asked.

"Yeah," Johnny said. "I guess he hears voices if he doesn't take his meds."

"Shit."

"And the voices told him to kill his feckin' grandmother?"

"They said, 'Kill the one you love the most.'"

Silence fell over us. Fraser took a drag from his cigarette and said, "Jesus."

Johnny said, "I heard he went up to the police station right before he did it."

"He did?" I asked.

"Yeah. I heard he walked into the police station and said, 'I'm Godzilla and I'm gonna burn down the town.' The cops were like, 'Yeah, okay Arthur, go home.' Then an hour or so later he came back all covered in blood and said, 'I just killed my fuckin' grandmother.'"

Johnny did his usual Dodo imitation, but no one laughed. We all stood around for a moment, spitting or making divots in the grass with our sneakers. I was thinking about all the times Dodo had stood just two feet away from me.

Johnny finally said, "They'll probably send him up to the mental hospital in Bridgewater."

"Not Medfield?" Fraser asked.

"Naw," Johnny said. "They don't keep murderers up there anymore."

"He wasn't staying with you, was he?" I asked.

"No, no," Johnny said. "That was awhile ago. I think he was over in Norwood. I guess the psych unit gave him a one-day pass."

"Bad move," Fraser said.

"He didn't seem crazy," I said. "Definitely not homicidal. I just thought he was retarded."

No one said anything. We just stood in our circle, arms folded, glancing over our shoulders at nothing in particular. Johnny mentioned that Clete knew more about what had happened and that he might stop by.

He never did, though.

And I never saw him in Medfield again.

A police cruiser drove by and all of us looked up. Each of us tensed. We were always ready to run. Harper took one last drag from his cigarette, threw it on the ground, and stamped it out. Eventually the cruiser just turned the corner and we watched it pass.

Fraser said, "I guess he has better things to do tonight."

Whitey

MCMXCIII

You are now about to witness the strength of street knowledge.

—N.W.A.

"Yo, WHERE'S THIS skinhead friend of yours?"

"He's not really my friend," I said.

"Well, whatevah. Where is he?"

"I have no idea."

Troy seemed satisfied with my answer for the time being. He stepped away from my personal space and started pacing back and forth by the pay phones. I watched him as he grabbed the crotch of his baggy jeans and adjusted the red bandana around his head. He was tall and muscular and the second black person I had ever met.

Part of me felt bad for saying that Whitey wasn't my friend. He wasn't a close friend, but he was definitely a friend. I had been over to his house, but he had never been over to mine. We hung out together only in groups, never one-on-one. He was aggressive and foolish, but we both loved heavy metal and horror movies and he was always cool to me. Although Whitey wasn't someone I would have willfully chosen to hang out with, I had no substantial reason to really dislike him either.

But I certainly distanced myself from Whitey the summer he decided to become a Nazi skinhead. After that, I began thinking about him less as a friend and more as an acquaintance. Prior to shaving his head, Whitey had had a full head of long, blond hair that was practically albino-white. Combined with the fact that his last name was Whitehall, it was as if Whitey was simply destined to have the nickname that he did.

Whitey decided to become a skinhead after one semester at the Tri-County vocational school, where he was learning to be an auto mechanic. Apparently there was a group of skinheads there, and for some reason, Whitey had gravitated to them. Even as a teenager, I sort of knew that Whitey's newfound identity had little to do with his racial beliefs, and more to do with the fact that he was at a new school where he didn't know anyone. Before he left Medfield High, I couldn't recall ever hearing him griping about minorities, or praising the virtues of der Führer. I just figured that Whitey had "fallen in with the wrong crowd." I also wondered whether the skinheads at Tri-County had sought him out simply because he looked so unquestionably Aryan.

Medfield was more than 96 percent white. Once, during dinner, my mother, just out of curiosity, asked me how many black kids there were at the high school.

"One," I said.

She said, "Well, that's one more than when I was there."

Thomas Okeke was a senior when I was a freshman. His parents were Nigerian, or, as the people in town would say, "Africa African." I didn't know him well, but sometimes when my friends and I were hanging out at the basketball courts he was there practicing free throws and listening to rap music from a boom box. Not having any interest in sports, I would forgo shooting hoops with my friends and sit by the bench and ask Thomas whether I could look through his tapes. He always said "Sure," and I would peruse his collection of Beastie Boys, Run-D.M.C., and LL Cool J. I was never a fan of rap, until one day when I picked up a tape by a group called N.W.A., which I would later find out stood for "Niggers with Attitude." Reading the back of the tape, I noticed a song called "Fuck tha Police."

I held the cassette up and said, "Hey, Thomas, do you mind if I play this?"

Thomas stopped dribbling, saw what I was holding, and said, "Yeah, but keep it low."

I put the tape in, turned down the volume, and clicked Play.

And immediately became a fan.

The song "Straight outta Compton" wasn't metal, but it was as intense as any metal song I had ever heard. It sounded ominous and dangerous. Though I wasn't black or urban, "Fuck tha Police" resonated so strongly with me that it felt like I was as close to those things as I could possibly be. Having long hair and loitering uptown in Medfield meant that my friends and I were constantly being harassed by the cops—flashlights in the face at nighttime, stalking behind you during the day, and endless strings of insults and intimidation for no reason at all. Hearing

N.W.A. for the first time made me realize that in the lily white suburbs, *we* were the "Niggers with Attitude."

Thomas was very different from Troy. Thomas wore nice sweaters and never got into trouble. He had a laid-back personality, and everybody liked him. In the thirty seconds I had known him, I could see that Troy was a raging inferno. He was wearing a red tank top and the veins underneath his skin looked like bulging water pipes about to burst through papier-mâché. Troy was the sort of black guy I heard about on rap albums or saw on MTV. Though he was only the second black person I had ever met, he was the first one who seemed to fit all the stereotypes I heard in music or saw on television.

Troy was from one of the worst neighborhoods in Boston, Dorchester—a place far away from Medfield in every imaginable way. He had been brought to town by a girl named Heather. Heather and her girlfriends hung out with us at Baker's. The girls my friends and I spent time with had distinct personalities, but they all looked the same—slightly overweight with high, teased bangs that puffed around their heads. They wore Adidas windbreakers and reeked of Kool cigarettes and Aqua Net hairspray. They got into more fistfights than the boys did.

Sometimes the girls attended parties near the city, which was where Heather met Troy. I never knew why Heather and her friends went to places like Dorchester to hang out, although maybe it was because the jocks and preppies at Medfield High had no interest in aggressive chicks who smoked cigarettes and listened to Salt-N-Pepa. I also had no idea how they even got to the city, as all of us were just shy of driving age.

But I was suddenly face-to-face with Troy, who had obviously heard about Whitey's newfound racial convictions.

Something was going to happen.

Worlds were going to collide.

Shit was about to go down.

"My man, is he comin' up here or what?"

"I don't really know," I said. "He's usually here."

Heather came up next to me and elbowed Johnny and I away from the pay phone that sat just across the street from Baker's Pond and the white Unitarian Church. "I'll call him," she said, placing a quarter in the slot.

I wasn't sure what beef Heather had with Whitey. It seemed unlikely that she was instigating a fight for social justice, but anything was possible. I figured there was some drama I was unaware of, or she just wanted to see a fight. Heather impatiently turned and twisted while she held the receiver. She bit her bottom lip and rolled her eyes. Eventually she slammed the phone down. "There's no answer," she said.

Troy got close to me again and said, "Yo, is it true he carries around a stick that he calls a 'nigger-beater'?"

"That's true," I said.

"Man, I can't wait to meet this mothahfuckah!"

One of the accessories that came along with Whitey's new persona was a shortened hockey stick that he did, in fact, call a "nigger-beater." He showed it to us one day at Baker's. It was about a foot long with a red bandana tied to the end.

"Wanna see my nigger-beater?" Whitey asked us.

We all laughed, somewhat uneasily, and said, "What?"

He took the stick out from his knapsack and held it up with a snicker. "Check this out. I keep it in my locker at school."

All of us burst out laughing, especially Johnny. He said, "You're a fucking idiot, Whitey."

Whitey just shrugged and put the stick back in his knapsack. "Whatever," he said. "You guys don't know what it's like at Fry High."

Back by the pay phones, Troy said, "Does he always carry it with him?"

"He keeps it in his knapsack," I said. "But today is Saturday, so I don't know."

Troy began to look around, frantically. "What can I use?" he said. "I ain't got no blade on me right now."

I tried not to show panic. Johnny, who had been unusually quiet, laughed nervously. "I wouldn't worry about it," he said to Troy. "It's a little piece of a hockey stick."

Troy tried to remove one of the posts from the white farmer's fence we were all sitting on, but it wouldn't budge. Then he walked over to an oak tree and began snapping off branches. "I'll hit 'im with this mothahfuckah."

Johnny laughed nervously again and said, "Hey man, you're not going to mess him up too bad, are you?"

Troy shot a look at Johnny and said, "Why? Are you his boy?"

I stepped away from Johnny.

"No, no," Johnny said.

Troy looked at him.

"I mean, kind of. He's my friend, but I'm not into that skinhead shit. Maybe you'll straighten him out."

Troy eyeballed Johnny for a moment and went back to snapping a branch down to size. I began biting my nails, a habit I thought I had left behind. I felt nervous, but exhilarated. Though I didn't vocalize it, I shared Johnny's sentiment. Whitey deserved an ass-kicking, but neither of us wanted to see him permanently damaged. I had witnessed numerous fistfights, but Troy's intensity was new to me. It bordered on homicidal. All of a sudden, Whitey seemed like a harmless poseur and Medfield seemed like a harmless place. Troy seemed like a raging comet that had fallen from some alternate reality and landed in our tiny little world.

While I was contemplating all this, Whitey emerged from behind the Unitarian Church across the street from where we were sitting. He was empty-handed, had a smile on his face, and was very clearly sans nigger-beater. He waved, but none of us waved back. The sun was glistening off his freshly shaved head.

"Oh, god," Johnny said.

"Is that him?" Troy asked. "That's him, right?"

I said, "Yeah," figuring Whitey's appearance left no reason to lie.

Troy threw down the tree branch and walked across North Street without paying any attention to traffic. Mothers in station wagons slowed and stopped. Troy marched over to the sidewalk and onto the bright-green grass in front of the bright-white church. "Oh, god," Johnny repeated. As Troy approached him, Whitey stopped walking and gave him a bewildered look.

Troy went up to Whitey and extended his hand.

Whitey cautiously took it.

Burned into my memory forever is the image of Whitey and Troy shaking hands. It was like I was living inside a historic photograph. I saw the girl at Kent State University crying over the dead body of her fallen comrade. I saw the Hindenburg explode.

Troy and Whitey began talking. Whitey's face remained bewildered while Troy began hulking up. He was inching closer.

Just then, Harper came out of nowhere and stood next to Johnny and me. Neither of us noticed he was there until he took an unlit cigarette out of his mouth and said, "What's up?"

Johnny pointed across the street and said, "Look."

Harper took in the scene and calmly said, "Oh, shit."

Though we couldn't hear the words he was saying, Troy's voice began to rise. Whitey was stepping back and trying to circle around him, but Troy kept blocking him. Whitey held up his hands in quick surrender.

"I have no problem with you," I finally heard him say.

Troy got in his face. Whitey backed off and scurried up the stairs of the church. Troy followed right up after him. With his back against the large wooden doors, Whitey help up his hands again.

"I have no fuckin' problem with you!" he yelled in Troy's face.

Troy shoved him, which caused the large antique doors of the church to boom and buckle. Whitey bounced off them and Troy shoved him back again.

Troy put his face against Whitey's and screamed, "Call me a niggah, mothahfuckah!"

Whitey kept his hands up and shouted, "I have no problem with you!"

One last time, Troy grabbed Whitey by his denim jacket and threw him against the doors. Eventually, Troy backed off while he stared Whitey down. He walked away, glancing over his shoulder with each step. Whitey looked down at Troy and then across the street to us. There were no tears, but his eyes were filled with hurt.

We all looked away.

Troy crossed the street and adjusted the bandana on his head. "He's a fuckin' pussy," he said.

Johnny, Harper, and I just stared at our sneakers. An old man with a coffee in his hand walked past us on the sidewalk and gave us a friendly smile. I nodded politely and finally looked up at Whitey.

He shook his head, turned around, and left the way he'd come.

"Fuckin' pussy," Troy repeated.

I squinted my eyes and looked up at the tall steeple on the Unitarian Church. It was new. The original one had blown off during a hurricane in 1938. I recalled seeing an old black-and-white photograph of it in a book about Medfield. During the hurricane, the steeple had toppled over and literally stabbed the roof of the church, sticking straight out of it like a knife in a wedding cake. I remember thinking it didn't look real.

"Fuckin' Whitey," Johnny said with a laugh. "Thanks for not hurting him, man."

Troy said, "He's a pussy. He wasn't gonna do shit. I ain't gonna swing on nobody that ain't gonna swing on me. He learned his lesson."

In my mind, I was thinking about the fact that Whitey actually *wasn't* a pussy. I had seen Whitey get into his fair share of dustups, and he always came away the victor, even against older kids twice his size. Whitey was scrappy and vicious, and he never cared about the fountain of blood that flowed from his mouth whenever a punch to his braces sliced open his gums like razor-blades. He came away from each fight looking like a vampire, crimson red drooling down his chin and streaking the swollen strings of his white hair.

Whitey was tough as hell, but Troy's mere existence was too much.

Shit had gone down and worlds had collided. Something had happened, but like so often in Medfield, nothing had happened. I wondered why Troy had decided not to throw the first punch. Maybe because he was aware of his surroundings. If the Medfield cops had gotten involved, Troy would have been screwed. Experienced street fighters always knew that who threw the first punch was legally vital. I also wondered whether Whitey's encounter with Troy would bolster his racist convictions, or make him abandon them altogether.

I assumed the latter.

Harper stamped out his cigarette and said, "I'm going over to the gas station to get matches."

We all just nodded.

"Anyone want anything?"

"Get me a soda, faggot."

Making the Grade

MCMXCIV

I would prefer even to fail with honor than win by cheating.

—Sophocles

Chance never helps those who do not help themselves.

—Sophocles

"Hey, Mr. Brock, have you ever worn a dress?"

Mr. Brock straightened his spine, looked at me grimly, and said, "No."

No one laughed.

Brown had dared me to do it. The thought of someone like Mr. Brock wearing a dress was so preposterous that asking him if he had ever worn one seemed hilarious...at the time. Brock stared at me for a moment to see whether there would be some stupid follow-up to my stupid question. When he saw there wasn't, he bent back down and continued helping someone with their classwork.

Brown and I went back to doing nothing.

Electronics class was impossible. There was no way I was going to pass it. I shouldn't have even been there, but it was a college-level course, and I needed it to graduate at the "college level" so I could go to college. Since September, I had gloriously failed every test and quiz. The math was so far beyond my comprehension that I felt like a chimpanzee trying to do physics. By November, I had decided to just gleefully accept every F that Brock placed on my desk. After each red "F" at the top of the page, I used my blue pen to write: *U-C-K I-T.*

Brown was in the same boat, but on a slightly different deck. The class didn't mean as much to him, since he wasn't going to college. Dan Brown and I had sat next to each other since fifth-grade social studies, and he and Fraser were my two closest friends. Through the years, Brown and I had endured subjects like math and science taught by psychotic middle-aged women who wore frightening amounts of eye makeup and would scream like a lunatic if someone forgot a ruler. We had fought in the academic trenches side by side for years, but we both knew that twelfth-grade Electronics was our Waterloo. Together, we would go down in a hail of scholastic bullets.

Brown liked Norwegian death metal, video games, and M&Ms. He wore thick eyeglasses and had long brown hair he kept in a ponytail. He didn't talk much, but when he did, he often said something thoughtful, pithy, and hilarious. In junior high, he started hanging out with us at Baker's Pond, just outside the circle we always stood in. He'd just stand there, smoking cigarettes, drinking from a bottle of Coke, and listening to the rest of us talk, occasionally laughing at dirty jokes or telling one himself. Though the most introverted of us all, he was, in some ways, the coolest. Brown didn't pretend to not give a shit—he legitimately didn't.

Mr. Brock was brand-new to Medfield High and stood out from the rest of the teachers in every possible way. He was young and enormously thick—over six feet tall with the largest neck and forearms I had ever seen on a human being. His jet-black hair was practically shaved, and the only thing that prevented him from looking like a total badass were the large, nerdy glasses he wore. Beyond the spectacles, it looked like he could (and would) snap someone in half.

It also seemed like he himself might snap in half. Mr. Brock's hands were always clenched, his posture was always straight, and he never smiled. No one in his class fucked around. When Brock introduced himself on the first day of school, he told us that he used to coach wrestling at the high school he had just come from. "Medfield does not have a wrestling team," he said with a baritone timbre. "But hopefully that will soon change." He then got right down to business, abruptly explaining the difference between amps and volts. Everyone hurriedly opened their notebooks and began scribbling.

"You," he said that first day, pointing to me. "Come up here."

I put down my pen and hesitantly walked to the front of the classroom.

Brock went over to a cabinet and took out some antique device made of four U-shaped magnets and a crank. It looked like a large pencil sharpener. He placed the heavy device on a desk and uncoiled two copper wires.

"Here," he said to me. "Hold these wires."

I held a wire in each hand.

"Hold on as tight as you can."

I nodded.

Without warning, Brock rapidly turned the crank, which sent a painful surge of electricity through my arms. I jumped back and dropped the wires. The class laughed.

Brock turned to the students and said, "It's volts that jolt and mills that kill. Remember that."

The class wrote it down. My hands felt like they were asleep. I shook them out, trying to get feeling back.

"Go sit down," Mr. Brock said to me.

I sat.

Brock then went to the blackboard and began explaining Ohm's law. He drew a diagram with letters and squiggly lines. "The current through a conductor between two points is directly proportional to the potential difference across the two points."

My eyes glazed over for the next three months.

I had never actually failed a class in my entire life. D's showed up on my report card sporadically throughout grade school and junior high (always in math or science), but by high school I was a solid A/B student who still occasionally disrupted the classroom with a joke or an outburst. On my report cards, the phrase *conscientious and diligent* was often followed by *lacks self-control*. Though I planned on entering college as a creative writing major, I knew an F in any subject was catastrophic. The guidance counselors had told us that colleges could (and would) rescind an acceptance if someone's grades tanked during senior year. I tried to come off as not caring, but in truth, this kept me awake at night. Brown, on the other hand, just sat in class indifferently, casually popping M&Ms into his mouth from the bag he kept in the cubby hole beneath our lab desk.

We took our midterm on the last day before Thanksgiving break. The test was multiple choice and given on the new Scantron computer sheets the school had just started using. After looking over the test, I quickly realized that I would never remember the things I had never known. So I began randomly filling in bubbles with a No. 2 pencil, trying to create patterns that looked both artistic and *not* random. I finished in minutes, but waited to bring the test up. I didn't want to be the first, but I didn't want to be the last. When I finally did turn in my test, Brock looked at me harshly, his fists clenched so tightly that his knuckles were red and white.

I nodded and smiled.

He didn't.

When the class bell finally rang, the rest of the students frantically bubbled in their final answers. Brock rose from his desk and said, "Time is up. Put your pencils down."

Everyone did. Sighs were let out, arms were stretched, fingers were run through frazzled hair. Brock went to the front of the class and said, "I hope everyone did well. I will have the results for you when we return from Thanksgiving recess."

Everyone just stared at him.

"You may go."

"Mr. Brock won't be returning."

A voice from the side of the classroom said, "What?"

Mrs. Beaumont gave us a wince and shrugged her shoulders. She said, "I guess he decided to take a job somewhere else."

"So you're our teacher now?" another voice called out.

"No, I'm your substitute until the school finds a permanent replacement."

Everyone looked at each other. Brown and I looked at each other.

Mrs. Beaumont walked over to what used to be Mr. Brock's desk and picked up our textbook. "So," she said, "what chapter did you leave off on?"

The class just stared at her.

"Anyone?"

The tapping of a pen. A cough. The tearing of a sheet of a paper.

"Okay," she finally said. "I'll just take a look at some of the questions on your midterm and see if I can figure it out. One moment please."

Quiet conversations broke out around the classroom. I watched Mrs. Beaumont walk behind the tall lab desk and start flipping through the pages of our midterm. She picked up her pencil and began making notes. She was left-handed and curled her wrist arthritically as she scribbled.

A kid named Mike said, "So, wait, Mr. Brock is seriously not coming back?"

Without looking up, Mrs. Beaumont said, "He's seriously not."

More chatter broke out, this time louder. Again without looking up, Mrs. Beaumont shushed us with a long, soft "shhhh," but the silence only lasted a minute.

Brown said, "I can't believe they sent Mrs. Beaumont here."

"I know," I said.

All of us had known Mrs. Beaumont since the first grade. She was one of four women on constant substitute-teacher rotation throughout all of elementary school. She was tall and narrow and—no matter what season it was—always wore a turtleneck sweater and a long skirt that went down to her ankles. I hadn't seen her in years, but aside from a few more gray strands of hair that sprung out of her temples like cat whiskers, she looked exactly the same.

Mrs. Beaumont was pleasant and patient. Like Brown, I was surprised to see her taking over. Her wispy stature and kind disposition seemed appropriate for third-grade multiplication, but totally wrong for a college-level course in electronics.

"I think I found it," she finally said. "Chapter twenty. Here we go…"

Everyone opened their books, but remained fixated on Mrs. Beaumont.

A kid named Parker Campbell asked, "So where did Mr. Brock go?"

"I have no idea."

"He just quit?"

"Apparently so."

"Can you do that?" Parker asked.

Mrs. Beaumont shrugged her shoulders the same way she had before. "I guess so," she said.

"What a freak of nature," Parker said.

The class laughed.

I didn't like Parker, but he was right. Brock had seemed way off-kilter. I was sure if a stethoscope had been placed on his chest, the ticking of a time bomb would've been heard. The serial killer glasses he wore didn't help either. Although I had no confidence in Mrs. Beaumont as an electronics teacher, I was glad Mr. Brock was gone. He taught like an android. All the data was there, but the humanity was not. He couldn't have cared less whether Brown and I passed or failed. His job was to transmit information. Whether or not we received it was not his concern.

Parker Campbell was a worm. It was no surprise he only felt comfortable badmouthing Mr. Brock when he wasn't around and was certain he wasn't coming back. Parker and his friends hung out with my friends from time to time. Our cliques occasionally converged at house parties or uptown at Baker's. He and his buddies were all rich kids, but they dressed like gangster rappers and thought they were thugs because they shoplifted clothes from the mall. They sauntered down the hallways at school wearing crooked baseball caps and hundred-dollar Girbaud jeans that were two sizes too big. Everyone called them "wiggers" when they weren't around, and I always wondered whether they ever knew or cared.

Parker was part of a small contingent of troubled rich kids at Medfield High. They were smart and attractive and totally fucked up. They drove drunk and crashed their hand-me-down BMWs into trees. They dealt pot and acid, and some even burglarized the large homes in their own neighborhoods. Their fathers were business executives who were never around, and their mothers stayed home all day zonked out on Stoli and Prozac. Although they caused more trouble than any of my friends or me, they suffered none of the same consequences we did. If they were arrested, nothing ever came of it. They never got suspended. They never had to talk to the school psychologist. They did stupid things, but they weren't stupid. Most were actually in honors classes and went off to good colleges after graduation. It seemed like as long as their grades were good, everything else was, too. By my senior year of high school, I could see that so much of Medfield was based on perception instead of reality.

Parker bullied anyone who could easily be bullied. In Electronics, his target was Patty Jablonski. She was the only girl in the class. Patty was pale and quiet and had the body of a middle-aged woman. Her hair was frizzy and she had a snaggletooth.

One day before the bell rang, Parker was riding Patty about her irritable bowel syndrome, which she openly talked about, oblivious to the fact that she was committing social suicide. Brown and I sat on the opposite side of the room, so we couldn't hear what Parker was saying to her. We could just see that Parker was laughing and she was not. Eventually, Patty stood up from her desk and screamed, "Parker, you think that the things you say don't affect me, but they do affect me! It hurts, Parker! It really hurts!"

Time stopped. Oxygen left the room.

Patty ran out to the hallway with her hands over her face. Parker just let out a hiss and leaned back in his chair. Brock, who had been writing something on the blackboard, turned his head.

"I don't know what her problem is," Parker said to him.

Mr. Brock put down his piece of chalk and walked over to the classroom door. He stepped into the hallway, looked left, then right. He came back inside and pressed the intercom button to call the office.

"Yes?" the secretary's voice said through the speaker.

Brock said, "Patty Jablonski just bolted out of my classroom."

There was a pause.

"Okay," the secretary finally said.

"That is all," Brock said.

Another pause.

"Okay, thank you."

Brock went back to the board, picked up his chalk, and started writing again.

Patty never came back that day, or any other day.

Mrs. Beaumont read from the textbook and occasionally wrote something on the board. When she asked a question, no one raised their hand. Eventually, she just gave the answer. Brown ate M&Ms. I scribbled song lyrics. When the bell finally rang, everyone jumped up from their seat and sprinted for the door.

For the next month, Electronics class played out just as it had on Mrs. Beaumont's first day. It wasn't much different from Mr. Brock's class, except people occasionally screwed around. Paper airplanes glided across the room and fart noises were made. Mrs. Beaumont just gave disapproving looks, which surprisingly worked. All of us were in the throes of puberty, but we had all known Mrs. Beaumont since we were six years old. We were adolescents who pushed boundaries, but when Mrs. Beaumont shamed us for it, we shrunk in our desks like embarrassed little boys.

We never took tests or quizzes in Mrs. Beaumont's class. Brown and I caught on to this fairly quickly. We figured that since Mrs. Beaumont was not a real teacher, she couldn't technically grade us. No one ever asked about tests, probably for fear of Mrs. Beaumont suddenly realizing we needed them. My anxiety dwindled as the weeks went on. When it came to grades, receiving nothing was better than receiving something. I figured I would end up with a harmless "Incomplete." Strangely, I actually began to pay attention.

On the last day before Christmas break, Mrs. Beaumont brought us sugar cookies shaped like angels. She opened the tin and placed them on the lab desk. "Help yourselves," she said. A horde of boys ran to the tin and took one each.

Parker took two handfuls.

An old man dressed in full naval regalia walked into the classroom.

Everyone burst out laughing.

The man took off his white cap and tossed it on the lab desk like a Frisbee. His hair was iron gray and severely matted down on his head in a peculiar way. "Well," he said with a large smile that brightened his ham-pink cheeks, "I was going to wear this to get some respect on my first day, but I guess that didn't work!"

Brown looked at me and quietly said, "What the fuck?"

"You're our new teacher?" Parker asked him.

"You got it." The man saluted us and said, "Captain Upham at your service, but you can call me Mr. Upham."

"You're really a captain?" I asked.

"Retired," he said. "Being a schoolteacher was something I've always wanted to do, so here I am."

"Where did they find you?" Parker asked.

"I found *them*," Upham said. "Your school placed an ad in *The Globe*. It said: 'Electronics Teacher. Immediate Availability.'"

I said, "So you've never been a teacher?"

Upham clapped his hands and said, "Nope! First day on the job!" He undid the button on his naval jacket, revealing a gut that looked like the result of many decades with Budweiser. Four yellow stripes adorned the cuffs of his jacket, and the shiny visor of his hat had a lot of gold leaves that looked like scrambled eggs.

"I guess I'll tell you a little bit about myself," Upham said as he walked over to the blackboard. He searched for a piece of chalk, then wrote his name on the board. I was sure everyone else was thinking that spelling out his name was totally unnecessary, especially since there was an Upham Road in Medfield, but we just let him carry on in silence. He wrote *Captain John Upham*. "It's pronounced 'Up-um,'" he said, even though he had just said it.

"What kind of boat did you captain?" Mike asked.

Upham finished writing, turned around, and said, "A sub—a nuclear sub."

"Really?"

"Yup. Out in the Pacific. We'd be submerged for weeks on end—couldn't come up until our missions were over. One time I had an officer die on me—a heart attack—and we had to stick him in the ship's freezer until we came back up."

He had every boy's attention.

"Been all over the world. Finally retired two years ago. Got bored and decided to teach before I kicked the ol' bucket myself." Upham winked and said, "I think the wife was happy to have me out of the house, too."

45

We laughed. Upham looked around and noticed something. "No girls in this class, huh?" He laughed and winked again. "Good," he said. "We can talk like men."

More laughter as Parker said, "Can we drink booze?"

Upham chuckled and said, "Hey, as long as I don't see it, I don't care what you do."

We looked at each other in disbelief.

"But anyway," he said, "I've had a lot of experience with electronics—radios, radar, and sonar. So, I guess your principal thought I was qualified." Upham looked over at a piece of paper that was sitting on Brock's old desk. He said, "Well, I guess I should take roll call."

Mr. Upham was nothing like any teacher we had ever seen. None of our history teachers had ever traveled. None of our math teachers had ever engineered. And none of our English teachers had ever written. For the first time, we actually had a teacher who could tell us something about the real world.

After taking attendance, Upham spent most of the first class talking about himself—where he was from, where he had been, and the things he had done. He answered any question anyone asked him, and not long after he started talking, it became clear that all of us were far more interested in Captain John Upham than we were in electronics. As class was coming to an end, Upham recounted a story about his crewmen getting the clap while they were stationed in Thailand. "Half of my men ended up in the infirmary," he said, laughing at the memory.

The bell rang.

Upham looked up at the clock and said, "Oops. Well, I guess we'll have to start with the electronics tomorrow."

Brown and I gathered up our things and headed to the cafeteria. I left the class feeling good about Mr. Upham as a teacher, but my anxiety about passing Electronics returned. Playtime with Mrs. Beaumont was over. I knew it wouldn't be long before F's started showing up on my desk again.

My fears were realized the following day when Mr. Upham started teaching us binary code. As soon as he went to the blackboard and wrote *10001110101*, my eyes glazed over again and remained that way until the end of class. I looked over at Brown, who was writing down everything Upham was saying.

"What are you doing?" I whispered.

Brown said softy, "Hmm? I'm writing this down. I'd like to know this."

I just nodded.

I respected Brown's practicality. He was interested in what Upham was saying because he liked computers and video games and wanted to know how they worked. He couldn't have cared less about transistors and Ohm's law. He didn't give a shit about college or grades. He was interested in the things he might face in the real world.

Which was coming fast.

I had been accepted to Emerson College, but they accepted me provisionally, which upped my anxiety even more. I was on my way to college, but I felt nothing like college material. My criminal record was more impressive than my academic one. I didn't understand what a sorority or a fraternity was and I didn't know the difference between a bachelor's and a master's. I applied to Emerson as a lark. In Medfield, higher education was pushed on us by teachers and guidance counselors as if there was no other option in life. And we were told that if we didn't go to college, we would mostly certainly work at a gas station for the rest of our lives and die a lonely death. I applied to Emerson because I believed the threat and also because I couldn't think of a better plan.

Even my major, creative writing, was chosen without any real consideration. I had originally applied as a film major. After seeing *Pulp Fiction* in the theater seven times, I considered Quentin Tarantino a huge inspiration. If a geeky guy who worked at a video store could make such an awesome movie and be such a huge success, so could I.

But during my tour of Emerson, a film instructor named Pete Chvany took me aside, looked me straight in the eye, and said, "Are your parents rich?"

"No," I said, looking into the intense blue eyes of a white-haired Mark Twain lookalike.

He put his index finger into my chest and said, "Then *you* should *not* be a film major. Film and film-making costs a lot of money, and it all comes out of *your* pocket."

I said, "Okay."

I changed my major to creative writing the following day.

By my senior year of high school, I was looking further down the road, wondering what I was actually going to do in the real world. Even though I had not been to college yet, I knew that college wasn't the real world. My pipe dream was that I would become a rock star author. I would write books and then travel the world on book tours. I would be rich and famous, and sleep with lots of women.

My reality, however, was oblivion. I was completely clueless as to how I was going to make a living. The only thing I knew was what I *didn't* want to do. Slinging pizzas after school at a new chain restaurant in town called Papa Gino's affirmed that I didn't want to work with food, or do anything else for a big corporation. And seventeen years in a small town made me want to run toward a big city. Beyond that, my future was a vacuum of empty space.

Upham announced our first test a few weeks after his first class. I shut my textbook with a frustrated slap, realizing that my grade-free run in Electronics was finally over. If Emerson saw an F on my transcript, I was dead in the water. I might end up working at a gas station and dying a lonely death after all.

Henry O'Neil flew way under the social radar at Medfield High. He was a bright kid who had already taken physics, which meant that for him, Electronics was a breeze. He was the only one in class who knew what he was doing and was always the first to hand in his test. He was short and his ears stuck out. He looked like Alfred E. Neuman, except he had a thick head of Brillo hair, which earned him the nickname Muffin.

At some point, Parker Campbell decided that rubbing Henry's head was good luck. Before our first test with Upham, Parker yelled, "Time to rub the Muffin!" He then leapt over his desk, put O'Neil in a headlock, and knuckled his skull. Everyone laughed, including Upham. Henry just smiled and shrugged it off by saying, "Whatever helps you, Parker." Much as I disliked

Parker, I thought it was funny, especially after seeing how Henry just took Parker's teasing in stride, unlike the now forgotten Patty Jablonski.

Upham began handing out our tests and said, "You can use your textbooks if you'd like."

Mike said, "This is an open-book test? Are you serious?"

"Sure!" Upham said.

I said, "I still don't think that's going to help me."

Upham said, "I don't know what to tell ya."

"Me either," Parker said.

Upham just shrugged his shoulders.

"Can I just copy off of Muffin?" Parker asked.

"Sure!" Upham exclaimed.

"Are you serious?" Parker asked.

Upham said, "It's your education, not mine."

"Can I copy off of Parker, then?" I asked.

Upham smiled at me. "Go ahead!"

Brown and I looked at each other with suspicion. We were not sure this was actually happening, or if it was maybe some kind of sting operation—if the principal and superintendent would suddenly break down the classroom door and yell, "Freeze!" Figuring we had nothing left to lose, Brown finally said to me, "Well, I'll just copy off you, then, if you don't mind."

"No problem," I told him.

Parker and I stood up with our tests and pencils and slowly walked over to Henry's desk. The two of us eyeballed Upham the whole time, waiting for him to stop us, but he never did. Parker and I grabbed two empty chairs and pulled them up alongside

Henry. The rest of the class looked on in astonishment. Everyone seemed to be waiting for Upham to say something, but he just sat down, clasped his hands behind his head, and put his feet up on his desk. Henry casually flipped through the pages of the test and looked over some things. Then he reached into his knapsack and took out his textbook and graphing calculator.

Finally, he got to work...as did Parker and I.

Henry wrote out equations and formulas, occasionally erasing and starting again. "Come on, Muffin," Parker said. "Don't let me down." Each time Henry finished a problem, Parker wrote it down and then slid his paper over to me and said, "Here you go." I would say, "Thanks," and copy the copy. We were speaking in hushed tones, but I wasn't sure why. We were cheating in legal anarchy, but we all knew that anarchy applied only to Room 103. Real life and Medfield High were still outside the door.

The rest of the class did not engage in the all-out copying that Parker and I did, but a few other students did walk up to Henry's desk to double-check their work. Henry eventually finished and went over his answers. Once he was satisfied, he gave Parker and me an affirmative nod.

"Thanks, Muffin," Parker said.

I said, "Thank you," and Henry just nodded and politely smiled.

I brought my test over to Brown. He closed the issue of *Nintendo Power* he had been reading and got to work copying. As he wrote, I looked over at Upham. The whole time we had been cheating, he either just stared out the window or read the newspaper, occasionally whistling some jaunty maritime song that sounded very similar to "I'm Popeye the Sailor Man."

The bell rang. Everyone turned in the tests. Upham stood up and collected them with a placid smile.

"Thanks, Upham," Parker said.

"My pleasure."

"Thanks, Captain," I said.

"See you tomorrow."

"Good news! Everyone passed!"

Some guys laughed and some others just looked dumbfounded. There was still a part of me that thought the whole thing was a put-on—as if Upham was actually going to show up and tell us that he had reported us all to the principal and we would receive suspensions. Instead, he just merrily handed back our tests without saying a word.

Brown and I both got A-minuses for Henry O'Neil's efforts. We showed each other the grades with looks of unearned gratification.

"Well," Brown said, "at least I know how to cheat."

Not everyone had cheated, though. As Upham passed back the tests, I studied the handful of guys who didn't copy off Henry or check their work against his. They got B's and C's. Their honesty was curious, which drew out an odd feeling from me. Even though they'd had a free pass to cheat, I wondered why they hadn't. As I looked at my A-minus, part of me felt guilty, but part of me didn't. Cheating was dishonorable, but it was the only way I was going to pass a subject that I didn't care about. I needed to pass Electronics to get into college, even though Electronics had nothing to do with my college major. As I opened my notebook and filed away my undeserved grade, I convinced myself that cheating was an acceptable tactic in an academic bureaucracy.

After handing back our tests, Upham was walking to the front of the classroom when Mike, completely out of nowhere, said, "Hey, Upham, is that a rug?"

Upham spun around and said, "Yeah!"

The entire class burst out laughing and a few kids half-fell out of their chairs. Although it had been obvious since day one that Upham was wearing a hairpiece, no one had ever mentioned it (to his face). What was more surprising was that Mike was the one who'd brought it up. He was a soft-spoken, athletic guy who loved baseball. He was one of the people who hadn't cheated off of Henry. Mike barely spoke in class, and I found it interesting that calling out Upham on his hairpiece was the thing he'd decided to speak up about.

Over the laughter, Upham pointed to the steel gray hair that was matted to his skull and said, "Yeah, there's a glue that holds it on. It takes about ten minutes in the morning."

Just then, the door from the next classroom opened. Everyone turned and saw Ms. Marino with a sour look on her already humorless face. She glared at Upham and said, "Is everything all right in here?"

Upham, surprised by the question, smiled and said, "Yeah, of course."

Marino gave him a stern look and said, "Fine, then."

She closed the door, quietly. The laughter died.

Upham, with a guilty grin on his face, said, "Try to keep it down, huh?"

We all nodded.

"Why do you wear it?" Parker asked.

Upham shrugged and said, "I don't know. I just think it looks better."

I surprisingly agreed. Even though I thought hairpieces were stupid on most people, Upham was a guy who just wouldn't have looked right with a bald head. I was expecting a battery of questions about Upham's hairpiece from the class, but after admitting that he wore one and the reason why, the discussion was over.

I raised my hand.

"Yes?"

"So," I said, "will we be able to copy off of Mr. O'Neil for the rest of the year, or was that just a onetime deal?"

Upham held out his hands and said, "Like I said, it's your education, not mine." Then he smiled and said, "I don't really give a shit!"

The class broke out into boisterous laughter again. This time, the door to Ms. Marino's classroom swung open, hard.

She looked over at Upham and shouted, "May I see you for a minute?"

Several guys let out collective "Oooohs" and Ms. Marino turned around and yelled, "*Hey!*" The guys turned their heads, continuing to laugh quietly. Marino marched into our classroom and walked over to the hallway door. "Out here, please," she said to him, opening the door. Upham followed behind her like a man going to the gallows. Once the door was closed, we put our heads down and buried our faces into our arms, guiltily laughing like children.

Ms. Marino taught biology. I had had her the year before. She was a short woman with short hair who was built like a fire hydrant. She talked about her ex-husband in a very angry and *very* past-tense way. Ms. Marino's moods swayed with the wind. One minute, she could be totally congenial, talking about her weekend at the tennis club and planting flowers in her garden. The next minute, she could go haywire, ranting feverishly that we didn't know the material and weren't paying attention.

And she hated boys. If girls were chatting in class, they would get a stern look, but the boys would be screamed at and sent to the office. Having dealt with her kind since kindergarten, I was able to navigate her emotional tides and did surprisingly well in her class. She actually seemed to like me, and I often wondered whether maybe she felt some sort of empathy because I was a little different from the other boys. Ms. Marino could be an unstable bitch, but I really didn't mind her, especially since (mood swings aside) she had been a fairly good teacher. I would just never for the life of me understand why so many of the women who taught me throughout my childhood and adolescence all seemed to fit the same general personality type—emotionally unhinged and angry almost all of the time.

The door opened and Upham walked back into the room with his hands in his pockets and his head hung low. Marino marched back to her classroom and closed the door with a moderate slam.

Upham said, "Guys, do me a favor and keep it down, huh? I don't want to listen to that fuckin' lady again."

We laughed loudly, caught ourselves, and then simmered right down.

Electronics class continued as a circus for the rest of the year. Sometimes Upham taught and sometimes he didn't. If he didn't feel like lecturing, he would simply stand in front of the class and tell us war stories from peacetime. Other times, he'd just lay some personal or political philosophy on us. One of his impromptu lectures on what was wrong with America made it into my journal one night: *Our electronics' teacher, who is from the navy and slowly losing his marbles, went on a tangent and told us how the downfall of America would come about. I was all ears. His main point was that there were too many people taking too much from the government and not giving anything back. All worldly empires fail. The United States is no exception.*

One day, Mike asked him whether he remembered any of the nuclear launch codes from his old submarine. Upham said, "I sure do." Then he walked over to the board and wrote down a series of numbers and letters.

"Is that seriously a launch code?" I asked.

Upham looked back at the board and silently counted out the letters and numbers. He said, "Yup. That's it."

"I mean, is it still active?" I asked.

Upham shrugged and said, "No, probably not. They change them." He looked back at the board and said, "Maybe it is, though. I honestly can't remember."

We all looked at the blackboard with wide eyes and uneasy smiles. Brown was frantically jotting down the code before Upham, perhaps realizing he had just mistakenly divulged a legitimate nuclear launch code to a group of teenage boys, started erasing it from the board.

For the next few months, sometimes I went to class and sometimes I didn't. Since Electronics was during the school's mixed lunch periods, I would occasionally skip class and hang out in the cafeteria with a group of girls I was trying to impress.

"Don't you ever get in trouble for not going to class?" one of them asked me one day.

I took a bite of an apple and casually said, "Eh, I've got it worked out."

After their lunch was over, and I showed up late for class, Upham would ask me where I had been.

"In the cafeteria."

He'd just shrug one shoulder and go back to teaching.

Brown and I told very few of our friends about the mayhem in Electronics. The two of us knew that if rumors spread about what was going on in Room 103, the party would be over. Medfield High School was one of the best high schools in the state of Massachusetts. If the principal or administrators ever learned about what was happening, there would have been a small town uproar. I imagined meetings and hearings and lawyers.

On the last day of school, Upham brought in his high school yearbook. "Thought I might show you how I looked back then," he said. All of us gathered around one of the lab tables as he flipped through the pages and found himself. We looked at the black-and-white photograph showing a slender Mr. Upham, the same friendly smile, even more of a gleam in his younger eye.

Parker said, "Hey, Mr. Upham, show us some of the bitches you tagged."

"Sure!"

We broke out into the same volume of laughter that had brought Ms. Marino into the classroom months before. I glanced over at her door, expecting her to come charging in, but nothing happened. Upham flipped through some pages before stopping on a picture of an attractive young woman with a pearl necklace and a beehive hairdo.

Upham pointed to the photograph and said, "I got her *and*..." he flipped to another page and said, "...then I got her sister, too!"

We laughed louder and harder, this time with Upham joining in. The door to Ms. Marino's classroom flung open. Still laughing, we all looked over and saw her standing there, her face a combination of shock and anger. Upham looked over at her, still laughing himself. Just as Marino was about to speak, Upham wiped joyous moisture from his eyes and then gestured to her with his hand in what appeared to be both a wave and a brush-off.

Marino stared at him, waiting for him to say something, but he never did. Instead, Upham just looked back down at the yearbook and said, "This guy here was a buddy of mine..." Marino kept waiting for Upham to engage her, but when it was obvious he wasn't going to, she just shook her head and slammed the door.

After Upham finished telling us some high school stories, he told us we could hang out and talk until the bell rang. "And," he said, pointing his thumb toward Marino's classroom, "try to keep the noise down so I don't have to deal with what's-her-name over there."

I looked over at the empty seat next to me.

Brown was gone.

With only weeks to go until graduation, Brown just stopped showing up for school. His absences started randomly in April. He would come in on Monday, but then be gone until Friday. When I asked him where he was, he would just say, "Hmm? I wasn't feeling well." Even though he looked perfectly fine, I never pressed it. He was obviously just ditching school.

But I didn't know why. We were practically at the finish line. It seemed insane to me that someone would just drop out of the race so close to the end. The only thing I could think of was that maybe Brown didn't have enough credits to graduate, so he decided to just quit before he was fired. I also considered the fact that Brown hated school and instead of just talking the talk, he stood up and walked the walk. If education in America was nothing more than a race to the end, Brown decided that he was tired of running like a rat. On one hand, I thought Brown was foolish for not graduating, because, in many ways, he was smarter than I was. On the other hand, I respected him for having the balls to legitimately say "Fuck this."

I ended up passing Electronics. Cheating off Henry since the winter had given me straight A's, but the D's and F's from Brock's time had brought down my overall average to a B-plus, which was both adequate and strangely gratifying. The only time I ever felt truly guilty about how I passed was when my mother looked at my final report card and said, "Wow, you really turned it around in Electronics, huh?"

In class that last day, I turned my chair toward the window and looked outside. It was a sunny day and a light wind was blowing yellow tree pollen through the air, which gave reality the sort of sepia tint that some old pictures had. Seeing I was by myself, Upham came over and stood next to me.

He put his hands in his pockets and said, "So, what are you doing after graduation?"

"Going to Emerson," I said.

"Good school. For what?"

"Writing."

Upham nodded.

"I guess that's not very practical, huh?"

Upham looked out the window and said, "Eh, not many people can write. It's a good skill to have."

"Well," I told Upham, "thanks for letting me pass this class."

Upham waved me off and turned back toward the window. "Ah, I didn't come here to give grades," he said. "Like I told you, I went right into the Navy after high school, so I never had a chance to become a teacher. It's something I've always wanted to do and now I've done it."

"So you won't be coming back next year?" I asked.

"Naw," he said with a sniff and a wipe of his nose.

"Fair enough," I said. "I wish I knew what I wanted to do after high school like you did."

Still gazing out the window, Upham said, "Ah, I didn't really know. I had nothing else to do."

"Should I go?" I asked.

Upham looked down at me and said, "Go where? To college?"

"Yeah."

"Why not?" he said. "Even if you don't do anything with writing, it'll keep you out of the job market for four years. Just don't take on too much debt. You'll have a good time."

For a moment, I felt good about nearly everything.

The last of the final bells rang. I gathered my things and stood up. Everyone walked to where Upham and I were standing. Each boy offered his hand, which Upham gladly shook.

"Good luck out there," he called out.

"Thanks, Upham," each one said as they walked away for the last time.

"Good luck out there," Upham said to me with a wink.

"Thanks, Captain."

A Turning of the Blue Tides

MCMXCV

The measure of a man is what he does with power.

—Plato

"Do you hear me? I'll be back in five minutes and you better be gone."

We just looked at the cop. He drove away.

"Fuck him," Fraser said. "We're not loitering—we're patrons."

"I'm not going anywhere," I said.

Brown drank from the straw in his soda cup and said, "Nope."

The three of us went back to opening our bags of Burger King and unwrapping our food. We were sitting on the hood of Fraser's mother's car—a brand-new green Toyota. Fraser's own car, a battered old station wagon covered with bumper stickers, had not passed inspection. His mom had let him borrow her car so we could grab some late-night food after finishing up at our dead-end jobs.

It was the last summer before my first year of college. I was working full-time at my part-time job, trying to save money before school. I slung pizzas at Papa Gino's while Fraser and Brown worked at a local bookstore. Because I was headed to school as a creative writing major, I was envious of the fact that Fraser and Brown were surrounded by books all day. They assured me I shouldn't have been.

"It might be books," Fraser said, "but it's still retail. It blows."

Since junior high and all throughout most of high school, our battles with the police had not let up. Before getting our licenses, the battles took place on foot. Infractions such as jaywalking were treated as if it were 1939 and we had just invaded Poland. We got harassed almost every weekend while walking through the center of town. "What are *you* doin'?" was the common salutation from the open window of a cop car. After telling the officer we were just walking uptown, we were met with the same interrogation: Who were we going to be with? (No idea.) Did we have drugs on us? (No.) Did we know who smashed the windows at the library/church/school? (Probably not.) I *may* have known who was to blame, but I *definitely knew* who didn't do it.

The rest of our evenings always played out the same. If we were hanging out in a public park, we would inevitably get chased away, scattering through town while the cruisers searched for us with spotlights until all of us just went home out of exasperation or exhaustion. If we were walking down the train tracks, a cop was usually waiting at a railroad crossing, ready to jump out of his car and run at us. He rarely caught up, but if he did, he would take down our names, never telling us why or what for. It went nowhere, but it was enough to put us all into a slow panic for the next few days at school.

By eighteen, my days as an adolescent vandal were far behind me. The young, cancerous anger that had been growing in the pit of my stomach since I was thirteen had gone into remission. I had distanced myself from my stepfather so much that we only passed by each other in the kitchen on weekend mornings. I had dated a girl and fallen in love so hard that I suffered from all the cliché ailments: the butterflies, the insomnia, the inability to eat. And, more important than anything, I was on my way out of Medfield. I no longer felt a need to destroy everything around me. After high school, Fraser, Brown, and I had gone back to being suburban nerds—we never broke the law, because we didn't have time, and what little time we had was spent doing nothing. Our lives consisted of work, listening to metal, and shooting the shit in parking lots after work. By eighteen, all the crap we took from the police was exceptionally unwarranted, and exceptionally infuriating, especially in other towns besides Medfield where the cops didn't even know who we were, or the bad reputations we supposedly had.

After getting our licenses, the harassment from the cops that used to take place on foot now took place in cars. The three of us all drove shit boxes, which was entirely just cause to get pulled over every weekend. Getting pulled over became so commonplace that every night before we got in one of our cars, one of us would say, "Think we'll be seeing the blues tonight?" And the reply was always "Is grass green?" We would get stopped for anything and everything: broken taillights, squeaky fan belts, five miles over the speed limit, not "coming to a complete stop."

Slow nights for the cops were bad nights for us—the nights when our cars were searched. The cops never found anything, but they were so desperate to score that they usually called in another officer to help tear through our stuff. Searches could take close to an hour while the three of us just sat on the curb, staring at our Chuck Taylors, wondering whether anything might be planted on us. By the end, the cops would just give us back our registration and insult us, before finally (and begrudgingly) letting us go.

By senior year of high school, the three of us had developed a white-hot hatred for the police. Whenever Fraser got pulled over by an overbearing and disrespectful officer, he would put on "Cop Killer" by Ice-T after the blue lights turned off and the guy drove away. "Fuckin' pigs," he'd say, putting his car in drive and white-knuckling his steering wheel. "I swear to Christ, someday I'm gonna fuckin' snap."

By senior year, the three of us had also started to resist. The older we got, the less shit we took from the police. One night while I was waiting for a friend after my shift outside of Papa Gino's, a cop pulled up alongside me.

"Get out of here," he said.

I pointed to my red shirt and said, "I work here."

"Are you working right now?"

"No," I said. "I'm done. I'm waiting for someone."

"Then I just told you to get the fuck outta here."

"I'm not fuckin' going anywhere."

"Oh yeah, tough guy?" the cop said to me. "Are you driving tonight?"

"Yeah."

"Good," he said. "I'll be waiting for you. Just remember, the pen is mightier than the sword."

With that, the officer threw his cruiser in reverse, then gunned it toward me, just barely missing me with his bumper.

I didn't move.

Just as I knew the cop that night had nothing, we all knew the cop harassing us in the Burger King parking lot had nothing. Fraser was right—we weren't loitering; we were patrons. We would have eaten our food inside, but we had gotten to Burger King just as it was about to close. The girl at the register, who looked exactly our age, told us we could order, but had to get our food to go.

"You can eat outside," she told us.

"No problem at all," Fraser said.

We had just taken our white bags out to the car when the cop showed up telling us to leave. He was overweight, with red hair and a young, freckled face. The writing on the side of his cruiser read: *K-9 Unit*, and a German shepherd in the backseat barked at us from behind a closed window. We didn't know the officer. We were two towns away, in Medway, where the nearest Burger King was. Unlike in Medfield, where we knew every cop and their general temperament, we had no idea how this cop was going to handle us. But as soon as he pulled up with his attitude, he was instantly familiar and we were ready to lock horns.

Fraser and I were sitting on the hood of the car, our feet resting on the bumper. Brown was standing next to us, meticulously setting up his food on the outlaid burger wrapper. Fraser and I had just torn everything open and begun scarfing down our Whoppers. Medfield had no fast food restaurants, and while there was a McDonald's nearer to us, in Millis, we always drove the extra miles to Medway because we all thought that when it came to fast food, Burger King was somehow "better."

After the cop left, we practically forgot about him. Between mouthfuls of food, the three of us talked about music. We were hostile to everything Kurt Cobain had represented and created. Though we liked some grunge music, we hated the depressing aesthetic of it, to the point where we would openly make fun of people who wore flannel. As teenagers, the three of us were raised on a weekly diet of *Headbangers Ball*—the MTV show that played endless metal videos into the midnight hour every Saturday night. To us, metal was about sex, death, and destruction—not moping around because your parents were mean to you. In our music, you killed your parents if they were mean to you.

The popularity of grunge in the mid-'90s had driven the three of us underground and put us on a constant search for new bands. We were at the local record store every Thursday after cashing our paychecks. After coming through the door, the three of us went off in our own directions, flipping through rows of CDs, literally judging albums by their covers. I chose my selections carefully. One album was worth two hours of my minimally-waged time. Instead of going to big rock concerts at big arenas like we had before, Fraser, Brown, and I started driving into Boston on the weekends to see local bands at filthy dives like the Rathskeller— Boston's version of CBGB's, affectionately known as "The Rat."

I liked where the three of us were. Getting more into under-ground music gave us an air of coolness, though, still within the confines of rural Medfield, we were anything but cool. I liked wearing a band T-shirt that made someone point and say, "Who is that?" I liked finding my own music, instead of listening to whatever FM radio or MTV found for me.

Neither Fraser nor Brown had graduated high school. The three of us celebrated their lack of achievement one afternoon in Fraser's backyard by hanging his cap and gown on a tall makeshift cross and burning it with gasoline and a lighter. Whatever the synthetic blue fabric was, it went up in clear, shimmery flames and dripped away like candle wax. We thought it was hilarious until the cap and gown was gone and all that remained was the tall, burning cross. We quickly ran to fetch the garden hose before any of the neighbors looked over and got the wrong idea.

At the time, I looked upon Fraser and Brown's not graduating with a mixture of ambivalence and acceptance. In May, I wrote in my journal: *Graduation is less than one week away. Fraser and Brown didn't make it. And who gives a shit if they get a diploma or not? I saw an education become less and less important to them as time went by. They stopped caring. I stopped caring for them. Whatever they do, whatever.*

Regardless of the ceremonial pomp and circumstance, Fraser still planned on getting his diploma. He was only a few credits short, and in between shifts at the bookstore, he was going to summer school.

Brown had no interest in getting his diploma. It was an unspoken topic among the three of us, which was odd because we had always talked about anything. For me, not talking with Brown about his decision to drop out was all about avoiding discomfort. It was uncomfortable to say that high school was mostly easy, even though intelligence was definitely not the thing that hindered Brown (or Fraser). It was also uncomfortable to say that getting a high school diploma was important, because I never wanted to lecture Brown in some awkward, fatherly way. As a result, the most important conversation was always left unsaid.

When the cop pulled back into the parking lot, Fraser looked over and said, "Here we go." Brown put down his soda and Fraser and I put down our burgers and wiped our hands. As the cop entered the lot, he put on his blue lights and revved his engine.

None of us moved. Brown stood right where he had been, next to the front tire of Fraser's mom's car. Fraser and I remained on the hood, waiting to see what the cop's big move was going to be. As the cruiser raced toward us, the door flew open. The cop yelled, "I told you guys to..." He swung his left foot out of the car and it dragged along the pavement as the cruiser raced straight for us.

"Whoa!" Fraser yelled. "Whoa!"

The cop threw the shifter into park, harshly grinding the gears. Brown dashed out of the way, just as the cruiser slammed into the side of Fraser's mother's car, catapulting Fraser and I from the hood in a half-jolt/half-jump.

"What the fuck?!"

The cruiser stopped. The officer, his face even redder, pursed his lips and put it in reverse. As he did, the shocks on Fraser's mother's car lowered down. The three of us walked around to survey the damage.

There was a large crater in the door.

The cruiser was unscathed.

We looked over at the cop. He was staring blankly at his dashboard, wiping sweat from his forehead. Fraser started walking toward him with his soda in his hand. For some instinctual reason, he had grabbed it when the two of us were thrown off the hood. Fraser's pace was slow and deliberate.

"Oh, shit," Brown muttered.

The cop, seeing Fraser coming toward him, got out of his cruiser. The German shepherd in the backseat was wild, the hot breath from its snapping jaws fogging up the window.

"Whose car is this?" the officer stammered.

Fraser threw his soda against the pavement, where an explosion of ice and Dr. Pepper erupted just close enough to the cop's feet to make a point.

"That's my mother's brand-new car you just fucking hit!" he screamed.

The cop looked at him fearfully and quietly said, "Can I have your license and registration please?"

Fraser stared at him. After a few tense moments, he finally hissed and shook his head. He went to the driver's side of his mother's car, but when he lifted the handle to open it, he realized that the crater in the door had sealed it shut. Jerking the handle in frustration, he hissed again and walked around to the passenger's side and got the registration out of the glove box.

"Thank you," the cop said as Fraser handed it to him.

"Yeah," Fraser said.

The cop went back to his cruiser and got inside. The dog in the back was still barking, but the officer never made any attempt to quiet him. Instead, he picked up the receiver for his CB and began speaking. We couldn't hear what he was saying. Fraser and Brown both lit cigarettes.

We watched intently. A cop asking for a license and registration usually meant a ticket was on the way. Although it seemed unlikely that Fraser was getting a ticket, after all the negative interactions we had had with the police, it didn't seem impossible, either. In trying to look like a hard-ass, the cop had come away looking like a complete ass.

I wondered whether the officer was going to try and save face by charging us with loitering. I wondered whether he was going to hand us tickets and say, "This wouldn't have happened if you had just done what I told you." I had seen the police break the law enough times to know this was entirely possible. I also wondered whether the cop was going to somehow say that Fraser had caused the accident, but given the nature of the damage, that seemed doubtful, unless Fraser had figured out some miraculous way to drive a car sideways.

The cop talked back and forth with someone on the CB. Fraser smoked multiple cigarettes. Brown and I quietly ate the rest of our food. When the two of us crushed up our bags to throw them away, I asked Fraser whether he wanted his food, to which he firmly said, "No." His eyes were still sharply focused on the officer. I gathered up Fraser's food and threw it in the trash barrel by the Burger King door.

Ten minutes later, another cruiser pulled into the parking lot. An older cop with smooth, olive skin and black hair styled with mousse got out of his car. He was on the shorter side, but in good shape. He had the sort of finely tuned arm muscles that were achieved by long hours on a Nautilus machine. There were three gold Vs on his uniform. He walked over to the redheaded officer, who stayed inside his cruiser. Before they spoke, the younger officer looked at the agitated German shepherd and calmed him by gently shushing him. "That's a good boy," he said pleasantly. The dog stopped barking, but remained sitting, ears pointed upright.

The two officers talked and exchanged pieces of white paper. Fraser, Brown, and I just leaned against the Toyota with our arms folded. I wondered what sort of bullshit story the redheaded officer was telling. "The car slipped out of park," or "My foot slipped off the brake." Either way, I figured he wasn't saying, "I was trying to spring into action like a tough guy so I could intimidate these kids." I shook my head and looked at the asphalt. It was almost midnight. If the cop had just left us alone, the three of us would have been home already, probably in bed.

The older cop finally walked over to us. "Good evening, gentlemen," he said, showing a perfectly white smile. "I'm Sergeant Pacella." He pointed at Fraser and said, "This is your car, right?"

"My mother's car."

The sergeant nodded and said, "Ah, right. Yes, please apologize to your mom for me."

I looked over at the redheaded cop. He was still in his cruiser, filling out paperwork. The sergeant handed Fraser a piece of white paper, about the size of an index card.

He said, "This is the insurance information for the Medway Police Department. Please give this to your mom so she can file a claim. I've already filled out an accident report." He handed Fraser a business card. "And this is my number. If she has any questions, please have her call me."

Fraser took everything and said, "Okay."

The sergeant looked the three of us over and said, "By the way, I take it you guys are okay. No one is hurt, right?"

"No," we all mumbled.

"Good," he said. "Did you guys have a chance to finish your dinner?"

"Yeah," we all mumbled.

"Good," he said. "Thank you for your patience, gentlemen. Enjoy the rest of your evening."

The sergeant waved and walked back to the cruisers. He spoke with the other officer for just a moment before the red-headed cop nodded somberly and closed his door. Fraser was staring him down, but he avoided all eye contact as he drove past us. The German shepherd was happily panting, his long tongue hung out to the side. Sergeant Pacella smiled and waved one last time as he drove away. Crickets chirped from the woods behind the Burger King dumpsters.

"Oh," Brown said, "I guess we can stay here now."

Fraser, calmer now, said, "I'm pretty sure we could stay here all night if we wanted to."

I said, "Let's come back next weekend."

An Education

MCMXCV

The paradox of education is precisely this—that as one begins to become conscious, one begins to examine the society in which he is being educated.

—James Baldwin

"Stop talking about me!"

We all looked up at my roommate, Sam. Then we looked at each other.

Someone said, "What?"

"I can hear you from the other room! Stop talking about me!"

We all looked at each other again. Silence. Sam studied us with his intense sapphire eyes. Then he shuffled back to his bedroom without closing the door. The three of us exchanged confused looks. Danielle held out her hands and shrugged her shoulders. We tried to not to laugh, but eventually did. Sam came back out.

Sam shook his long index finger. "I mean it!" he shouted. "Stop talking about me!"

Danielle said, "Sam, no one was talking about you."

"I can hear you! Now stop it!"

We all looked at the floor.

"I mean it!"

We continued looking at the floor. Eventually, Sam shuffled back to his bedroom again. The sound of his blue slippers scuffing against the floor tiles was the only sound to be heard. Once he was gone, we all stood up and quietly made our way from the common room to the hallway. As soon as the heavy door swung closed behind us, we started laughing at full volume.

"What the fuck?" my other roommate, Jake, said.

"Was someone talking about him?" I asked. "Did I miss something?"

"*No one* was talking about him!" Danielle exclaimed.

"Dude," I said, "that kid is fucked. No wonder he's a theater major."

In the first few weeks of college, Sam was becoming the quintessential "nightmare roommate." He was technically Jake's roommate, because they bunked together in the same bedroom, but we shared a five-person suite, so I was able to watch Sam unravel too. Sharing a bedroom with Sam meant that Jake was taking the full brunt of it, though. On the third day of school, Jake came out of his room snickering, informing us that Sam would only brush his teeth while sitting at his desk and not in the bathroom.

But we were all noticing his mental decline. Sam was always coming into the common room and just standing in a daze. Tall and thin with wild black hair, we'd all look up at him and wait for him to say something. After several moments of uncomfortable silence, Danielle would finally ask, "Sam, is everything okay?"

Sam, snapping out of his fog in a somewhat dramatic way, would return to his senses and say, "Oh…yeah…fine, fine…I just have a migraine. I'm just, you know, kind of out of it right now. Oh, sorry, sorry. Sorry to interrupt you guys." Then he would shamble back to his room in his bathrobe and slippers.

One day, Sam looked up at the ceiling of our dorm room and told us that he was "allergic to the fire alarm."

There was another long silence before I finally said, "What?"

He pointed to the little red box affixed high on the wall and said, "*That*. I'm allergic to *that*."

We looked up at the fire alarm and then back at Sam. Since I had already engaged him, I felt obligated to continue down the rabbit hole. "You're allergic to smoke *or…*?"

Sam stood up quickly and said, "If that thing goes off, I'm just…I'm just in big trouble, that's all." He turned to go to his room and said, "I just can't…I just can't."

The thing that made Sam even more strange was the fact that he wasn't always strange. Some days he would stride into our suite with a big smile on his face. "Hey, guys! How's everyone doing today?" We'd all respond with equal (yet curious) enthusiasm and then wait for him to say something insane.

But he wouldn't. He'd just sit down and talk to us as if he (and everything) was totally fine—as if he had never told us that he was allergic to the fire alarm, or heard things that didn't exist. I started wondering whether Sam was on psych meds that he didn't always take. I had also read about people having "spells" in Victorian novels and assumed that was maybe what Sam suffered from. Whenever I saw him act normally, I just figured that his odd behavior was the result of nerves because he was away from home for the first time, which was something we were all dealing with during the first few weeks of our freshman year.

The campus of Emerson College was simply downtown Boston. Each fall on Boylston Street, thousands of eighteen-year-olds were plucked from the comfort of their suburban homes and dropped into the heart of a major metropolitan city. Emerson's campus sat on the edge of what had once been called the Combat Zone. "The Zone" had been the red-light district in Boston for decades—rows of porn theaters, strip joints, and roughhouse bars. By 1995, its roughness was becoming gentrified. Only a handful of the seedy places remained. One of them, a gay porn theater called the Naked Eye, was directly across the street from our dining hall. Danielle and I would sit by the window, eating our grilled cheese sandwiches, and clock the average time it took for a patron to enter and exit (20 minutes).

Danielle became my best friend and not-quite girlfriend during my first few months at school. We both loved books, horror movies, and heavy metal. Danielle was gorgeous—a tall, slim Jersey girl, blonde-haired, and blue-eyed. She was a theater major and had done some modeling in high school. We were both dorky outsiders from rural suburbs, but it seemed totally inconceivable to me that such an attractive girl would wear a Megadeth T-shirt or want to sleep with me. Like most freshmen, the two of us had left our significant others back home with the best intentions of staying together, but collegiate life, distance, and hormones had other plans. After the two of us finally broke things off with our high school sweethearts, we hurriedly stripped out of our clothes and did away with some serious sexual tension.

Because of my average grades and poor class ranking in high school, Emerson accepted me provisionally. During orientation, they gathered the "provisional students" into an old Puritan church on Marlborough Street, far away from the main Emerson buildings. The church rented their space to the college for large lectures during the afternoon hours, when parishioners weren't there. As I shifted my bony rear end in the harsh wooden pew, a woman walked up to the altar and began to speak.

"Take a look at the other students around you," the woman said, her voice echoing off the walls. "Half of you will not be here next semester."

Everyone actually looked around. I suddenly felt the same way I had the summer before fifth grade, when I'd found out I that my teacher was going to be a horrendous old woman named Mrs. Prescott. She was the one teacher everyone dreaded getting—the one with the reputation—and she lived up to that reputation in spades. Mrs. Prescott taught by ridicule and humiliation, and she got on my case so badly that I began suffering from serious anxiety, causing my grades to fall so severely that by winter I was dangerously close to repeating the grade. For several weeks, I was pulled out of class for IQ tests and psychological evaluations. The tests were given downstairs in a place called the Resource Room. Each time I was called out of class to go down for my tests, a jock named Trevor would whisper, "Time for the Retard Room, Sean."

Emerson's accepting me provisionally felt like the Resource Room all over again. It was like I had spent grades five through twelve trying to prove that I was smart and capable, only to have it all dashed by grade thirteen. To make things worse, the woman up at the altar went on to tell us that Emerson had a place we could go to get help called the Academic Resource Center.

I could have cried and the inner-child inside me probably was.

I squirmed in the wooden pew for every minute of the half-hour I sat there. The woman finally concluded her talk by telling us, somewhat ominously, that our grades "would be closely monitored by the administration." After she was done, we all stood up and walked out of the church with our backpacks slung over our shoulders and our heads slung low to the ground.

Later that night, the fire alarm went off back at the dorm. Danielle and I had been in my room listening to Alanis Morissette and sharing teen angst stories. A small strobe light began to flash while a piercing whoop repeated in threes. The two of us groaned, rolled our eyes, and put on our Doc Martens. Our dormitory was newly renovated and still under construction, and the fire alarm was tripped by workmen nearly everyday, but usually around lunchtime. This was the first one at night, when everyone was home from class.

As soon as I opened my door, Jake flung his bedroom door open and sprinted toward the hallway.

"Is there really a fire?" I called out.

He ignored me and kept running.

"What's going on?" Danielle said from behind me.

I peeked into Jake and Sam's bedroom and saw Sam convulsing on the floor, his eyes rolled back into his head. Snorting and grunting sounds were coming from the back of his clenched teeth.

"Oh, shit."

Danielle came up behind me, saw what was happening, and slapped a hand over her mouth.

Jake came running back into the suite with our two RAs, Darcey and Dylan. Darcey was an attractive cheerleader type and Dylan was an attractive football player type. I incorrectly assumed that the situation was beyond their capabilities, but to my surprise, the two of them sprang into action. Dylan pointed at Darcey and said, "Go downstairs and get the paramedics—they should be here anyway." Darcey ran back out while Dylan got down on the floor and put his hand on Sam's shoulder.

"Sam, can you hear me?" he yelled over the fire alarm. "You're going to be okay. Help is coming."

Danielle, Jake, and I stepped away from the action. We stood in the common room with our arms folded, nervously shifting our weight from foot to foot.

"Should we go outside?" Jake asked.

"There's no fire," I said. "Is there ever a fire?"

Darcey came back into the room with two paramedics and a firefighter. Darcey's bun had come loose and her hair was frazzled with static. She gnawed at her pink fingernails. The paramedics went into the bedroom with a stretcher while the firefighter turned to the three of us.

"Is he epileptic?" he asked.

The three of us either said nothing, or shook our heads.

"Is this the first time this has happened?"

"Yeah," Jake said.

"Does he have a problem with these strobes?" the fireman asked, pointing at the flashing light.

The three of us just stood there, looking baffled.

Seeing that we were no help, the fireman turned and walked into the bedroom. Darcey said, "You guys should go outside."

"Is there a fire?" I asked.

Darcey shouted, "It doesn't matter! Go outside!"

We stared at each other, angrily. The tension finally broke. I had disliked Darcey since orientation, where I sat indignantly thinking that Darcey and Dylan were like characters from *Saved by the Bell*. Old high school politics were still in play—Darcey was a preppy and I was not. She thought I was weird. I thought she was boring.

I shook my head, turned, and left with Danielle and Jake. More than seven hundred students filled the south side of Boston Common, a lush green park in the heart of the city. Kids lit up cigarettes and joints and a pair of guys with long dreadlocks banged on bongo drums. Girls danced around in the cool night air. A chicken fight broke out above the crowd. Jake, Danielle, and I stood with our arms folded, looking up at the eighth floor. We had forgotten our jackets.

Jake said, "I think I might request a transfer."

We laughed. I said, "I don't blame you."

Jake smiled and said, "I can't take this shit."

It was impossible to not like Jake. He was from New Hampshire and, like most people I had ever met from north of

Massachusetts, was extremely polite and friendly. He wore smart eyeglasses and liked *Star Trek*, but he wasn't what most people would call "nerdy." He was actually a well-spoken, good-looking guy. Between his genuine politeness and warmth, more than one girl in our dorm had taken an interest in him. In some ways, he was the perfect roommate for Sam. Most kids would have lost their patience with him long ago (I certainly would have).

Outside on the Common, Danielle said, "I don't know. Informing your roommates that you're epileptic seems like a good idea."

"You think he is?" I asked.

Danielle said, "You think he was faking it?"

"I hate to sound callous, but it wouldn't surprise me."

"It wouldn't surprise me either," Jake said. "He lies a lot."

"Really?"

Jake looked away from the building and said, "Well, he lied about his religion."

"He did?"

"I didn't tell you? He told me he was Jewish and then a few days later he said he was Mormon."

"That's quite a difference," I said.

Jake laughed and shook his head. "I can't take this shit."

After a few minutes, the paramedics wheeled Sam into an ambulance. He was upright on the stretcher and looked alert. The fire trucks eventually turned off their red lights and pulled away from the dorm. The three of us began filing back into the building with the hundreds of other students. Once inside the lobby, I saw the resident director, a pleasant woman in her thirties named Francesca.

"Was there a fire?" I asked.

"No," she said, "it was a false alarm."

Three weeks later, Sam came into the common room with two large bandages on his nose and chin. Both of his eyes were blackened.

Danielle said, "Holy shit! Sam, what happened?"

"Oh, oh," he said. "Nothing. It's nothing. I just, ah…" Sam took two steps toward his room, but then took two steps back. We waited for him to finish. He finally said, "It's just that, umm, well, I got mugged today."

Jake said, "Really? Where?"

Sam pointed to nothing in particular and said, "Over by Brimmer. It was just, you know…I don't know."

"Are you all right?" Danielle asked.

"Yeah, I'm fine. I mean, I'll be fine. I just, you know…I just need to lie down."

Sam ambled off to his room and closed the door. We all looked at each other with both bewilderment and skepticism. We were getting used to Sam's weirdness and lies, but seeing him legitimately banged up like this raised legitimate questions. He had clearly been assaulted, but by whom? Had he really been mugged? I probably wasn't the only one who was wondering whether he had punched himself in the face just for attention. We had never gotten to the bottom of the epilepsy. After the fire alarm incident, Jake had asked Sam whether he was epileptic and Sam had said no. Jake asked what the problem was and Sam just told him that he "needed to be more careful."

After the first few weeks of school, Jake had given up on Sam. We all had. We were meeting new people and adapting to college life. We were learning how to live on our own—when to eat, when to go to bed, and when to do laundry. No one had time to orbit around Sam's insanity.

I was also learning that Emerson's accepting me on a provisional basis was at least questionable and at most bullshit. After a week of classes, I realized not only that could I handle the work, but that my aptitude was on par with, and often above, my classmate's. I hadn't read every book that was assigned, but I wasn't unfamiliar with any of them, either. A class in expository writing, mandatory for every freshman, was where I saw that my skills were better than average. At first I felt cocky about it in an "I told you so" sort of way, but I was mostly surprised. The number of college students who couldn't write a sentence or craft a paragraph was astounding to me. I found myself admitting (somewhat begrudgingly) that all the boasting my old high school had done about preparing us well for college had been entirely true.

Though technically ready for battle, the artistic combat I stepped into most cautiously was in the trenches of the writing workshop. I very much felt like a soldier in those first few days. Outwardly, I was poised and determined, but inwardly, I was downright terrified and uncertain. I had taken a creative writing class in high school, but it was a fluffy love fest. No matter how terrible someone's story was, no one ever said anything negative about it. I knew Emerson would be different. Winning a few writing awards in high school meant nothing. At Emerson, I was sitting in a judgment circle with a dozen other kids who had achieved the exact same thing. We were all new fish in a bigger pond, but our sizes wouldn't be determined until the first Xeroxed copies of our work were passed around.

By pure luck, the first writing teacher I had was Andre Dubus III. He was the first writer I ever met, and he defied all the expectations of what I thought one would be. On the first day of class, he strode into the room like a gunslinger. "Hello, lovely people!" he called out. Andre was Hollywood handsome, with a chiseled jaw and a thick mane of dark hair that was just short enough in the back to *not* be called a mullet. The girl next to me referred to it as "sensitive-man hair." If someone had told me that Patrick Swayze was Andre's brother, I would have believed it. When he stood in front of the class, Andre put one foot up on a chair, revealing a pair of black cowboy boots.

Before we went around the room giving our paltry teenage bios, Andre told us a little about himself—how his father was a famous writer (I had never heard of him), how he came to be a writer himself, and how he had been a boxer, a bounty hunter, and a carpenter. Everyone was awestruck, especially the girls. Andre also told us about the book he was writing about an Iranian immigrant who buys a home in America. He was writing it out longhand inside his car between carpentry jobs and teaching school. "It's the only place I can find quiet," he said. "I'm not quite sure where the story's going yet," he told us. Then, as if something had just occurred to him, Andre picked up a blue marker and began drawing on the whiteboard behind him.

He drew a picture of a stick figure man holding a pen. The man was sketching a line underneath himself, like a tightrope walker drawing his own wire. "I never know how a story is going to end," Andre said. "I just write." He drew a vertical line to the right of the man, indicating a destination. "Just like this guy here," he said, slowly drawing out the rest of the wire. "I just write toward the end. I write 'til I get there."

I jotted the image down in my notebook.

It was the first and best piece of writing advice I've ever been given.

Andre gave us two writing exercises to do on the first day of class. First, we needed to describe a beautiful, sunny day in a meadow...from the perspective of someone with a migraine headache. Second, we had to describe a violent scene. "Anything," he told us. "Just use that wonderful imagination you all have."

My description of the sunny meadow through the eyes of a migraine sufferer was okay, but when I read my violent scene out loud to the class, I felt like a performer in the center of the spotlight. I wrote a quick story off the top of my head about a man beating another man, tying him to a chair, and pulling out his teeth with a pair of pliers. *A crack and a twist*, I wrote, *and the blood began to flow.* As I read, Andre winced and grabbed the side of his jaw. I could barely get the words out because everyone was squirming in their seats and letting out cries of imagined pain. After I finished reading, the class laughed and, to my utter surprise, applauded. In one fell swoop of emotions, I was gratified, humbled, and embarrassed. It wasn't the first time in my life I felt like I might have a talent for something, but it was one of the few and most significant. Once the applause died down, a kid from Southern California named Diego said both sarcastically and sincerely, "Yeah, I think Sean really understood the essence of this exercise."

I was proud of what I could do. For years, I had always thought that my ability to pen a half-decent sentence was just some innate ability or genetic inheritance from my mother. Some of it may have been, but after seeing my classmates react so positively to my writing at Emerson, I gave it more thought and realized that most of it came from good old-fashioned woodshedding. And my mother *had* played a huge role. She never hesitated to buy me regular books when I was a child, but the other things she always bought me—the things I loved even more—were the read-along storybooks that came with a seven-inch vinyl record. You read along while you listened along. *Star Wars* was my favorite. In a world before VCRs, I saw *Star Wars* before I ever saw the movie because I had seen it in my mind. The record played the orchestral music from the film while a narrator read the story and voice actors played out the dialogue. I read along with every word, every paragraph, every comma, and every period. And at Emerson I was beginning to see what a hugely beneficial pastime that had been. I wasn't just reading the words on the page—I was hearing the words on the page. I was hearing their cadence and their rhythm. I was seeing the right words and how they described the right scenes. Without knowing it, I was learning how to craft a compelling narrative—how to arc a story, how to keep a reader moving. The read-along storybooks were an all-encompassing mental experience that utilized two of my physical senses and invigorated my imagination. For hours, I would sit cross-legged on my bedroom floor in front of a little record player, reading and listening, observing and examining, anxiously awaiting the next beep from R2-D2 that told you it was time to turn the page. What I didn't know at the time—and what I finally came to realize at Emerson—was that all of those hours of joy had also been lessons. And they were probably some of the best lessons any future writer could have. For the rest of my life, my mind would be crammed with stories, and characters, and *words...words...words*.

But even as I sat in creative writing classes doing well, there was a voice in the back of my head telling me that creative writing couldn't really be taught. It was the voice of my earlier teenage self—the kid who sat in his bedroom reading novels and scribbling away in a notebook. As valuable as some of Andre's wisdom was, part of me felt like the only way to become a good writer was to sit in a quiet room and read a lot and write a lot.

The End.

All of the writing professors at Emerson had published books, but none of them made their living just by writing. Academia subsidized their careers. I smiled with wry amusement each time I received a syllabus and saw that the professor had assigned one of his own books. I knew there was no money in the arts, so I understood why writers taught, but sometimes during class I wondered whether the whole thing was a racket. Many writing professors walked around campus with their heads in the ozone. Sometimes I looked at them and thought that the academic world of creative writing had been invented simply because the real world wouldn't have them.

And I wondered about Emerson, too. Not long after being there, I saw it less as a college and more as a business, especially when I had to fight with the financial aid office for pennies, or was forced to pay eighty dollars for a textbook that was probably worth the pennies I was fighting for. And I wasn't alone in that thinking or that battle. Each time Jake went out the door to argue with the financial aid office, he would say, "Hey, Sean, do you have any Vaseline? I was just wondering because I'm off to financial aid to get a good, hard fucking."

Emerson had lured all of my starry-eyed classmates into its writing program with the hope that they would all become famous novelists, but how many of them really would? I had the same starry eyes, and while sometimes my own head floated in the ozone, the working-class background I had come from always kept my feet planted on terra firma. Because of that, I never saw myself as a college student—I saw myself as college customer. I never lost sight of my writerly ambition, but I never lost sight of that, either. Another voice in the back of my mind was that of Matt Damon from *Good Will Hunting*—the scene in the Harvard pub when he tells a pompous, ponytailed grad student: "You dropped a hundred and fifty grand on a fuckin' education you coulda got for a dollah-fifty in late charges at the public library."

Before long, I also saw that some people in the creative writing program were so far off their rocker that it was hard to imagine they even had a rocker to go off of in the first place. Though none were as crazy as Sam, a lot of the young would-be authors I sat amongst in workshops had peculiar habits and bizarre personalities. Just a week into class, a girl named Zoë submitted a story about two men exploring a cave in the Ozarks. When the kid next to me used the word *spelunking* to describe what they were doing, Zoë threw off her glasses, stood up, and screamed, "Spelunking!? Spelunking!? That's how you describe my story!?" The kid next to me held up his palms in confused surrender and Zöe stormed out of the classroom. "Okay," the professor finally said. "Let's move on." After class, while everyone was gathering their things, Zoë came back in, went up to the professor's desk, and told her that she needed a break and was dropping out of school. The professor just nervously nodded and told her that was fine, and we never saw Zoë again.

A kid from Vermont sat next to me in Andre's class on the first day and, after deciding that my writing met his approval, gravitated toward me every day.

And I practically cringed each time he did.

His name was Alastair Bailey. I remembered him from orientation—he was hard to miss. He was over six feet tall, and during the meet-and-greet for writing majors, he was decked out in full goth regalia, complete with a long black velvet cape, and pale white vampire makeup, which was starting to smear from the beading sweat behind his eyeglasses. Unlike most goth kids, Alastair wasn't shy or introverted. On the contrary, he was oppressively sociable. The corduroy-clad professors he introduced himself to had to shake his hand and pretend like they weren't talking to someone dressed like Dracula.

I disliked Alastair, but he liked me. He was one of those people who decided we were friends whether I liked it or not. Within minutes of meeting, Alastair needed to inform me that he was working on a horror trilogy (something I could have guessed before he even said it) and had sent excerpts of it to Stephen King, who responded with glowing encouragement. Part of me believed him, because Alastair was a decent writer, but I was mentally rolling my eyes after each masturbatory sentence he spoke. One time in the library, Alastair sat down next to me while I was attempting to study and told me that he was trying to work out a schedule with his professors so that he could just turn in his stories and not actually attend class. "I'm nocturnal," he said. I just nodded, gathered up my things, and said, "Cool, man. Speaking of which, I have to get to class."

I politely dodged Alastair as best I could, but after Andre caught him playing solitaire on his laptop while a girl was sharing her story, I avoided him like the plague that Stephen King wrote about in *The Stand*. "Alastair, what the hell are you doing!?" Andre shouted. I legitimately thought he was going to punch him. Alastair slapped his computer shut and just looked down in red-faced embarrassment while Andre told him what an asshole he was. When it was over, Andre took a few laps around the room to calm himself. From then on, I made sure I got to class early and chose a seat between two people, so Alastair couldn't get near me.

Most days I ended up next to Thomas Libby, a bookish, handsome guy from Maine. He had the air of a man twice our age, and it wasn't just the oval eyeglasses he wore. One day, Thomas came into class with an old hardbound book he had just picked up from an antique bookshop near campus. He sat down and studied its spine like an archeologist. I watched him slowly run his hand over the leather cover the way a blind man might read braille. Then he blew between the tanned pages, which sent off a fine puff of dust that hung midair in a sunbeam. With a pleased grin, Thomas opened the book and smelled its pages.

I smiled and said, "I smell books too."

Thomas looked at me over the top of his glasses and said, "I always knew that deep down you were a hopeless romantic, Gorman."

He and I ended up playing poker together on the weekends.

I caught on to the social politics of the writing workshop fairly quickly. After a few weeks, it became obvious which fish were going to go belly-up and which were going to swim. Only a handful of students had any real, discernible talent. The rest were either wistful imposters, or kids from other majors who were just taking a writing class to fill credits. Whenever these students critiqued my work, I zoned out and doodled in my notebook. But when people like Thomas spoke, I tuned in carefully. I might have been developing the same arrogance as Alastair, but I was determined not to show it. I had no idea what I was doing. I was writing toward the writer I would become, still trying to find my own voice. Like everyone else, I was faking it until I made it.

After a few weeks of classes, all of us in the writing program became intrigued by one of our classmates named Leslie Ann Carver. What was intriguing about Leslie was that she literally couldn't write. The first time she passed around one of her stories, all of us read the opening lines, stopped in confusion, and then flipped through the rest of the pages. Leslie's text was incomprehensible. Sentences were garbled, words were scrambled, commas and semicolons were strewn everywhere. It was like a fourth-grader was trying to write Margaret Atwood. And I was certain that her insistence on having a three-name moniker was because she envisioned herself as a Louisa May Alcott or Joyce Carol Oats.

I felt horrible for Leslie. Aside from having an obvious love of literature, yet being completely incapable of writing it, she was also the most physically awkward person I had ever seen. Her face was riddled with blackheads and her greasy brown hair was parted so severely down the middle that it looked like her skull had been struck with a hatchet. Leslie's voice was deeply masculine and when she spoke, a line of drool often fell from her bottom lip, which protruded out like a salival birdbath. She was constantly slurping and wiping. Her childhood must have been hell, which I knew was the creative black coffee for any great artist. I used to sit in class thinking that if she could only jog the part of her brain that prevented her from writing, her stuff would probably be brilliant.

One day in Expository Writing, the instructor—a snarky M.F.A. student who *actually* wore tweed jackets with elbow patches—took Leslie aside and told her that she really needed to go to the Academic Resource Center to get help with her writing.

"I'm dyslexic," Leslie said, point-blank. This got the attention of the entire class. Not everyone was looking, but everyone was listening.

The instructor pointed at one of Leslie's essays, which was covered in scribbles of red ink. He said, "I understand that, but what about spelling? Half the words in this are spelled wrong. Don't you have a spell-check?"

Leslie began contorting nervously and shaking her head back and forth. I was waiting for her answer just as eagerly as the instructor, and everyone else in class.

She said nothing.

Finally, the instructor said, "Listen, you really need to go down there and get some help. I literally cannot grade this." He handed the paper back to her and Leslie bowed her head and sat down next to me, flushed red and full of tears. I glanced sideways at her and tried to remember whether I had seen her at the meeting for provisional students. I was certain I would have remembered and I was certain I had not. Leslie came back to class only a few times after the instructor took her to task. She sat even further to the back of the room and never said another word.

After another two weeks, she disappeared altogether.

"Guys, come look at this," Jake said in a whisper as he came out of his bedroom. He was laughing under his breath. Danielle and I stood up and we all tiptoed, even though Sam wasn't home. Jake pointed to Sam's desk, which had nothing on it, except one piece of paper set precisely in the middle.

"What is it?" Danielle whispered.

"Read it,' Jake said.

It was a consent form for plastic surgery. Sam had gotten a nose job and a chin enhancement. We now knew what the bandages and black eyes were all about.

"Apparently he didn't get mugged," I said, matter-of-factly and without whispering.

"Unbelievable," Danielle said, dropping her whisper as well.

We walked back out to the common room and sat down. Jake put his head in his hands. "I can't take this shit," he said.

"Aw, it's okay, Jake," Danielle said.

"Obviously he wanted us to see that," I said.

"What a fucking whacko," Danielle said. "Seriously."

"Why would you lie and then put that out there for everyone to see?" I asked.

"I can't take this shit."

A week later, I came home from class to find Sam's parents in his bedroom. They were packing. Jake was standing in the common room. He gave me a large, excited smile as I came through the door.

"What's happening?" I asked, somewhat loudly.

Sam's parents put down the boxes they were holding and came out of the bedroom. With his back to them, Jake quickly retracted his smile and put on a somber face. Sam's dad was un-assuming, but his mother was dressed in a poncho stitched with Native American designs. They looked like they may have been hippies in a previous life.

"Sam's in the hospital," his mother said to me.

"Oh."

"We don't know what's wrong with him."

"Yeah."

"Is he on drugs?"

I shifted my eyes to his father and then back to his mother. "Not that I'm aware of," I said.

"He's taking a leave of absence from school," his mother told us. "He just needs some time."

"Right."

She raised her hand and made a dramatic sweeping gesture around the room. She said, "I just don't think he's ready for all… for all *this*."

The Rapture

MCMXCVI

*Beloved, believe not every spirit, but try the spirits
whether they are of God: because many false
prophets are gone into the world.*

—1 John 4:1

"So you're in a cult, right?"

"What?"

"I heard that you were in a satanic cult."

"Who told you that?"

"I just heard that from some people."

I looked over at Larry, the diesel mechanic. He was quietly laughing behind Stanley's back.

"No," I said. "I'm not in a cult."

Stanley put his large paw on my left shoulder and said, "Okay. I just wanted to be sure." He walked away. I looked over at Larry and rolled my eyes. He kept laughing, but straightened up and walked into the garage as soon as Stanley turned around.

Larry had a Ph.D. in ball-breaking. He lived across the street from my parents and I had known him my whole life. In the summer, he waxed his Corvette in the driveway wearing nothing but denim shorts and tan work boots. His static comb-over was gray and his eyes were so crystal blue they were nearly white. Larry was the head mechanic at the Medfield Highway Department, which was my new summer job between my freshman and sophomore year of college. When Larry wasn't fixing a dump truck or a street sweeper, he sat on a chair in front of the town garage with his arms crossed, calling everyone an idiot and hilariously pointing out everything that was wrong with them. At work, he kept to himself, other than occasionally chatting with whoever stopped by the garage, usually the cops or paramedics who came to get gas.

One time, Larry and I were standing in front of the garage when an older woman named Mildred drove up in the ambulance to get diesel fuel. Although Mildred was a paramedic, she never drove the ambulance to emergencies and had apparently just been sent out on an errand since there was nothing going on. Larry and I watched as she put the ambulance in reverse and began slowly rolling toward the pump. As the back-up alarm beeped, Larry pointed from his chair and said, "Watch this." The two of us looked on as Mildred—a small woman driving an enormously large vehicle—cautiously maneuvered backwards, nervously using the side mirrors to see where she was going. The windows on the ambulance were down, and I almost hollered to Mildred to stop after it became clear that she was going to hit the steel guardrail that protected the fuel pumps from being hit.

Mildred hit the guardrail.

After a loud, metal crunch, I started laughing, though somewhat guiltily. Mildred hit the brakes and frantically looked around. Larry, without missing a beat, calmly said, "That's good, Mildred. All set."

Larry had obviously told Stanley that I was in a satanic cult because he knew I'd never hear the end of it. Stanley was a devout Christian and Larry knew that telling him I worshipped Satan was going to be an endless source of amusement all summer (for Larry). Larry probably concocted the scheme because I wore heavy metal T-shirts and had long, dark hair and a goatee. If someone saw me as demonic, I couldn't exactly complain. Part of it was my own doing.

My stepfather had gotten me the job as a laborer for the Highway Department. One night while I was home for spring break, he mentioned to me that there was an opening for summer help. He casually offered the job and I casually accepted it. "Yeah, I guess so," was my exact response. Since jobs for teenagers in Medfield were scarce, I took whatever I could get. I wasn't thrilled about working for the town, but the money was a lot better than the minimum wage job I had at Papa Gino's throughout high school. I worked with two other college kids, both of whom were older and both of whom had fathers who also worked for the town. On the social ladder of the Medfield Highway Department, we were on the rung just above the garbage we picked up on the side of the road: "fuckin' summah help."

I met Stanley in June when we started paving. A subcontractor who operated the large road grader, he was a master of the machine. Once while we were paving Hartford Street, a guy named Jack said to me, "Watch how precisely Stanley grades this." I watched Stanley steer the twelve-ton machine slowly, without looking forward, his eyes intensely focused on the curb. He maneuvered the blade underneath the machine to create a perfect edge to the road. After the grader passed by us, Jack said, "That's why Stanley gets seventy-five dollars an hour and you get shit." Once Stanley graded the road, it was our job to smooth out the hot asphalt with what I thought were rakes until I heard all the other guys call them lutes. It was also the time when the older guys told the "summah help" that we didn't know what we were doing and were going too slow.

I didn't mind the abuse—it was good-spirited and to be expected. I didn't like the work, however. Although I liked being outdoors in the sunshine, the physical labor was monotonous and seemed to have little reward. As always, I was the smallest in stature and found it hard to keep up. I never complained and always finished, but I knew my first summer working for the Highway Department was going to be my last. I was looking forward to September.

Stanley was a tall and immense sixty-seven-year-old. My hand barely fit around his when I shook it. Rather than wearing tank tops or T-shirts like the other guys, Stanley wore collared dress shirts tucked firmly into his jeans. He was composed and polite and had gentle eyes and a kind smile. During the extra-hot days, he bought cold sodas for the rest of us, and the only time I ever saw him angry was when a motorist drove by the work site too fast. He'd holler "Slow down!" and then calmly go back to whatever he had just been saying.

I had had little interaction with Stanley until Larry told him I was in a satanic cult. After that, Stanley was all over me. He stopped and talked with me every chance he got—during coffee breaks or whenever we were waiting for another truckload of asphalt. I'd practically wince each time he climbed out of the grader and started toward me.

"Have you read the Bible?"

"I have."

"And what did you make of it?"

"I had to read it for two classes in school."

"So what did you make of it?"

"It's an important book."

"Are you prepared for the rapture?"

"What's that?"

"The end of the world. You need to prepare for it."

"So, like, bottled water and canned goods?"

"No, no," Stanley said. He put his index finger into my chest and said, "You need to prepare your soul."

"Oh."

"I'm going to give you some literature," he said. "I want you to read it." He pronounced *literature* as "lit-rat-sure."

I said, "Okay," with a hesitation I hoped Stanley didn't notice. I was thankfully saved when the orange and black dump truck with a new load of steaming asphalt arrived. Stanley said, "Okay," and climbed back into the grader.

Brandon, the other college kid I worked with, came up to me and said, "Man, that guy really has a hard-on for you."

I said, "Fucking Larry told him I was in a cult or worshipped the devil or something."

Brandon laughed and said, "Fucking Larry."

Everything I'd told Stanley about my relationship to the Bible was true. What I left out was that I thought it was bullshit. That's what my rebellious teenage intellect made of it—a rebellious teenage intellect now bolstered by some freshmen knowledge of Nietzsche, Schopenhauer, and Mill. I couldn't believe that human beings in the twentieth century hadn't lost their gills and cast off their primordial tails. Religion was another thing I had always looked at from the outside in.

I was raised nothing. When my mother was a child, she was forced to go to church every Sunday while my grandparents stayed home. She always resented this, and kept me as far away from religion as she could. My grandmother supported her in her decision, but for more pragmatic and simplistic reasons—she thought the new head priest at the local church was an asshole. As a child, I was only "Christian" in the sense that my family celebrated two Christian holidays. But every aspect of religion was taken out of them. Christmas was about Santa Claus and Easter was about the Easter Bunny. The only time Christ's name was ever uttered in my house was if someone stubbed their toe.

As a teenager, resistance to Christianity wasn't second nature to me, but first. Belief in a sky deity seemed foolish. Morals from the Bronze Age seemed antiquated. Christianity's doctrines on sex and women and "love for all" could not have been more diametrically opposed to everything I had come to believe by just growing naturally in the world. At nineteen years old, I could see that nearly every Christian I knew had been indoctrinated as a child, which made perfect sense to me. I couldn't imagine a grown adult reading the Bible and saying, "Well, this explains everything."

As opposed to the philosophy of Christianity as I was, I didn't actively hate Christians. My first girlfriend in high school was a faithful Catholic, and I adored her. Her faith didn't matter and it didn't bother me. I didn't care what anyone believed as long as they didn't interrupt my day with it. The only time I had a problem with religion was when people started saying, "God thinks you suck," or when people proselytized, which was why Stanley was making me uneasy.

The next day, Stanley handed me three books. They looked low-budget. There were no pictures on the covers, just bold, dramatic text. The titles were simplistic: *The Rapture* and *The Word*. They were all written by reverends or "doctors."

Stanley pointed to the third one, *The Demon Inside*, and said, "This one is about demonic possession."

"Okay."

"You know my daughter has had problems with demonic possession, right?"

"No," I said. "*Really?*"

"She's had a very hard time of it. We've taken her to a lot of specialists."

"What do they do?"

"Well, the last priest we took her to was down in South Carolina. He has the possessed sit in a room with their loved ones. My wife and I were there with her. So you sit and pray while the priest reads scripture and eventually the possessed start vomiting."

"On the floor?"

"No, no. They have buckets. But, anyway, they all start vomiting and eventually they're free of the demon. That has worked so far, but it's an ongoing process. You see, once you've been possessed, it weakens your soul forever. After you're possessed the first time, you're much more susceptible to being possessed again."

"Oh."

"She's always fighting off spirits. A few weeks ago, she was walking down the stairs at the house and she just stopped before the last few steps. She couldn't move. She was paralyzed. As soon as I saw her, I knew a demon was trying to take possession. So, I got down on my knees and started praying and it worked. He freed her and she was able to walk down the rest of the stairs."

I just nodded my head. As Stanley spoke, I considered the possibility that he and Larry were in on the joke together. I kept waiting for Stanley to slap me on the arm and say, "Boy, Larry and I got you good, didn't we?!"

But he never did.

On the contrary, Stanley was alarmingly serious. I had never heard anyone say such insane things with such somber conviction. He was as serious as a heart attack. He meant every word.

I held up the books and said, "Okay, I'll take a look at these."

"Good boy," he said.

That night, I got home, flopped myself on my bed, and flipped through the books, which were printed in a large font with wide gutter margins. I knew little about publishing, but enough to know that this meant the books were high in effect and low in content. I thought about actually reading them for the fun of it, but after skimming a few dull paragraphs, I could see that there was no humor to be found, even ironically. I threw the books under my bedside table. I stared at the ceiling and tried to think of a suitable time to give the books back to Stanley so it would seem like I had actually read them. At first I thought a few days would suffice, but then I decided on a week so it would seem like I had really studied them. My fear was that Stanley was going to quiz me, but I had successfully bullshitted my way through enough book reports in school to fall asleep that night without much concern.

"What's up, peckah-head?"

"Good morning."

Luigi walked past me and sat down on a bench outside the office and opened up his newspaper. It was six-thirty and the sun was just starting to rise. The rattle of cicadas fired up from the woods behind the garage.

Like most of the guys in the Highway Department, Luigi had grown up in Medfield and lived there his whole life. He was a friend of the family, and I knew him the best. He had a mustache only slightly wider than Charlie Chaplin's and he wore thick eyeglasses, the lenses tinted blue. He was one of the most legitimately nice guys I had ever known. Anytime I worked with Luigi and we drove around in one of the town trucks, he'd always stop and buy a cup of twenty-five-cent lemonade from the kids who were selling it from a little stand in their front yard. He'd give them a dollar and tell them to keep the change.

Luigi took a sip of coffee from a Styrofoam cup and said, "So I heard Stanley's been giving you the gospel."

I adjusted the red bandana on my head and said, "Yeah. Fuckin' Larry."

Luigi chuckled and said, "He's such a miserable prick. He has to do shit like that because he has no fuckin' life. Imagine that, Sean. No wife. No kids. You just go home at the end of the day and shut the door."

I nodded. For some reason, Luigi and Larry didn't like each other. I figured there was some townie history behind it, but I never asked what it was. It was unfortunate, because the two of them were both good guys and both hilarious in their own ways.

"He's told you all that shit?" I asked.

"I've heard it all, Sean—the world's gonna end and his daughter is *The Exorcist*."

"Yeah, what's up with that?"

"The truth, Sean?"

"Yeah."

"His daughter was a fuckin' drug addict. I knew her. She was wild. I think she took one too many acid trips and never came back. You know what I mean?"

I rolled my eyes a bit and said, "Now it all makes sense."

Luigi said, "It's sad, but listen, just let him talk. He's a good guy. He'll eventually leave you alone."

"I hope so."

Brandon arrived as Luigi and I were talking. Feeling how hot the early-morning sun already was, he took off his T-shirt, revealing the same lithe, tanned body that I was getting from our hours of manual labor. "Damn," Brandon said as he sat down next to Luigi and cracked a can of Coke. "It's already fucking hot today." Luigi looked at him as he unwrapped a Snickers bar.

"That's your breakfast?"

Brandon chugged the soda and said, "Rocket fuel, Luigi."

Luigi chuckled to himself and said, "Peckah-head." He sipped his coffee and went back to the paper.

The cast of characters that made up the Medfield Highway Department all filed in, parking their pickups—all Fords or Chevys— next to the garage. Alphonso, the other mechanic, shuffled up to us and removed the Mack Truck cap from his bald head. He wiped the beaded sweat from his brow and said, "Hot one today, boy. Hot one today."

"Sure is, Fonzie," Luigi said.

Alphonso was an eighty-year-old widower who had worked for the town since he was a teenager back in the 1930s. His nose rivaled Jimmy Durante's. He wore the same green coveralls everyday and thought everything he worked on was a piece of junk. He called every truck engine a "shitty fuckin' setup," which he said so rapidly it sounded like one word. Alphonso had worked for the town for so long that he made less money by continuing to work than he would have by just collecting his retirement pension. The payroll office at the town hall used to complain because sometimes he wouldn't even pick up his paychecks. Everything in his life had been paid off a long time ago. He worked because he liked it and, I assumed, because he had nothing else to do.

Though a whiz with engines, I was told that Alphonso was illiterate. One time, Larry asked Alphonso to get him a can of WD-40 and he came back with hornet spray. As a result, Larry put a sign over the tool room door that read: *Nursing Home Annex.*

"You know what I like on a day like this?" Alphonso said to us. "A cucumber sandwich—two pieces of white bread with some sliced cucumber in the middle. A little oil and vinegar? It'll cool you right down. I'll have one for lunch today, boy."

"Sounds good, Fonzie," Luigi said, without looking up from his paper.

Brandon looked up, pensively. "Are we paving today? Isn't it supposed to rain?"

"Naw," Alphonso said. "Can't pave today. Weatherman said thundershowers this afternoon. Can't pave today."

I said, "Good. I get a break from Stanley."

Luigi folded his paper up and snickered. "Yeah, you peckah-heads will be digging ditches on the side of the road today."

Brandon said, "Are you serious?"

Luigi stood up and said, "Yup." Then, with a southern accent, he exclaimed, "Shakin' here, boss!"

"*Cool Hand Luke*," I said.

"Good fuckin' movie, Sean. Good fuckin' movie."

Brandon squinted his eyes and said, "So we're going to be digging ditches in a rainstorm. Nice."

Luigi snickered again and said, "Have fun, cocksuckahs."

The foreman finally arrived and told Brandon and me that we would indeed be digging ditches. New street signs were being put up along Route 27. Before the rain started, though, the boss told us we needed to go down Maplewood Road and Causeway Street to pick up some fallen branches. Brandon stood up and the two of us went to the tool room where, as always, I glanced up at the *Playboy* centerfolds from the 1980s that were hung on the dirty walls above the claw hammers and pipe wrenches. Though a little dog-eared at the corners, the old centerfolds still looked like they had been pinned up just yesterday. My eyes were always drawn to a blonde high up near the ceiling. Her wholly natural body put me in mind of the same *Playboy* magazines from the '80s I had first seen as a kid. She made me nostalgic for a time before collagen and silicon. After grabbing two shovels and a pickax, Brandon and I climbed into one of the small orange and black dump trucks and began our day.

Once we were away from the garage, we turned up the radio and began making fun of the town guys. We imitated their mannerisms and the way they spoke. We played out entire conversations like actors, especially the way they talked about the blizzard of '78 like it had been Armageddon. Brandon said, "Two hundred feet of snow that year, Sean. You don't remembah—too young." The harder we exaggerated, the harder we laughed.

"Shittyfuckin'setup!"

"Fuckin' summah help!"

Like me, Brandon had known the town guys his whole life. He went to Stonehill, a small college in nearby Easton, which was warmly called "Stoned Hill." He never mentioned what his major was. Brandon was a boyish sort of good-looking and laid back. His parents were divorced and he lived in another town with his mother, but I remembered seeing Brandon at a few summer parties, where he got a lot of attention from girls. His last name was well known in Medfield and it seemed like everyone was his cousin or uncle.

Brandon and I were the first in our families to go to college. In another reality, the two of us probably would have ended up working our way up the ladder at the Highway Department. We would have gone from summer help to full-time employees to eventually getting our CDL licenses and becoming truck drivers or heavy equipment operators. That way, we could have sat in the air-conditioned trucks and watched the new crop of "summah help" do all the grunt work we had to do.

Much as we made fun of the townies we worked with, we never saw ourselves as superior. On the contrary, sometimes we thought we were the stupid ones. Once, while eating our lunches under the shade of a maple tree near the center of town, Brandon remarked how our college degrees were probably going to be worthless since everyone our age was going to have one.

"Those guys are the smart ones," Brandon said, referring to the town guys. "They make good money and get an awesome pension. When they're retired down in Florida, we'll be up here, wiping our asses with our college degrees."

I nodded and said, "Yeah, I definitely think about that sometimes."

I enjoyed college, but after a year of it I began to wonder whether I had simply gotten roped in by a sales pitch. No part of me ever thought that a degree in creative writing would serve any practical purpose in the real world. I'd decided to attend college simply because I'd received a decent number of grants and scholarships and because, quite frankly, I'd had nothing better to do. After getting to know some of my professors, I could see that their trajectory was not so different from that of the town guys. They got their bachelor's degree, started as part-time faculty, got their master's degree, and then became full-time faculty. The only difference, however, was that the town guys owned everything they had, whereas the academics were saddled with lifelong debt from obtaining their degrees. It seemed like the only ones who really benefitted from collegiate life were the college administrators. The more I looked, the more I saw academia as some strange modern-day feudalism where the peasants actually paid to work.

When Brandon and I got to Maplewood Road, we saw a full-size tree lying across the street. Apparently the line of communication had broken down and somehow a tree had become a branch. I said, "That storm the other night must have brought it down."

Brandon looked at it incredulously and said, "So I guess you and I are supposed to just lift up this tree?"

"You better call it in," I said.

Brandon picked up the mic for the CB and said, "Unit Five to base."

A voice crackled, "Go ahead." We were calling the town garage, but really had no idea who we were speaking to. It was just a voice.

Brandon said, "Yeah, we're down here on Maplewood and there's a tree in the road."

"A big tree?"

Brandon thought about it for a second and said, "I mean, like, a medium-size tree. We can't move it."

"Okay. Is there anything else on the road?"

"Yeah," Brandon said. "There's, like, branches and shit." Just as the words left his mouth, Brandon winced and slapped the mic against his forehead.

Silence.

"Umm, anyway, we can pick all that up," Brandon finally said.

"All right, Unit Five."

Brandon hung up the mic. I laughed and said, "I don't think you're supposed to curse on the public scanner. Like, the whole town can hear that—the police, fire, and town hall."

Brandon shook his head, opened the door, and said, "Yeah, I know." He put the CB mic back in its cradle and said, "Whatever. Fuck it. Let's go."

The two of us got to work, picking up branches and tossing them into the back of the dump truck. We each took an end of the bigger ones and heaved them in with a "one, two, three." Once we were done, we climbed back into the truck, this time with me at the wheel. I tuned the radio to a classic rock station called the Eagle. Every morning before we left, Larry had the Eagle on in the garage and I would have '70s tunes stuck in my head for the rest of the day. Brandon and I chatted about girls over "Sweet Home Alabama."

I stopped at a red light in the center of town, listening to the music and thinking about a short story I wanted to write for the next semester. Brandon tapped his fingers on the side of the door as my mind wandered. Once a few cars passed, I started to turn. Brandon calmly looked down the street, even though vehicles were coming right at us at a fairly high rate of speed. He said, "A left on red, huh, Sean?"

I slammed on the brakes. But then I gassed it once I realized I was halfway through the intersection anyway.

Brandon started cracking up.

"Why the hell did I just do that?" I asked, looking in the rearview mirror.

Brandon shook his head and said, "I don't know, man. Summah fuckin' help."

I nervously looked in the side-views, expecting to see a cop, or worse, another orange and black town truck. There was nothing, however, except a maroon SUV, whose driver was probably thinking the idiots who worked for the Highway Department ran red lights just for kicks. As I drove down Main Street, I shook my head and said, "Seriously, I have no idea why I just did that."

Brandon shrugged his shoulders and took the last swig from his can of Coke.

Driving through the center of Medfield took about two minutes without hitting any other red lights. We passed the town hall, the barbershop, and the two rival pizza places that sat on opposite sides of Main Street. Traffic was light, as most residents had already vacated to their summer homes on Cape Cod. "Sweet Home Alabama" was followed by "Walk This Way."

I made a left onto Causeway Street, whose black asphalt was glistening with shimmery mirages in the hot morning sun. Causeway started as a winding back road that stretched into the neighboring town of Millis. After about half a mile, however, it became a straightaway gravel road that crossed over the swampy banks of the Stop River. Causeway Street always flooded in the summertime, and the residents had been petitioning the town to pave it for years. But the town was worried that paving a long straightaway would encourage teenagers to speed. I looked in the mirrors as the wheels of the truck left the smooth asphalt and bumped over the crunchy gravel. The tires kicked up a dust cloud, just like in the movies. I thought it looked cool, so I gave it a little gas to kick up some more.

Up ahead, Brandon and I could see the branches we needed to pick up. They had fallen from a pair of oak trees that stood just before the river. I slowed down as Brandon put on his work gloves. A white Buick was approaching from the opposite direction, dust kicking up from its tires as well. It started to slow once it saw us. The gravel part of Causeway Street was so narrow; it could barely fit two cars. Since the dump truck was large, I pulled to the side to let the other car pass.

We started to sink.

Brandon's eyes widened as our wheels slid down the embankment.

"Whoa! Whoa! Dude!"

I jerked the wheel in the other direction, but the truck only slid down further.

"Just stop!" Brandon yelled. "Just stop!"

I hit the brakes and yelled, "Fuck!"

The white Buick passed us in a cloud of dust, its driver giving me a quick glance through his dark sunglasses. The truck was so tilted, my ass began to slide down the pleather bench seat toward Brandon. I threw the gearshift into park and grabbed the door handle to steady myself. Brandon's body was practically hanging out the window.

Brandon and I sat in silence for a few moments. The cloud of gray dust settled.

Brandon said, "This fucker is gonna tip over."

"I'm afraid to get out."

"Your weight might be the only thing keeping it up."

"Fuck!"

Birds chirped in the distance.

"Fuck!" I yelled again.

"We need to get out," Brandon said. "We can't be in here if it goes."

"Yeah," I said. "But we can't get out on your side. This thing will crush us to death."

"Yeah."

I lifted the door handle. It unlocked and I pushed it open, but gravity shut it again. I steadied myself by holding the steering wheel and pushing the door open with my boot. Slowly, I twisted my body out of the truck. Brandon grabbed the steering wheel and pulled himself across the seat while I held the door. I offered my hand, but he said, "I've got it." He shimmied his body out and planted his feet on the gravel. The two of us walked down the road and looked back at the truck. It was at a ninety-degree angle. We were both panting, our hands on our hips.

Brandon said, "I can't believe that thing didn't tip over."

"Jesus Christ."

I looked down the road from where we had come from. I looked up the road to where we should have been.

"I guess I'll radio for help," I finally said.

I walked back to the truck and reached up for the door handle. I could just barely get my fingers around it. Seeing this, Brandon jogged over. While he held the door, I reached into the cab and lifted the CB mic from its cradle. The curly black cord stretched out straight as I pulled it toward my mouth.

I paused for a moment before pressing the button and saying, "Unit Five to base."

Brandon started to smile.

"Go ahead," the voice said.

"Yeah, umm, we're up on Causeway Street."

Silence.

"Okay."

"Yeah, umm, we need a tow."

"A what?"

"A tow," I repeated. "We slid off the embankment."

Silence.

"Okay."

"So we can't get the truck out. We're stuck."

Silence.

"All right, Unit Five."

I threw the mic back into the truck. Brandon couldn't stifle his laughter any longer. "Smooth move, Gorman," he finally said.

About twenty minutes later, a yellow front-end loader arrived with hooks and chains sitting in its bucket. It was driven by Harley, one of the few highway guys on the Highway Department who wasn't from Medfield. I was relieved to see him. Harley was a relaxed guy with white hair and a neatly trimmed white beard. He talked with a slow accent, and I could never tell whether it was from the deep South or high Maine. Harley came to work every morning on one of those large motorcycles with a curved windshield and built-in saddlebags. If he was going to give me shit, there would be a minimal amount of it.

Harley parked the loader, letting out a hiss from its airbrakes. He climbed down the ladder and walked over to us. He gave the truck a glance.

"Almost went over, huh?"

I said, "Yeah."

"Who was driving?"

"I was."

"What happened?"

"I was getting out of the way for another car."

Harley looked down the road and said, "Yeah, this road's pretty narrow, I guess."

"I didn't think we'd both fit."

"Yeah, you would have both fit. Just gotta go slow."

I looked at the ground and nodded.

Harley got back in the loader and brought it over to the back of the dump truck. He got out and hooked the chains somewhere underneath the chassis.

"Just let me pull it a little ways and steady it," he said to me. "Then get in it and put it in neutral."

"Okay."

Harley climbed back into the loader and backed it up. The loud beeping alarm for reverse sounded and I was glad that we were in a secluded area of swampland so none of the near-by residents could peek out their windows and see my stupid folly. Once the chains were taut, Harley nodded to me and I climbed back into the truck. I started the engine and put it in neutral.

The loader pulled it from the embankment with ease.

Harley got out again, collected the chains, and threw them back into the bucket. Brandon began picking up the branches we had originally come for.

"Thanks," I said to Harley.

"No problem," he said. "See you fellas later."

I got to work picking up the branches with Brandon. Harley took off in the loader. It was sunny, but dark storm clouds were coming in from the west. After filling half the truck with branches, I clapped my work gloves together and said, "Okay, let's go."

Brandon said, "I'll drive."

We drove to the landfill and dumped the branches into the brush pile. It was just about ten o'clock, so we went back to the town garage for the morning coffee break, though neither Brandon nor I drank coffee. Luigi pulled into the lot at the same time we did. He got out of his own dump truck and waited for us by the office door. He shook his head.

"What's the matter with you guys? Swearing on the fuckin' radio and tippin' over fuckin' dump trucks."

"Summah help," I said sarcastically.

Luigi chuckled and said, "Cocksuckahs."

It began to rain.

"You have to remove all satanic imagery from your life," Stanley said to me.

"Like what?"

Stanley pointed to a ceramic frog that was sitting in a small garden. It was in the front yard of one of the houses on the street we were paving. "Like that," he said. "That's an accursed image— it's divination."

"A frog?"

"Having stuff like that around your home is an invitation for evil spirits."

"Oh."

"My wife used to have this little owl on the windowsill of our kitchen." Stanley indicated about two inches with his thumb and index finger. "Just a little knickknack, you know? Anyway, one night I was sitting in my chair and I saw a bat fly through the living room wall. This is called satanic harassment, you see. The bat came out of one wall, flew across the room, and flew into another wall, like a ghost. I finally said to my wife, 'That's it, you've got to get that little owl out of here.' And she did. She threw it away. But you see what I mean? Stuff like that draws demons in."

All at once, Stanley's kind eyes looked unsettling. Rationalizing his daughter's drug problems with demonic possession was one thing, but hearing him recount stories about seeing spectral bats was something entirely different. Although I still considered Stanley fundamentally harmless, I suddenly felt that might not always be the case. Either Stanley was having legitimate hallucinations, or he believed so strongly in what he was saying that he made himself see what he wanted to see. It seemed like a dangerous state of mind.

"Have you read those books I gave you?"

"Yeah," I said. "I can give them back to you."

"No, no. You can keep them."

"That's okay," I said. "I can give them back to you."

"Keep them. Just make sure you understand what's in them."

"I do," I said. "Definitely."

Stanley put his hand on my shoulder and said, "Good. Good boy."

Brandon and Luigi walked over to where Stanley and I were standing. We were waiting for another truckload of asphalt.

"What's happening?" Brandon said.

"Not much," I told him.

Stanley said, "I'm gonna get a soda. Anyone want anything?"

"No thanks, Stanley," Luigi said.

"I'm good," Brandon said.

Stanley looked at me and pointed.

"No thanks," I told him.

Once Stanley was out of earshot, Luigi looked at me with a grin. "Praise the lord, huh Sean?"

"That guy just told me that he saw ghost bats in his house."

"*What?*" Brandon said.

"No," Luigi said. "Stanley's not that crazy."

"You think I just made that up?"

Luigi said, "*Ghost bats?*"

"Yeah, he said that frogs and owls are satanic and he saw a bat fly through his living room wall."

Luigi said, "Get the fuck outta here, Sean."

"I swear to God."

Luigi chuckled and said, "Ghost bats. What a cocksuckah."

"Jesus Christ," Brandon said.

The dump truck with the asphalt arrived. The three of us picked up our lutes. I looked down at the ceramic frog Stanley had been talking about and shook my head.

"Fuckin' Larry."

Stepping Forth

MCMXCIX

Times have not become more violent. They have just become more televised.

—Marilyn Manson, *Rolling Stone*

Look back, and smile on perils past.

—Sir Walter Scott, *Kenilworth*

"I can't believe this happened," she said.

"Are you kidding?" Ron said. "I can't believe this doesn't happen *everyday.*"

The first real discussion I ever had about Columbine was in a college poetry class. Like most of the students, one girl who'd spoken was utterly shocked and perplexed. Our teacher, a melancholy and unmotivated poet, seemed like he was humoring the class by letting us share our thoughts. He just nodded in agreement with everything being said as he arranged papers on his desk. I was afraid to say what I was really feeling. But once Ron, a good-looking, talented guy who sat across from me in our workshop circle, spoke up, I pointed to him and nodded.

"*Right?*" he said to me.

"Right."

News of Columbine had spread slowly around campus the day before. I didn't hear anything about it until the evening, after returning home from my work study job with the English Department. When I came through the door, someone hanging out in our common room just casually mentioned something about two kids shooting up their school in Colorado. My immediate reaction was ambivalent. I just said, "Really?" and put down my backpack. We talked for a few minutes and then went down to the dining hall for dinner. We didn't even put on the evening news that night. Instead, we watched *Felicity* and MTV.

It wasn't until the next morning, when I watched CNN, that I realized the largeness of it: the scope of the plan, the arsenal of weapons, the number of deaths. Down in the dining hall for breakfast, the volume on the large projection TV was turned up so everyone could hear. The room was quiet. I ate a bowl of Lucky Charms with my eyes glued to the set. The news wasn't going to end, so when the reporters started repeating themselves, I packed up and headed across campus to poetry.

A few things were turning in my mind as I walked through Boston's Public Garden. It was sixty degrees and sunny. People sat on blankets eating apples and reading books. Suburban families were waiting for the Swan Boats—avian-shaped pontoons that pedaled tourists in circles around a small pond inside the park. The Swan Boats had just opened for the season, so the lines of people waiting for them were ridiculously long. As a lifelong Massachusetts resident, I had never been on one, nor even entertained the idea. Though the scene around me was the postcard version of a springtime Boston day, my mind was in a dark place, conjuring images and emotions from a darker time.

I understood Columbine. I wasn't shocked and I wasn't perplexed. And I also knew that I was mostly alone with my thoughts. I felt ostracized again. For most of the world, a high school shooting was something unfathomable. For me, it was something evocative.

I recalled each time a teacher humiliated me in front of my classmates. I remembered being spastic with anxiety and slouched with insecurity. I remembered my bad skin and my braces. I recalled girls telling me I was ugly and vomiting the contents of my nervous stomach into the toilet bowls at school. I remembered Jeff Bozzelli telling me the only reason I made the Little League team was because not enough boys had tried out. I recalled the time some kids (who I thought were my friends) called me on the telephone and told me they didn't want to play with me anymore because I was too weird. I remembered a lot of time alone in my bedroom.

I recalled all the angst and all the rage.

And it was hard for me to not feel just a bit melodramatic.

It all seemed behind me, until Columbine made me realize the memories had just been asleep. I was twenty-one years old—no longer a teenager, but by American standards, not really a man. Old enough, however, to look back and see that the horrors of youth are seldom permanent and sometimes self-induced. Eventually my braces came off and my spine got straight. At some point during high school, I realized that solitary adolescence and public education were finally going to end. I began to see a light at the end of the tunnel. A light that, for whatever reason, was just not in focus for either Eric Harris or Dylan Klebold—two names now flashing across every television screen in America.

I passed by the Bull & Finch Pub, which was the bar in Boston used for the exterior shots on *Cheers*. On the way to class each day, I would wave off the tourists who asked me to take their picture in front of it. Midwesterners would look at me dejectedly as I ignored them, but not quite as dejectedly as they did when they walked *out* of the Bull & Finch, realizing the interior looked absolutely nothing like the bar on TV.

As I walked to class, I remembered being grounded one summer when I was fourteen years old. Though the infraction escaped me, the punishment did not. I remembered having to sit in my room for two days with no television or music. After reading every rock magazine I owned, I finally opened my bedroom door and started perusing the large collection of books that sat on my mother's bookshelf.

I ran my index finger along hardcover spines, seeing names like Robin Cook, Jackie Collins, and Judith Krantz. I pulled out a few to look at their covers, only to put them back just as quickly as I had pulled them out. A large black book caught my eye because I recognized the name emblazoned on the cover in large gray letters: Stephen King. There were no pictures or illustrations on the cover, just text: *The Bachman Books: Four Early Novels by Stephen King*. I didn't understand why it wasn't just a Stephen King book, but, knowing Stephen King wrote horror, I decided to take it into my bedroom and give it a try.

The first part of the book was an introduction, in which King explained why he had written under a penname. Even after reading it twice, I still didn't quite understand. The second part of the book was a novel called *Rage*, underneath which read: *A high school Show-and-Tell session explodes into a nightmare of evil...*

I started reading.

I was instantly pulled in. Unlike reading some of the books they assigned in school, this time I understood everything that was happening. The only things to see between the lines were the things I wanted to see between the lines. I liked the idea that a good story could be told with clarity. And because I was still in high school, the environment felt very real. *Rage* was my day-to-day life. I could smell the hallways and hear the slamming lockers.

The story revolved around an outcast named Charlie Decker who shoots two of his teachers and holds his algebra class hostage. It was written in the first person. It was like Stephen King was tapping into the darkest recesses of my adolescent psyche, and suddenly I didn't feel so alone. Even if Charlie Decker wasn't real, Stephen King was. He understood. Chapter Three opened with Charlie eating Ritz crackers to calm his stomach, which was not just something I could relate to, but something I actually *did*.

Rage was the first book I ever read cover to cover in one sitting. Something changed in me that day during my teenage imprisonment. It was the day I started preferring my own company and seeing solitary confinement as solitary refinement. My bedroom became a laboratory where I split literary atoms. Not only did I discover a love of books, but I discovered a kinship with King, if only an intangible one.

Other than the Columbine discussion that day, poetry class was standard workshop fare. Boys read poems about oak trees and chipped white fences. Girls read poems about the smell of their ex-boyfriends still lingering on their pillows. I read an allegorical poem about a narcoleptic bird. The professor looked like he was dying for a cigarette.

Outside on Beacon Street after class, Ron lit up a cigarette of his own. "Yeah, man," he said to me, "that shit isn't surprising. High school is fucking hell. Obviously what those kids did was fucked up, but most people don't know what it's like to be tormented every day of your fucking life. It's not surprising two dudes finally snapped."

"I'll be honest," I said. "It's not like I never thought about doing that."

Ron tapped me on the chest and said, "Man, everyone has."

There was a minor gap in our conversation as we glanced at the other kids around us.

"Okay," he conceded. "Maybe not *everyone*."

I knew nothing about Ron and had never really talked to him before. Looks-wise, he didn't strike me as someone who would have been tormented in high school, but at twenty-one, I probably didn't either. To any passerby on the sidewalk, the two of us undoubtedly just looked like a couple of young college guys. We talked for a while, shook hands, and went down the street in two different directions.

Back at the dorm, groups of people were in their rooms, huddled around their small TVs. As the week went on, we were strafed with black and white images from security cameras showing Harris and Klebold calmly shooting as they walked through the cafeteria. The news aired crying students and crying parents and helicopter footage of classmates running for their lives.

It didn't take long for something I had expected to happen to happen. Eventually, the talking heads on the news began speculating and finger pointing. My friends and I watched with keen interest. We knew what was coming.

Even though I had read on some news sites that Harris and Klebold hated Marilyn Manson, I knew Marilyn Manson—the"Antichrist Superstar"—was going to find himself in the crosshairs of the American public. He did, after all, have a song called "Get Your Gunn" (though not about school shootings) and another song, "Lunchbox," about the state of Florida banning metal lunchboxes because kids were using them as weapons. It all seemed ridiculous to me, but I was not oblivious to the fact that the lyrics for "Lunchbox" could easily be interpreted as a bullied child shooting up his school: "Next motherfucker gonna get my metal…pow, pow, pow."

Though not surprised it was happening, I was still disappointed with the witch hunt against Marilyn Manson. My friends and I watched the talking heads with either mocking laughter or indignant frustration. Having been metal fans in the late '80s, we all vividly remembered the witch hunt against heavy metal that spawned Tipper Gore's Parents Music Resource Center. As teenagers, Fraser, Brown, and I loved watching daytime talk shows about "the satanic influence of heavy metal." One of Fraser's favorite bands, Judas Priest, was actually put on trial because two teenagers attempted suicide (one succeeded) after supposedly hearing the subliminal message "Do it" in one of their songs.

Priest was acquitted.

Fraser and I thought the whole thing was stupid. In high school, the two of us would leaf through the PMRC pamphlets in the guidance office and make fun of them. I remembered one pamphlet with an illustration of a stoned teenager wearing headphones with the title: *Music. A Health Issue?* Fraser and I laughed, tore up the pamphlets, and went on listening to heavy metal without ever once attempting suicide or homicide.

The other "influence" the media set their sights on after Columbine were violent video games, which was something new that I couldn't quite relate to. I had grown up with simplistic arcade endeavors like Pac-Man and Q*bert. Unlike new video games, most old video games didn't have the complex scenarios that could hold a kid's attention for an entire afternoon. After an hour or two of smashing bricks on Super Mario Brothers, I was always ready to go outside and do something else.

The news kept mentioning a computer game that Harris and Klebold were obsessed with called *Doom,* and I recalled the first time I had ever seen it. I also remembered the kid I grew up with who used to play it. I hadn't thought of him in a while, but after one incident during our senior year, no one in my high school would ever forget him.

In the fifth grade, Jonas Damita had the coolest BMX ramps in town. They were yellow and red, and so large that I never attempted to do any of Jonas's stunts on them. I'd just pedal my bike up and coast back down and repeat the process again. Jonas, though, was without fear. He would pedal up the ramps as fast he could, fly into the air, twist on his bike, and glide back down to the earth. Fraser and I would just watch from the sidelines, straddling our Huffys like we might give it a go, but we never did.

All of us lived within walking distance of Jonas's house. Fraser and I usually stopped by whenever we saw Jonas and his older brother out in the driveway, which was often. There was never an invitation, but it was never odd to just show up. Jonas was a friend, but none of us ever called him, or had his phone number. We were at the age where you just left the house with a group of friends and met up with another group of friends.

Jonas and his brother, Eran, lived with their mother in an old duplex. We never went inside and his mother rarely came out. If we had to go to the bathroom, we went out back and peed in the woods. Even though we were all "the weird kids," Jonas was weird in a different way. He was composed and still, and when he spoke, his tone was deliberate and exact. He was athletically built and walked with a military-like posture. Both his brother and his mother walked the same way.

Jonas also had extremely high brain-wattage. In school, seeing anything on his papers besides an A-plus was rare. He was especially good at math, which I was envious of. In our eighth grade yearbook, Jonas was voted "Most Likely to Succeed." Being an overly-excited spastic—the polar-opposite of Jonas—he wrote in my yearbook: *Gorman, you are extremely screwed in many different ways.* Underneath his name, he drew the circled-A symbol for Anarchy.

Jonas continued to hang out on the periphery of our social circle all throughout high school. Sometimes he was around, sometimes he wasn't. Jonas enjoyed the mild criminal spirit of my friends and me. He could use his deadpan tone to break balls with the best of us. I always thought that Jonas saw hanging out with us as a useful way to have fun and blow off steam when he wasn't studying, which I assumed was often.

Jonas and I spent the most time together after we both turned sixteen and got jobs at Papa Gino's. Medfield had been in an uproar when Gino's moved into town during our junior year. Many residents were determined to preserve the town's rustic charm, and they didn't want a corporate chain restaurant to sully it. The old Greek men who owned the pizza place everyone had gone to for decades handed out petitions to stop Gino's from opening.

Although Jonas and I agreed with the local sentiment, the two of us resentfully took jobs at Gino's because Gino's was just about the only place in Medfield that hired teenagers. We hated Papa Gino's the minute we donned our respective green and red shirts. Jonas trained me in how to throw pizza dough, smear the sauce with a ladle, and spread the cheese with mathematically-precise measuring cups. He also taught me how to scam the punch-card system so we could get paid on our lunch breaks.

Jonas and I worked long hours side by side, openly talking about how stupid Gino's was. As we tossed pepperoni and chopped onions, it occurred to me how little I really knew about

Jonas, even though we had known each other for nearly a decade. I knew nothing about why his parents had divorced. I knew nothing about his father—Jonas never said a word about him. I knew nothing about his mother, or what she did for a living (if anything). I didn't know Jonas' ethnicity, even though he had an odd name and slightly darker features than everyone else in school. And even though I knew that Jonas had not lived in Medfield his whole life, I didn't know where he had come from.

One Saturday night after closing the restaurant, Jonas asked me whether there was anything going on.

"No," I said, pushing a wet mop over marooned-tiled floors. "Fraser and Brown went to some all-ages show in Boston."

"You can come to my house if you want," he said. "I'm bored."

I said, "Okay." There was probably a mild surprise in my tone.

The two of us punched out and walked to Jonas's house, all the while talking about how much school and Papa Gino's sucked. As Jonas put a key into his side door, I looked up and noticed a bedroom light on, which I assumed was his mother's room. It was late, but he never said anything about being quiet. He just walked in, and I followed him up the stairs, looking around curiously at every little thing.

Jonas's room was orderly and, not surprisingly, filled with disassembled computers and electronic equipment. There were no posters on the wall, except for one of an M. C. Escher painting. Some of his textbooks were stacked on a bedside table. They were all for advanced classes I would never set foot in: calculus, physics, and trigonometry.

"Have you heard of *Doom*?" he asked me, sitting down and flicking on his computer.

"No," I said, still looking around.

"It's a computer game where you shoot people. You might like it."

"Cool."

After the computer booted up, Jonas started playing the game while I sat on the bed behind him. I watched Jonas, in the first person, walk down endless gray hallways, shooting people at random. I asked Jonas what the object of the game was. He started to explain the plot, but then, as he shot another man on the screen, said, "I don't know. It doesn't really matter."

After showing me how to play, Jonas and I switched places and I took the helm in front of the screen. He gave instruction over my shoulder. I hunted and pecked at the keyboard as my character on the screen walked into walls. Instead of being the hunter, I became the hunted. Within minutes, I was dead.

I was also bored. I wasn't impressed with *Doom*. I didn't like that the game was on a computer instead of a console. I didn't like using a keyboard instead of a controller. I didn't like the lack of narrative or objective and was surprised that Jonas, who was far more intelligent than I was, enjoyed something so mindless. I figured *Doom* was just a way for him to not use his brain after a long day of heavy usage.

After coming back from the dead several times and trying again, I eventually pushed the keyboard away and said, "Eh, it's not really my thing."

Jonas grinned and said, "That's okay. It takes some getting used to."

Jonas and I switched places again and I watched him play for another hour before telling him I had to get home for curfew.

He paused the game, swiveled around in his desk chair, and said, "You have a curfew?"

"Well, yeah."

"You're old enough to have a job, but you have a curfew?"

"I guess so."

Jonas turned back around and saved his game. "That sucks," he said.

"Yeah," I said. "So, wait, you don't have a curfew?"

Jonas shook his head. "No."

"Like, at all?"

"No."

"Wow," I said. "I might bring this up with my parents."

Jonas stood up and said, "My mother trusts me. I don't get into trouble. I get good grades and I have a job. What's the point of a curfew?"

"That's what I'm saying."

Jonas said, "I'll come down with you. I have to lock the door."

We walked downstairs in the dark. I told Jonas I would see him tomorrow. He said, "See ya" and locked the deadbolt behind me. It was close to midnight. As I walked away from the house, I looked up and saw that Jonas's light was on, but his mother's was off.

Jonas and I continued to have the same relationship right up until our senior year. By that time, I had made my way into two honors classes, British literature and political science, which were the only two classes of mine that Jonas was in. The two of us sat next to each other in the back, but we didn't screw around. We did, however, zone out. I would write poems about killing people.

Jonas would sketch geometric shapes. We looked up and took notes only when we felt like it was worth it.

One day at our lockers, Jonas came up to me and handed me a piece of paper. It was a schematic but it wasn't labeled. I thought it was the circuit board for a radio.

"Did I tell you about this?" he asked me.

"I don't think so. What is it?"

"It's a bomb."

"It is?"

"Yeah," he said. "An ammonium nitrate bomb. It's from *The Anarchist Cookbook*."

"Oh. Are you going to build it?"

Jonas smiled. "No," he said. "I'm going to put it in the yearbook."

I held up the paper and said, "This diagram?"

"Yeah."

"How are you going to put it in the yearbook?"

"In the back," Jonas said. "You know how they have all those ads in the back for the local businesses? I'm going to buy a page and put that in."

"Oh," I said. "Why?"

Jonas shrugged his shoulders and said, "I don't know. As a prank. It's funny. Only we'll know what it is."

I let out a slight laugh and handed the schematic back to him. I said, "Oh, okay."

"So I'm collecting money. Are you in?"

"How much?" I asked.

"It's sixty dollars."

"Okay."

"So whatever you can give."

"Oh," I said. "Well, I don't really have any extra cash right now."

"Okay."

"I mean, we work at Papa Gino's, so you know."

"Right," Jonas said. "Well, okay. Let me know if you get some. I have to turn it in by Thursday."

"Okay," I said as Jonas walked away. "I'll let you know."

I was lying and was pretty sure Jonas knew I was lying. I didn't want to tell him that I thought it was a stupid idea. Sometimes after my Uncle Mike had a few beers in him at family parties, he would recount the senior pranks his class pulled off in the '70s. One year, he and his friends disassembled a Volkswagen and then reassembled it inside the enclosed courtyard of the school. Another year, they looped car tires up the entire length of the flagpole. I always asked him how they pulled off the tires stunt, but he would never tell me and he literally took the secret to his grave. By comparison, Jonas's bomb idea seemed lame. Plopping Volkswagens down in the courtyard and (somehow) getting a bunch of tires around a flagpole were stunts I could get behind. From a humor standpoint, putting a bomb schematic in the back pages of a yearbook was a dud. It didn't seem like anyone would care.

Until Oklahoma City.

I caught just a few minutes of the breaking news between getting home from school and going to work at Papa Gino's. I watched the television in my parent's living room as I put on my uniform and tied my black shoes. The image of the half-blown out building was shown repeatedly and quickly imprinted on my brain. As I pinned my nametag to my chest and got ready to leave, I knew that my high school memories would always be punctuated by two events: Oklahoma City and Kurt Cobain.

Jonas had recently quit Papa Gino's and gotten a job at a local warehouse that shipped electronic equipment. Before he left, he'd asked me whether I wanted an application for the place. "It's way more money," he told me. I asked him what I would be doing. After giving me the lowdown on what the job entailed (filing and stacking boxes), I politely declined. Even though Gino's was paying me minimum wage, I felt there was still some artistry involved with making pizza. Plus, it didn't sound like any girls worked at the warehouse. Gino's at least provided me with an environment in which to socialize with the opposite sex—something I was slowly getting comfortable with.

No one who knew anything about the bomb prank said anything about it after Oklahoma City. After asking for my donation, Jonas had collected the sixty dollars from some of his other friends—brainy kids who sat with Jonas in calculus, kids who I occasionally hung out with, but didn't really know. I asked Jonas what Mr. Hersch—the teacher who ran the yearbook staff—had said when Jonas gave him the bomb schematics.

"Nothing," Jonas said to me. "I just handed him the money and handed him the picture. I said, 'I'd like to put this in the ad section.' He just looked at it kind of funny and said, 'Well, okay.'"

"He didn't ask what it was?"

"Nope. That was literally it."

The two of us laughed. Even though Jonas and I differed on what we thought was funny, one thing we had agreed on forever was that authority was stupid. Even though we were never the closest of friends, we were always united in that.

The high school was practically empty the day the yearbooks came out. All the seniors were still in Cape Cod nursing post-prom hangovers. Each year, the principal warned the seniors that they would be disciplined for not coming to school on Monday and each year, everyone ignored him. Grades were in. Colleges had accepted. Prom was over. No one cared.

I didn't drink, so I was lively and alert that morning. The very first thing I did was go to the office to pick up my yearbook. The secretary took my money and handed it to me with a smile. I walked down the empty hallways to my first-period psychology class. The only people in the room besides me were two girls who were flipping through their own yearbooks and the teacher, Mr. Bishop, who read *The Boston Globe* with his feet up on his desk. I planted myself on the radiator by the windows and began flipping through the yearbook.

Looking for Jonas's bomb was not the first thing I did. I didn't even think of it. Instead, I opened to page one and started turning. Brown was in the book, but because he'd never had his senior pictures taken, the image over his name was just a stock, faceless silhouette and nothing else. Fraser wrote, *NON SERVIUM* in the final line of his bio—Latin for "I will not serve," which were Lucifer's last words before being cast into hell. I quoted Lemmy Kilmister from Motörhead: *Born to raise hell. We know how to do it, and we do it real well.*

Even before I was a senior, I had always liked yearbooks. I liked seeing the passage of time between the pages—the changing of hairstyles, of faces, of clothes. I liked seeing what people wrote—what band lyrics or lines of poetry were quoted. I liked the idea that everyone inside the pages was going their own separate way.

Unlike people from cities or big towns, the people I graduated high school with were not just faces in the hallway. I knew all of them. And they knew me. There were only a hundred fifteen of us. And we had not attended just four years of high school together. We had been together since kindergarten, some since preschool. We had spent thirteen of the most formative and tumultuous years of our lives with one another.

And it was over.

I was struck with a surprising sense of melancholy as I flipped through the yearbook. And I hated feeling something so cliché at such a cliché moment. There were names and faces on the pages that I would always truly despise—awful people who would probably never redeem themselves as humans. But for the most part, I saw a few close friends and a large number of people who had been indifferent at worst, but friendly at best. In our white, upper-class suburban town, I had always been the outcast, but as I looked at the final pages of our yearbook, I didn't feel quite so angsty about it. In this one small instance, I actually felt connected to something honestly pure and truly good.

I got to the back.

Jonas's bomb schematic was next to an ad for the local gas station. It appeared to be sideways, but I wasn't sure. I smiled and shook my head. I looked up at Mr. Bishop and the two girls. Jonas was right. People were oblivious. Seeing Jonas's bomb prank confirmed that my initial feeling had been right. It was lame. I wished that he and I had collaborated on something better. I figured that with his intelligence and my creativity, we could have pulled off something awesome. Maybe we could have even figured out how my uncle and his buddies had gotten those tires up the fucking flagpole.

About twenty minutes into first period, the chimes for a P.A. announcement echoed throughout the school. Everyone looked up at the wall speaker that sat just below the American flag. A button clicked and the secretary's voice came on: "May I have your attention, please? Would everyone who purchased a yearbook this morning please report to the office after first period? Again, would everyone who purchased a yearbook this morning please report to the office after first period? Thank you."

Mr. Bishop looked up from his paper and gave the girls a quizzical look, which the girls returned.

"What's that all about?" he asked.

The girls shrugged their shoulders and shook their heads. Mr. Bishop looked over at me.

"Sean?"

"I dunno."

"*Sean?*"

"I mean, I think I might know."

Mr. Bishop stared at me with a shit-eating grin.

I smiled back.

Mr. Bishop was one of my favorite teachers. My last year as a student was one of Mr. Bishop's last years as a teacher. He had been at Medfield High School since my mother was a student. I had seen pictures of him in her yearbook, looking only slightly younger, with slightly less gray hair. If Mr. Bishop saw me walking to work after school, he'd pull over and give me a lift. He was tall and lean and still had a passion for teaching…when he felt like it.

Imminent retirement after thirty years of teaching had given Mr. Bishop a laissez-fare attitude. He would often show up twenty minutes late for a forty-five minute class. One day, a fistfight broke out between two boys right in the middle of a lecture. I never knew what it was about, but after a few heated words, the two guys just stood up and started slugging away at each other, eventually grappling down to the floor. Two girls shrieked and jumped up from their seats, their desks thrown askew by flailing arms and legs. Mr. Bishop just calmly watched the brawl from the front of the classroom. The fight was short-lived and ended in a draw. After the two boys shoved off one another and wiped their bloody lips, Mr. Bishop casually walked over to them and pointed to the soccer field outside the window. He said, "Listen, if the two of you want to roll around with each other, go out on the grass." The boys just nodded, fixed the desks, and sat back down.

Mr. Bishop looked at me and said, "Sean, does it look like I give a shit? What happened?"

I let out a slight laugh and said, "Jonas Damita put a bomb in the yearbook."

"*What?*"

"Like, the blueprints for a bomb."

"What the hell did he do that for?"

"I dunno," I said. "As a prank, I guess."

141

"That's stupid."

"Yeah."

Mr. Bishop put his reading glasses back on, leaned back in his chair, and went back to his newspaper.

"Where is it?" one of the girls asked me.

"It's in the back," I said. "With the ads."

As they flipped through the pages, Mr. Pepperman gently knocked on Mr. Bishop's open door. Mr. Bishop folded down his newspaper and looked up.

"Sorry to bother you, Mr. Bishop," Pepperman said, "but I need Sean for a minute."

Mr. Bishop looked at me over the top his glasses and jerked his head toward the door. He straightened his paper out and went back to reading. As I stood up, Pepperman said, "Bring your yearbook." I grabbed the book off the radiator and walked to the door. Pepperman led me outside by placing his hand on my shoulder.

I had mixed feelings about Mr. Pepperman. When I was a freshman, he had been the gym teacher, but by my senior year he had become the dean of students, a new position. Prior to that, disciplinary matters were handled by our former principal—an old, humorless woman named Ms. Shaw. Ms. Shaw was a bitch, but she was direct. When I was in trouble, she sat me down, explained what I did wrong, gave me my punishment, and sent me on my way.

Pepperman, on the other hand, tried to be my friend. He'd sit me down and try to get me to talk about my feelings (he always failed). Then he'd lecture endlessly and emphasize his points by making slow karate gestures with his hands. His oversincerity came off as totally insincere. The memory of him in his short shorts and knee-high socks from freshman year also made it impossible for me to take much of what he said seriously. He reminded me of the overzealous principal in the *The Breakfast Club*—whenever I said something sarcastic to him (sometimes I just couldn't resist), I expected him to point at me with his index and pinky fingers and dramatically say, "Don't mess with the bull, young man—you'll get the horns."

"I need your yearbook," Pepperman told me once we were out by the lockers.

"Why?" I asked.

"You know why, Sean."

I handed him the yearbook. He put it under his arm. Then he took out a clipboard and crossed my name off a list.

"Am I going to get it back?" I asked.

"We don't know," he said. "We're either going to have to reprint the entire yearbook, or tear out the page with the bomb and refund the advertisers."

"So, that copy is like a souvenir," I said. "It might be worth something, like an old baseball card."

Pepperman looked up from his clipboard. "It's not funny, Sean."

"Okay."

"It's not funny at all. You know what happened in Oklahoma City, don't you?"

"Ah, yeah."

"That's why it's not funny. Did you know anything about this?"

"Yeah," I said.

"Did you help pay for the ad?"

"No."

"Jonas isn't in school today. Do you know where he is?"

"I have no idea."

Our eyes locked. Pepperman's gaze was intense, even through his oversize eyeglasses. He was trying to tell whether or not I was lying, which I wasn't. The moment was severe and awkward and one of the reasons my feelings about Pepperman were mixed. He could be excessively pleasant, but I had also seen him on more than one occasion really lose his temper with the boys in gym class—to the point where I thought he might actually slug them.

In this case, he seemed calm, and after seeing that I probably wasn't lying, he finally said, "Okay, Sean, go back to class."

I walked back into the classroom with Pepperman following behind me. "Girls," he said over my shoulder, "I'm sorry, but I need your yearbooks back." The two girls immediately stood up and handed them over.

I sat back in my desk and took out Kerouac's *On the Road*.

The Channel 7 news van was in front of the high school the next day. A brunette reporter whose face was painted heavily with makeup was surrounded by a mob of students. She was holding a microphone up to the face of Edgar Johnson, one of Jonas's friends who had helped pay for the ad. The interview was being filmed by a man holding a television camera with a large, glaring light attached to it. I was drawn to the scene by some sort of instinct, but by the time I walked over, the cameraman had switched off the light and lowered the camera. The reporter lowered her microphone. She looked at Edgar and said, "Okay, thank you."

Mr. Stone, our new principal, came out of the school from a side door. Stone seemed agreeable, but I hadn't had much interaction with him since Pepperman was put in charge of discipline.

He walked up to the reporter and said, "I need you off the school grounds."

The woman just looked at him.

"*Okay?*" he said, pointing to the street. "Anything past that curb is school property."

The reporter looked to where he was pointing and said, "Yeah." She and the cameraman packed up their equipment and climbed into their van. The cameraman drove right up to the curb Stone had just pointed to and parked. Mr. Stone shook his head and told us all to get inside.

I turned to Edgar and said, "So what happened?"

Edgar slung his backpack over his shoulder and said, "I just told her that I helped pay for the ad and that I didn't think we did anything wrong."

"Is Jonas here?"

"No. I think he's suspended. He might actually get expelled."

"Shit."

"It's stupid," Edgar said, adjusting his glasses. "No one would care if Oklahoma City hadn't happened."

As we walked, a slew of other kids ran up to Edgar and started asking him questions. I said, "See ya" over the din and walked away. He didn't hear me and went on talking to some girl about his television interview. I had only hung out with Edgar a handful of times with Jonas. He was a nondescript, intelligent kid whom no one paid much attention to...until everyone saw him talking to a television reporter.

The news van stayed parked in the same spot all day. During lunch, a few guys went up to the large windows of the cafeteria and pressed their buttocks against the glass. A few other students flipped it the bird. Unfortunately, the windows of the news van were blacked out, so no one could see a reaction.

My last period class was Home Ec. Like most seniors, I had taken it just to fill credit requirements before graduation. The class was easy, but I got C's. Fraser and I decided it would be funny to make everything we cooked blue. We used food coloring in every conceivable recipe: blue muffins, blue cake, blue chicken tetrazzini. Although everything we made tasted just fine, the teacher gave us low grades because of our "inability to follow instruction."

As class was winding down, a bunch of us took seats on the long radiator near the windows. We chatted and looked out at the news van, still parked where it had been since morning, its blackened windows still rolled up.

"How long are they going to sit there?" Fraser asked.

I said, "They're probably waiting for school to end so they can nab people on the way out."

I turned toward the window and waved dramatically. To my surprise, the tinted window on the van slowly rolled halfway down. The reporter, sitting in the passenger's seat, motioned with her finger for me to come out. She was wearing large, dark sunglasses, and the way she motioned in a "come hither" sort of way came off as a bit sexual. The other boys in the class let out a collective "Ooooooh!" The teacher, Mrs. Faucher, looked up from her desk.

"What's going on?" she asked.

Before I could answer, a kid named Todd said, "That news reporter wants to talk to Gorman."

"Don't do it, Sean," Mrs. Faucher said.

I turned back toward the window and pointed at my chest: *Me?*

The reporter nodded slowly. The class "Ooooooh!"ed again.

"Don't do it, Sean," Faucher repeated.

I walked to the door and said, "I'll be right back."

The class started laughing. Faucher just shook her head and went back to grading papers. Everyone was ready for summer.

I walked through the double doors of the school and onto the grass that separated South Street from the "school property" Mr. Stone had outlined earlier. As I approached the van, the reporter rolled down the rest of her darkened window.

"Hello," she said from behind her sunglasses.

I said, "Hey" and slung my elbow over the open window.

"What's your name?"

"Sean."

"And Sean, do you know Jonas?"

"I do."

"And did you know anything about him putting the bomb in the yearbook?"

"I did."

"Did you help pay for it?"

"I did not."

"And do you know where Jonas is today?"

"At his house?"

"He's not. We checked there this morning."

"Then I have no idea."

"I see."

The two of us stared at each other, but all I could see was the reflection of myself in her sunglasses. The cameraman in the driver's seat just stared gloomily through the windshield, looking like he might want a sandwich.

Finally I said, "You really think this is a news story?"

"Of course."

The reporter pointed to the Home Ec room and said, "Is there anyone in there who knows where Jonas is?"

I looked back and said, "I don't think so."

"Thank you," the woman said. "Nice meeting you."

I said, "Okay" as I moved my elbow. The reporter stared at me until the window was rolled up and she disappeared behind the black. I turned and walked back to the school. Everyone inside was staring at me like excited dogs waiting for food.

"What happened?" Fraser asked me.

"Nothing," I said. "She's an idiot."

"Told you not to, Sean," Mrs. Faucher said without looking up from her papers.

I told her I was sorry.

Without looking at me, she just raised her eyebrows and pursed her lips.

Like everyone in Medfield, my mother and I tuned in to Channel 7 after dinner that night. I saw myself. Unbeknownst to me, the cameraman had snuck a quick, panning shot of me while Edgar was being interviewed. The reporter's voice came into my living room in the form of a voiceover: "Seniors at Medfield High graduate next week, but their yearbook signing session is going to have to wait." Then she explained how a group of seniors paid for the ad back in November. Then they showed a dramatic picture of the blown-out federal building in Oklahoma. The voice became solemn. She said, "It's a painful reminder of the deadly April 19th bombing in Oklahoma City that killed one hundred and sixty-seven people."

I started laughing, as did my mother.

"You've got to be kidding me," my mom said.

They showed a brief clip of Edgar saying, "I'm not sorry about it. I still don't think that we did anything wrong." Underneath his face, the caption read: *Edgar Goodman. Paid for Ad.* They showed a clip of Vicky Scaramuzzo—a friend of mine who lived up the street—saying, "We should just rip out the page and get the yearbooks. Everyone just wants their yearbook. They don't care what's in it." The voiceover then went through some of the school's options: "The school could send the books back for reprinting, remove or black out the offending ad, or reissue the yearbook as is. There are tricky legal issues that school administrators say are best handled by lawyers."

The story ended.

For whatever reason, there was no mention of Jonas.

An interview with Bruce Willis was coming up next.

I didn't see Jonas for a while, in school or otherwise. The *Boston Herald* ran a story about the prank with a small picture of Jonas looking more intense than he really was. Small town gossip was raging. Jonas received a week's suspension. I heard lawyers were involved. I heard Mr. Hersch was in trouble. I heard that MIT was thinking about revoking Jonas's acceptance. Some of the rumors were true. Some were not.

Eventually Jonas came back to school. The first thing he did when he came up to me and my friends at our lockers was say, "I can't talk about it, so don't even ask." It was the most emotion I had ever seen come out of him. We all nodded solemnly and went back to getting books from our lockers.

And we never spoke of it again.

In the last few days, the school decided to give our yearbooks back with the bomb schematics torn out, just as Vicky had suggested on the news. The other advertisers on the page were refunded.

Yearbooks were signed.

Long hugs were given.

White and blue caps were thrown into the air.

I came back to my dorm room after poetry class and unlocked the large black trunk I had taken with me from home. I took out the photo albums and the pages of writing from high school that I sometimes handed into my college workshops when I was either too lazy or too overloaded with reading to do the real assignment. Underneath was my yearbook.

The book always opened itself to the back, where Jonas's bomb page had been torn out. Page 162 was followed by page 165. I ran my fingers along the torn page and noticed something I had never seen before, or had at least forgotten. On page 162, there was a "Best Wishes" note from the assistant superintendent. Below it was a poem called "Stepping Forth" by a girl in our class, Courtney Johnson. Although our class was small, Courtney was someone I had only an awareness of. I knew she was into art and drama and I knew her group of friends. I definitely didn't know she wrote poetry, but it didn't surprise me. It seemed like clandestine poetry writing was something almost all teenagers engaged in from time to time. I read her words:

STEPPING FORTH

Climbing another step
I cannot help but look back
down the hallway
behind me
To the first day
we stepped into the school as freshmen
afraid to let go of each other's hands
and venture forth
into the crowd
But today
we are the seniors
making and leaving memories behind
our final year of familiarity
of noisy hallways littered with
streamers and candy wrappers

of cheers at basketball games
of friendships that grew
stronger this year
of the streams of blue and white
taking silent steps across the stage.
And tomorrow
we step alone into the path of life
releasing each other's hands
but never forgetting the security
they held.

The poem was shit. I imagined Courtney's poem being work-shopped in one of my classes and cringed for her.

But it affected me. I suddenly remembered the way I had felt when I first opened the yearbook in Mr. Bishop's class. No matter where I went in the world, in some way, the people I grew up with would always come with me. Unlike the student poems I was reading in college, Courtney's poem was unadulterated by technique. Though trite and sentimental, it was heartfelt and honest, written in the language only a teenager can write in. In that sense, her poem was the realest shit.

I flipped to the page with Jonas's photo. He looked dignified—staring off camera into some imaginary horizon. I read his bio, which I hadn't done since high school, but when I did I was taken aback all over again. Jonas quoted Psalm 23:1: "The Lord is my shepherd, I shall not want". My surprise came from the fact that Jonas had never once discussed being a Christian. Never, in the years hanging out at this house, or the long hours at Papa

Gino's, had Jonas ever once said anything about Jesus, God, or the Bible. As far as I knew, he never attended church. Looking at the quote again, I remembered discussing Jonas's Bible quote and Fraser saying, "Yeah, what's up with that God shit?"

I wasn't surprised, however, to see that one of Jonas's other quotes was "Question Authority." This made me smile. He also wrote: "hacking is 'bad.'" Looking back at our yearbook, I could see that Jonas and I had always had different philosophical vehicles, but our engines always ran on the same basic fuel.

I was put to mind of a boring late night early on in high school near Fraser's house when Jonas and a group of our friends were hanging out at the playground behind the Dale Street School. We were sitting on the swings, staring at our feet, when for some reason we got on the subject of the Greek and Roman empires. After a few minutes of historical talk, we all wondered what might become of America. Fraser remarked that the only reason the U.S. hadn't been attacked since Pearl Harbor was because we had the most nuclear weapons. Everyone agreed. Another one of our friends said that there was no way any country could ever take the United States in a fight. Jonas, the only one of us standing, was leaning against the swing set with his arms folded. He said, "America is just another empire. Eventually, it'll fall."

I thought about Jonas one last time. I wondered what became of him and I also wondered what he and I had been. While I may have *thought* about shooting up the high school, I was never going to do it. While Jonas may have *thought* about blowing up the high school, he was never going to do it. They were dark thoughts, but they were just that—thoughts. Jonas and I were nothing more than two high school misfits trying to navigate ourselves through the vast Nowhereland of twentieth-century America. We were neither Harris nor Klebold. We might have been odd and just a little touched, but no one was going to die by our hands. I looked at the yearbook once more before I locked it away again. One more thing Jonas had written put a grin on my face. It was a Robert Steele quote.

"Education in America is nonexistent."

A Joke

MCMXCIX

Beware all enterprises that require new clothes.

—HENRY DAVID THOREAU, *WALDEN*

*A serious and good philosophical work could be
written consisting entirely of jokes.*

—LUDWIG WITTGENSTEIN

"YOU'LL HAVE TO wear a tie now that you're a supervisor."

"Really?"

Grayson looked at me and sarcastically said. "Sean, you haven't noticed that all the other supervisors are wearing ties?"

"I have," I said. "I just didn't know it was a thing. I mean, isn't *The Phoenix* supposed to be this cool, hip place?"

Grayson smirked, reached for his mouse, and looked at his computer screen. "Not down here, it's not."

"Yeah, I've definitely noticed that."

Grayson looked back toward me. "So is that a problem, or not?"

"It might be," I said.

"How so?"

I said, "I don't own any neckties. I find it pretty ironic that I work in a place where I have to wear a tie, but I can't afford to buy one."

Grayson looked at me incredulously. "Sean," he said, "you can get a necktie at Marshalls for, like, seven dollars. Would you like me to come with you and help you pick one out?"

I said, "No, thank you. I'll figure it out."

I was sitting across the desk from my philosophical antagonist, my sworn enemy, and my occupational archnemesis. I hated my boss, Grayson, more than I had ever hated anyone in my entire life. And it wasn't just because he was my superior. In fact, I had had great relationships with every boss I had ever worked for all throughout my high school and college years.

I hated Grayson because he was a fucking asshole.

My first job out of college was at an alternative newspaper called *The Boston Phoenix*, but I quickly found out that *alternative newspaper* was a misnomer. Because it listed live dates for local bands and show times for art house cinemas, nearly everyone I knew in Boston just assumed that *The Phoenix* was a small, independent newspaper. But in reality it was part of a larger corporation called the Phoenix Media Communications Group.

Working at *The Phoenix* was my first venture into office life in the corporate world. A career in journalism seemed like a logical path for someone with a degree in writing, and although I wasn't thrilled about my new surroundings, I was willing to pay my dues. *The Phoenix* initially hired me at a rate just above minimum wage, and I survived mainly on Top Ramen noodles and whatever cheap vegetables I could get from the produce vendors in Haymarket Square.

A friend from Emerson, Krista, had suggested that I apply at *The Phoenix*. She worked there part-time while still in school. This was my "safety" job. I knew I would probably be hired, so I saved it for last. I applied for entry-level jobs all over Boston and was universally rejected. Not long into my first-ever real world job search, I discovered two things: One, a college degree meant nothing, especially in Boston. And two, the booming economy of the late '90s meant that there were lots of jobs, but that lots of qualified people were applying for those jobs.

For the first time in my life, I had rent, and bills, and debt. After moving into a drafty apartment with four weeks of no income, I finally gave up and went to *The Phoenix* for an interview. I was immediately hired. I was given an ad-taker position in the personals department, which was where divorcées and alcoholics tried to find romance before Internet dating existed. My days were spent tethered to a cubicle by a headset, taking phone calls from forty-something women trashing their ex-husbands, and forty-something men telling me how much they hated their ex-wives.

Grayson promoted me to supervisor just as I was ready to quit. Apparently, right before I was hired, a supervisor named Brad had had to take a leave of absence after getting run over by a garbage truck while he was on his bicycle. His foot had practically been severed, but the doctors were able to reattach it. He wouldn't be back for a while.

Being made a supervisor meant that I would be working more closely with Grayson, which made my skin crawl. Though not my only boss, from just the limited interactions I had had with him as an ad-taker, I knew we weren't going to get along. Grayson was a thirty-something urbanite who had worked at *The Phoenix* for most of his adult life. Years of office work had given him the posture of a seahorse. His dark hair was receding, but he kept what he had left styled in short spikes. He had buckteeth that protruded from a downturned mouth. Whenever he ate a tuna fish sandwich, globs of mayonnaise collected at the corners.

Grayson was gay. Unlike some of the younger gay people in the office, he wasn't flamboyant, but he wore a lot of pastels and spoke in a moderately effeminate tone, depending on who was around. If he was speaking with his superiors, he turned it down. If he was speaking with his subordinates, he turned it up. Rather than a yuppie, Grayson referred to himself as a "guppie."

During the workday, Grayson was constantly coming out of his office and scolding everyone for surfing the web. "I see a lot of you on the Internet," he'd call out with his hands on his hips. Everyone would groan and close out LiveJournal or Napster. When I went into his office just minutes later, Grayson would quickly grab his mouse and close out whatever gay porn site was on his screen. Grayson looked at porn so much during work it became a joke around the office: "Make sure you knock on Grayson's door before you go in...even if it's open."

Grayson ogled the young men we worked with. As soon as some editor or intern walked out of his office, Grayson would turn to me and say, "His chest is so gorgeous," to which I would reply, "Okay." I didn't mind it, but just to try him, I began doing the same with women, which Grayson found disgusting. He'd then give me a lecture about professionalism. "Straight men are just so typical," he'd say. "You're all the same."

Someone like Grayson, and the office environment he thrived in, was completely foreign to me. Prior to working at *The Phoenix*, I had done nothing but manual labor. His sexuality aside, if anyone at my previous jobs had ever been as demeaning or condescending as Grayson, they would have been served a swift ass-kicking. Sometimes, while sitting at my desk, I recalled the no-nonsense guys I had worked with at the DPW back home and smiled at the idea of Grayson getting his nose bloodied for making some snide remark. In the world I came from, Grayson would have been dead in the water, which made it extremely difficult for me to take his shit.

The only person who had the free rein to *not* take Grayson's shit was Pat, the janitor. Pat was almost fifty years old, but had the body of someone half his age. His broad chest bulked out from beneath his Pink Floyd T-shirts and his thick arms were curled with muscles. He wore blue-tinted eyeglasses and kept his black Italian hair slicked straight back. He was from Winthrop and spoke with the legitimate Boston accent that seemed to be going extinct in the actual city of Boston.

When Pat came in to vacuum the office, he practically kicked down the door. He had no regard for office employees, and would slam the vacuum against their cubicles, making whoever was on the phone cover their open ear and start yelling into the receiver. No one ever said a word in protest. My favorite Pat move was when he came into Grayson's office to vacuum when Grayson was on the phone. Pat would grab Grayson by the back of his chair and wheel him away from his desk, like Grayson was some inanimate object. Then he would vacuum the small area where Grayson's feet had been, and shove him back into position. Grayson would hurriedly grab the base of his phone so it didn't fall off his desk. Pat always did this with a wink and a smile in my direction.

I hung out with Pat sometimes during breaks. I usually found him standing on the sidewalk of Brookline Avenue, leaning against the building with one foot against the brick wall. He would stand confidently with his arms folded, watching traffic go by. We talked a lot about pro wrestling. I would tell Pat about what was currently going on, and he would tell me about what had gone on in the '70s. One day, he turned to me as I was walking by.

"Hey, kid," he said to me, stroking his face. "I see you shaved off that goatee."

"Yeah," I said. "I've had it for, like, five years. Time for a change."

"Yeah," Pat said. "You know, when you're all clean-shaven like that…you look like a fuckin' pussy."

I laughed, and he laughed too. "You know what I mean?" he said. Pat then gave my skinny frame a once-over and said, "Kid, you gotta work out."

"I do sit-ups and push-ups," I said. "I'm telling you, I don't gain weight."

"Get a weight bench, kid." Pat flexed his bicep and said, "That's all I do. You can do everything with dumbbells and a bench. Don't listen to all those pussies at gyms. All those Nautilus machines are bullshit. Get some weights and a bench and fuckin' eat—you'll gain weight."

"I don't know," I said. "I like having definition, but I don't really want to gain weight."

Pat looked at me through his darkened glasses and said, "That's because you're a fuckin' pussy, kid."

He laughed, and I laughed too, and he said, "You know what I mean?"

Pat and I never hung out outside of work. Aside from being more than twice my age, he didn't drink, which, besides writing, was pretty much all I did in my spare time. I enjoyed the camaraderie I had with Pat, but our conversations were limited to classic rock, pro wrestling, and ball-breaking.

My closest friend at *The Phoenix* was Patrick. Patrick and I had practically nothing in common. I was from the country and he was from the city. I liked Metallica and he liked Madonna. I liked women and he liked men.

Although I had gone to a college with a notably large number of gay students, I had never really become friends with any of them. Most of them were theater majors, which put us in two very different campus worlds, both literally and figuratively. Not only were the drama classes on the very opposite side of campus from the writing classes, but I knew nothing about show tunes or acting or Hollywood glamour. And the theater kids certainly didn't know anything about pro wrestling, heavy metal, or Jack Daniel's. The gay guys at Emerson more or less stayed in their own environment, hanging out only with other gay guys, or the straight girls in the theater department, whom everyone (including the gay guys) referred to as "fag hags." In the first few weeks of college, it became very clear to me that all the drama kids who had felt totally ostracized in their small town high schools had come to Emerson and found Shangri-La. And after finding it, they found very little reason to leave it. I had always felt a little disappointed about the social politics of Emerson. I may not have had the same interests as the theater kids, but since I had always felt like an outcast and a minority in my own right, I felt that the gay guys and I must have had at least one thing in common.

I turned out to be right. Feeling ostracized in high school was something Patrick and I did have in common. It was during discussions about this facet of our lives that he and I really bonded, over after-work drinks. While I had been alone in my bedroom listening to Slayer because most of the girls didn't like me, Patrick had been alone in his bedroom listening to Kylie Minogue because *none* of the boys liked him.

Patrick was short and had bunny cheeks that all the girls in the office adored. He was bald at twenty-three, but this didn't seem to bother him, and he wore it well by keeping the sides neat and short. He was sarcastic and soft-spoken. We both thought *The Phoenix* was ridiculous, but stayed there because we had to— me, because I had an apartment and utilities; Patrick, because he was working his way through school. We drank after work at a bar right next door to *The Phoenix* called Boston Billiards. It was a chic pool hall with dim, fancy lights and billiard tables adorned with red felt. Patrick drank cocktails. I drank beer.

Because Patrick was my first gay friend, I had to get all my preliminary questions about homosexuality out of the way, which he graciously answered, always with a laugh and a smile.

"So how did you know you were gay?"

"How did you know you were straight?"

I narrowed my eyes and nodded. "Good point," I said. "Good point."

"You're so funny, Sean."

"Did you ever date a girl?"

Patrick pursed his lips and stared at the ceiling. "Not really, no."

"Okay, have you ever messed around with a girl?"

"That's the question you really wanted to ask, isn't it?"

"Not really," I said. "Kind of, I guess."

Patrick chuckled and said, "Yes, Sean, I've messed around with a girl."

"Who was it?"

"A friend."

"And what did you do?"

"We made out."

"Did you feel her up?"

Patrick rolled his eyes and sipped from his straw. "*Yes*, Sean, I felt her up."

"And you didn't like it?"

"It was okay."

"How do you feel about boobs?"

Patrick said, "I mean, they're, like, whatever."

"You don't like them?"

Patrick held up his hands and pantomimed as if he were awkwardly fluffing two pillows. He said, "I don't know. They're just, like, whatever. They're boobs."

"Boobs are awesome," I said.

Patrick sipped from his straw. "Yes, Sean, I know."

"And you like how a penis looks?"

"I call it a cock."

I grabbed my beer. "Right, okay."

Patrick smiled and said, "Oh, yeah. I like how a cock looks."

"Really?"

"Yup."

"That's interesting," I said, taking a sip from my pint.

"Why?" Patrick asked. "What do you see when you see a cock?"

I thought about it for a moment. "A mailbox."

Patrick laughed. "A *what*?"

I leaned into the table to make my point. "I don't know," I said. "I mean, obviously I've seen a lot of penises in porn."

"*Right.*"

"And to me, they're just like this utilitarian thing. I mean, I understand they have to be there in order for the porn to happen, but I'm not really paying that much attention to them, other than to recognize that they're serving a purpose, sort of like a mailbox."

"Well, now you know how I feel about tits," Patrick said.

I sipped my beer. "I see what you mean."

Patrick looked at me mischievously and said, "So have you ever watched gay porn?"

"I'm not gay."

Patrick smiled. "I didn't say you were."

After a few moments, I finally looked up at the ceiling and said, "Yes, I've seen gay porn."

"*Really?*" Patrick exclaimed. "Well...?"

"Okay," I said, "here's what happened."

Patrick sipped his drink and said, "Do tell."

I told Patrick about how after turning eighteen, my buddies and I would go to a porn shop in Dedham, just outside of Boston. Our trips to the porn shop were random; we went out of boredom, or if one of us was in need of something new. Even after going for several times and being totally familiar with the place, I never got comfortable walking through the blacked-out doors. Perusing rows of glossy, oversize VHS covers featuring nothing but flesh and penetration made me feel sleazy. And although the other patrons looked as normal as any regular guy on the street, it always felt awkward never making eye-contact with them, or engaging in small talk just to break the deafening silence of the place. I had been to public libraries with more ambient chatter.

"So anyway," I told Patrick, "this one buddy of mine went a little more regularly than the rest of us. So he had this, like, frequent-shopper card. It had numbers on it and they would punch a hole in it like a ticket stub whenever he bought a movie. If he bought, like, five movies, he would get the next one free."

Patrick said, "Okay."

"So one night we went in and it was time for his free movie, so he got a gay porn."

"Really?" Patrick said.

"I don't know," I said. "He came up to us in the store and said, 'I'm going to get this.' My other buddy and I were like, 'Umm, *okay*. Why?' He said, 'I don't know. Just for a joke.'"

"Riiiight," Patrick said.

"Listen," I said, "I'm pretty sure the dude wasn't gay."

Patrick sipped from his straw and shrugged his shoulders. "Okay," he said.

"He's not," I insisted.

"He just buys gay porn."

"But he didn't actually buy it."

Patrick said, "Right, I know. He got it 'for free.'" When he said, "for free," he made air-quotes with his fingers.

"ANYWAY," I said, "he got this gay porn."

"Right. And you watched it."

"Yeah," I said. "We went back to his place and he put it on."

Patrick burst out laughing. "Are you serious? How many of you were there?"

I clutched my pint and said, "Listen, he only put it on for a minute."

Patrick's cheeks were shiny red with laughter. "Right," he said. "Okay. A bunch of straight dudes just sittin' around, watchin' gay porn."

"I'm telling you…"

"How many of you were there?"

"Four."

Patrick, through a fit of laughter, said, "Yeah, I don't even think my gay friends and I have done that."

I shrugged with one shoulder and said, "What can I tell ya? I guess we just had some curiosity to see what it was like, but this was before the Internet, so we couldn't just turn on a computer and click on a website."

Patrick conceded this point, composed himself, and said, "Okay, so what was this movie about?"

I thought about it for a second and said, "I'm pretty sure it didn't have a plot. I think it was just a collection of scenes."

"So what did you see?"

I laughed and said, "I remember the first scene was these two, like, gay cowboys. It was funny because they looked nothing like cowboys. Like, they were all shaved down and their hair was perfectly styled."

"Sounds about right for gay porn," Patrick said.

"Anyway, they were in a barn and they fucked on this bale of hay."

Patrick laughed and said, "Yup. No plot needed. We like to just get right down to it."

"Well," I said, "that's where I envy you. I wish women were like that."

"So what did you think?" Patrick asked, looking mischievous again.

"Honestly," I said, "it definitely confirmed I'm not gay. We turned it off after a few minutes."

"I'll bet your friend watched it later," Patrick said.

I chuckled, took a sip of my beer, and said, "Who knows? I doubt it, though."

"Did it gross you out?"

I thought about it. "Kind of. Not really, I guess." I said, "You know what's weird though? I didn't have a problem with the actual sex, but before that, when they were kissing? That's when I had to look away."

Patrick looked at me curiously and said, "Really? Why do you think that is?"

I stared off in thought. "I don't know," I said. "I mean, fucking is sort of an animalistic act. To me, it was like watching two lions do it on the Discovery Channel. Like, it didn't turn me on, but it made sense. I guess kissing is more intimate, which was why I turned away. I think that's why I say it sort of confirmed I'm not gay."

Patrick nodded. "Yeah, that makes sense."

"So that's my story with the gay porn," I said.

Patrick's smile came back. He said, "Oh, I think there's still hope for you, Sean."

Spending more time with Patrick and Grayson had made me aware that gay guys converting straight guys was considered a badge of honor and, I was pretty sure, a major turn on. I didn't quite understand it, but I likened it to the infatuation that some straight guys had with taking a girl's virginity. Being Patrick's friend did away with any preconceived notions I may have had about gay people and straight people being different. Patrick, who was in the midst of a breakup, argued with his boyfriend in the same way and for the same reasons I had fought with all my ex-girlfriends. In the office, I could often hear him on the phone with his boyfriend speaking in hushed, angry tones. A few times, he stood up from his desk, wiping tears from his eyes. I said nothing as he made his way past me toward the bathroom. I felt bad. I wanted to console him, but my masculinity wouldn't allow it.

Patrick was my friend, but comforting a crying adult man was something I was totally incapable of.

Patrick went to Grayson when he was upset. Although he fully recognized that Grayson could be an ass, he didn't outright despise him as much as I did. Whenever I complained about some underhanded thing Grayson had done, Patrick would just shake his head and say, "Oh, Grayson." One time after work, I was ranting about the way Grayson brownnosed his superiors, but talked down to his subordinates.

"Doesn't that drive you nuts?" I asked Patrick.

Patrick conceded that Grayson did in fact do that, but just held out his hands and said, "He is who he is."

I said, "Who he is is an asshole."

Patrick laughed and said, "Oh, Sean."

One day, while Patrick and I were sitting in Grayson's office, Grayson offhandedly said, "Do you guys want to grab a drink after work tonight?"

Patrick and I looked at each other. Grayson looked at us.

"Sure," Patrick said. "I'm not doing anything."

Grayson looked at me and waited for my answer.

"Sure," I finally said. "I have no plans."

"Great," Grayson said. "I just need to destress tonight."

"Wait a second," I said. "We're not going to a gay bar, are we?"

Grayson and Patrick smiled at each other. "Would that make you uncomfortable, Sean?" Grayson said to me.

"It might," I said. "I mean, I don't want to be put in an awkward position where I have to explain to some dude that I'm not gay."

Grayson said, "Well, what would you do if a woman was hitting on you and you weren't interested?"

I thought about it and said, "I'm not sure that's ever happened. I mean, women don't generally pursue guys at bars."

Patrick said, "Oh, I definitely have some girlfriends who pursue guys at bars."

"Me too," Grayson said.

I said, "Well, why don't you bring them along tonight?"

Grayson and Patrick laughed. Grayson said, "Sean, trust me, none of my straight girlfriends would be interested in someone like you."

I shot Grayson an angry look and said, "Oh, yeah?" It was the look I might give someone I was moments away from punching.

Grayson held up his hands and said, "I'm sorry. I'm sorry. I'm just kidding." He smiled with thin sincerity.

"Yeah."

Patrick said, "Oh, this should be a fun night."

I withdrew my stare and said, "Definitely."

"Okay," Grayson said. "We don't have to go to a gay bar. I don't *just* go to gay bars, you know."

"Whatever," I said. "It doesn't really matter."

"But," Grayson said, "I'm not going to any of the dives that you hang out in."

I looked at Grayson and said, "Oh, trust me Grayson, you wouldn't last a minute in those dives."

Patrick laughed again and said, "Oh, this should be a fun night—can't wait to just sit back and watch the show."

Grayson shook his head and said, "Sean and I will be fine. I know how to handle him. He's just like my brother."

"How so?" I asked.

"Typical straight man."

I said, "Right."

I left Grayson's office wondering why I had agreed to go out with him after work. I had no interest in being around him any more than I had to. I figured adding alcohol to the mix would yield either some positive results, or some incredibly bad ones. On the one hand, Patrick was right—it might turn into a disaster. On the other hand, I wondered whether Grayson and I just relaxing socially could ease some of the tension between us. I thought that Grayson and I seeing each other as people, rather than coworkers, might lead us to some sort of peace. I didn't know what Grayson's intentions were, but I was much more interested in a good rapport than a bad one. Grayson and Patrick occasionally hung out after work, and I thought that maybe by doing so, I might also get closer to Patrick's easygoing attitude about him: "He is who he is."

The three of us left together right after work. I took off my tie as soon as we walked out the door. Patrick and Grayson did the same. It was mid-summer and there was a Red Sox game at Fenway Park. Working one block from Fenway was the bane of my existence. Patrick, Grayson, and I made our way through the hordes of fans like salmon swimming upstream. All of Kenmore Square reeked of beer, sweat, and grilling sausage. None of us spoke during our march through the horde. We just weaved and shoved our way through the baseball-capped humanity, side-stepping the drunks and the scalpers who barked in our faces: "Tickets!? Tickets, guys!? Tickets!?" Once we made it to the subway station, the three of us wiped sweat from our foreheads and groaned.

"God, I can't stand baseball season," Grayson said.

"It's the worst," I agreed.

I was feeling comfortable. Not liking sports and being annoyed by sports fans was at least one thing Grayson and I had in common. As we sat on the subway, unbuttoning the top buttons of our dress shirts, I looked around at the people my age who were either on their way home from work, or going to a summer night class at some local college. Some listened to music with giant headphones. Others read books with one hand while holding a metal pole with the other. Everyone was in their own world, swaying to the rhythm of the subway car and pulsing with the beat of the city.

Looking at them made me wish I were not in dress clothes. I wanted to be wearing the jeans, sneakers, and T-shirts they had on—the clothes I had always worn before working at *The Phoenix*. I also wanted to be back in school. Much as I had derided academic life, I was starting to miss it. I wanted to be learning, and reading, and hanging out with like-minded people. If Boston was a living thing, college students were the blood that kept it alive. The entire city thrived on academia, and for the first time since leaving college, I felt like I was no longer a part of its heartbeat.

I wondered whether the college kids on the subway looked at me as just another corporate fuckhead. It was probably how I would have looked at myself only a year before. I was uncomfortable with what I saw reflecting back at me in the dark window of the subway car. I hated the way I had to look. I hated my khakis. I hated my blue dress shirt. And I hated the necktie I had just cast off. Nothing about the clothes I wore reflected who I really was.

Though completely ill at ease with my appearance, I was happy with my environment. I had wanted to live in a city for as long as I could remember. Medfield had been nicknamed "Deadfield" for as long as I could remember. As a teenager, there was nothing to do, except loiter in the center of town and complain that there was nothing to do. There was no mall, no movie theater, and no arcade—all teenage hangouts my friends and I could clearly see in movies like *Sixteen Candles* and *Fast Times at Ridgemont High*.

And there was no culture except straight, white culture. Minorities and gay people were just characters in movies, or on TV. We knew they existed, but they weren't quite real. Although Medfield was ethnically devoid of anything but whiteness, very few kids I knew were legitimately racist. Even Whitey—our friend who had briefly become a Nazi skinhead—was just a temporary racist who went through a naïve teenage phase. Beyond that, the only time anything vaguely racist or homophobic was ever uttered was on the days when my friends would shoplift a series of small paperbacks from the local bookstore called *Truly Tasteless Jokes*.

The little books came in brightly colored volumes and could easily fit into your back pocket (which was why they were a preferred item for shoplifting). The author's name was Blanche Knott, which, even as a teenager, I thought was probably a pseudonym for someone who didn't want to be known. The chapters in each book were divided by topic: Polish, Jewish, Black, Handicapped, etc. My friends would steal the latest volume and we would sit on the steps of the public library, reading off the most terrible jokes in each category, rolling with orgastic laughter after each punchline.

"Why are Polish mothers so strong? From raising dumbbells."

"What's the difference between a Jewish girl and taxes? Taxes suck."

"Why did Helen Keller marry a black man? It was easy to read his lips."

"How do you find a blind man in a nudist colony? It's not hard."

No minority or majority was ever spared. If the person reading the jokes from the library steps touched upon a subject that applied to one us (usually Polish, Puerto Rican, or Catholic), the target of the joke would laugh as hard as everyone else and wait for the next one. Offense was never given or received. If anything, the offensive humor we batted around brought us closer: while people's ethnic quirks may have been different, the fact that we all had them made us alike. And when we broke each other's balls, nothing personal was ever off-limits—drunk parents, derelict siblings, white trash tendencies. Once an open wound became a scar, it became an anecdote or a punchline.

We'd pass around the *Truly Tasteless* books for an hour or so uptown before going back to drinking sodas, talking about girls, and toughening up our tanned emotional hides. Even though I never personally shoplifted the books, I would always wind up taking them home at the end of the afternoon since my friends knew I liked to read. In my bedroom, I only read the *Truly Tasteless* joke books only if I was truly bored. For the most part, they remained stashed underneath my bed alongside old copies of *Hustler* and *Penthouse*.

My friends and I might have told racist jokes from time to time, but it was never out of malice. In truth, we only cracked racist jokes because we weren't *supposed to* crack racist jokes—because the world felt that racist jokes were "inappropriate" and, well, "fuck the world." We also cracked racist jokes because some of them were witty and just plain funny. At the end of the day, we were all part of a generation raised on MTV, where diversity was celebrated and being racist was seen as the most uncool thing imaginable. Homophobia was a little more prevalent in high school, but that just stemmed from testosterone-fueled boys having no clue as to how anyone could not love tits. But the third season of MTV's *The Real World* legitimately changed our adolescent perspective. The season in San Francisco featured Pedro, a very likable gay man who died of AIDS. He helped convince almost everyone I knew that gay people were as normal as normal could be and that AIDS was a really awful thing.

Still, though, no one at Medfield High ever came out of the closet during high school. It always happened afterwards at college. A girl I graduated with named Shannon came out shortly after we graduated, which was a surprise to everyone in our class, but only at first. As soon we all took five seconds to think about it, it made perfect sense. No one cared, and I was quite certain no one would have cared back in high school, either. I always felt bad that Shannon didn't come out of the closet sooner, but Medfield just wasn't the right environment. Even if she had come out in high school, it wouldn't have mattered. She still would have ended up at the prom with a platonic guy friend.

Patrick fanned himself with his hand and said, "God, it's so hot in here."

I looked at the beads of sweat on Patrick's shiny head. "You're sweating pretty bad."

"Thanks, Sean, I'm aware."

"No problem."

"Maybe I should start caring a handkerchief," he said. "Can you imagine?"

"Why don't you?" Grayson asked.

"Handkerchiefs are gross," Patrick said. "I mean, why do people walk around all day with a piece of cloth that's covered in boogers? It's like, 'You know they invented these disposable things called tissues, right?'"

"I carry a handkerchief," Grayson said.

I said, "Why does that *not* surprise me?"

"Why?" Grayson said. "Does that offend you?"

I said, "It doesn't offend me, but it's like Patrick said—just use a tissue."

Grayson said, "Sometimes there's not a tissue around."

"We work in an office," I said. "When is there *not* a tissue around?"

"Well, I'm not always at work."

I said, "Yeah but…actually, never mind."

Patrick, still fanning himself, said, "I only see older people use handkerchiefs. Maybe it's a generational thing." He leaned forward and looked over at Grayson. "No offense, Grayson."

Grayson gave us a look and said, "I'm not *that* much older than the two of you."

"You're in your thirties," I said.

Grayson said, "I know to you that probably seems like a lifetime away, but trust me, you'll wake up tomorrow and suddenly *you'll* be thirty. Time starts to go by really fast."

"Yeah, you're probably right. I definitely won't wake up tomorrow and be thirty and still be working at *The Phoenix*, though."

Grayson looked at me.

"No offense," I said.

Grayson said, "I like my job, Sean."

"To each his own."

"Sean," he said, "if you don't like it, then why don't you just quit?"

"Don't tempt me."

"You're free to leave anytime."

I said, "And you're free to fire me anytime."

"Oh," Grayson said, "I know. Believe me, I know."

The three of us laughed. I was feeling all right. Grayson was more relaxed outside of the office. He wasn't more likable exactly, but he was easier to talk to. I was looking forward to having a drink.

We got off the subway at Arlington Street, which was just down the street from my recent alma mater. As we walked up the stairs, I was nervous at the thought of running into my old professors, especially the ones who had invested so much time in me—the ones who would take me aside after class, point to something I wrote and say, "This is really wonderful. This is why you need to become a writer."

But I hadn't become a writer.

I had become an office drone for a corporation. Seeing any of my old professors and explaining what I was doing with my life would have made me want to crawl back underground to the subway. They had all encouraged me to go to graduate school at either Emerson or the University of Iowa, but aside from picking up the applications and looking at them, I never gave it another thought. After four years of college and sixteen years of school, I was done with classroom life. I was also done with incurring any more debt that I knew I couldn't afford.

But the doldrums of *The Phoenix* had made me want to go running back to the safe shelter of academia, no matter what the cost might be. Although I was now in real life, the question of what to do with that life was the thing that kept me up at night and the reason I was drinking like the next day would never come…

…Except it always did.

Patrick, Grayson, and I walked over to Newbury Street, to a restaurant that had an outdoor patio. Every seat was filled with after-work professionals, all wearing sunglasses. The inside was packed with guys drinking craft beer and eating large plates of nachos. They were waiting for the Red Sox game to start on the televisions behind the bar.

"What do you think?" I asked.

Patrick and Grayson had sour looks on their faces.

"We can go somewhere else," I said.

Grayson said, "I wouldn't mind sitting on the patio, but we'll never get a table out there." He looked at the room full of blatantly straight men and said, "I definitely don't want to stay in here."

"Maybe just one drink?" Patrick said.

Grayson gave a conciliatory nod and said, "Yeah, that's fine."

We pushed our way up to the bar and ordered our drinks. Grayson and Patrick both ordered mojitos from the attractive blonde. Not recognizing anything they had on tap, I looked at the bartender and said, "Can you just give me a pint of beer-flavored beer?" She smiled and said, "Sure," and served me a pint of something light and frothy.

Grayson held up his drink and said, "Well, cheers, guys."

We clinked our glasses together, trying not to knock elbows with the throngs of people around us. Patrick and I conversed, but we were practically yelling. Patrick kept fanning himself with his hand. Grayson was quiet. He just held his drink up against his chest, eyeballing the taller men around him with a look of disdain.

"I don't think Grayson wants to stay here," Patrick said with a smile.

"I don't," Grayson said.

I took a long pull from my beer and said, "That's fine. This is not my scene anyway."

Patrick and Grayson killed their mojitos with long sips from their straws. Grayson put his empty glass on the bar and said, "Good. Let's go." As we were walking out, two pretty girls who looked just a bit older than me gave me a quick glance and a smile as they walked by.

One they were out of earshot, I said, "Guys, those two girls just smiled at me."

Patrick and Grayson looked over at them. Grayson rolled his eyes and said, "Who cares, Sean? They look stupid."

"They do?"

"Look at how much makeup they're wearing."

I gave a quick glance and noticed that the two brunettes were, in fact, wearing a good deal of makeup.

"Okay," I said. "And?"

"Sean," Grayson said, "they're whores."

I was taken aback by Grayson's abrupt hostility. "They are?"

Grayson rolled his eyes again. He pushed the door open and said, "Sean, we're leaving."

Once we were out on the sidewalk, Grayson said, "Let's go to Club Café."

"You're a hell of a wingman, Grayson."

"Oh, I am *definitely* not here to be your wingman tonight, Sean."

"Clearly."

"One of them was wearing capri pants."

"Okay."

"They were stupid whores."

I said, "Wow. Well, all right then."

Patrick said, "Club Café sounds good."

"Is this a gay bar?"

Patrick and Grayson looked at each other and smiled.

I said, "All right, fine. Whatever. I just want to sit down and have a fucking drink."

"It'll be relaxed," Grayson said.

"Fuck it," I said.

We walked a few blocks over to Columbus Avenue. It was hot and I was annoyed, as always, by the Red Sox game making everything in the city difficult. By the time we got to Club Café, whatever trepidation I had about going to a gay bar was gone. I just wanted to sit down and have a cold beverage.

The inside of Club Café was exactly as I expected it to be—dark and chic. The bottles of top-shelf liquor behind the bar were backlit with pinkish lighting. At first glance, there wasn't really anything that indicated this was a gay bar. It looked like any other stylish restaurant in Boston. At second glance, however, I did notice that the guy-to-girl ratio was a little skewed in favor of the guys. At third glance, I noticed that the men were dressed a bit nicer than the guys scarfing down nachos at the place we had just left.

We got a table by the windows. The waiter came over and greeted us. He had a European accent I couldn't quite place and when he asked me what I wanted to drink, I again said that I wanted a beer-flavored beer.

"I'm sorry, sir," the man said. "Does that mean you would like an ale, or a lager, or a porter, or…?"

"He wants a Pabst Blue Ribbon," Grayson said.

"Oh, I'm sorry, sir, but we don't—"

I held up my hand and said, "I'll just have what they're having."

The waiter smiled and said, "Three mojitos it is."

"When in Rome," I said.

"So do you feel comfortable here?" Grayson asked. He seemed genuinely concerned.

I looked around and said, "I do, actually."

"Good," Grayson said.

"To be honest," I said, "I am almost a little offended that no one checked me out when we came in."

Patrick said, "Oh yeah?"

"That's because they know you're not gay, Sean," Grayson said.

"They do?"

Grayson said, "You might be thin and neat in your appearance, but you don't walk like a gay man. You definitely walk like you're straight."

"Oh."

"Just trust me," Grayson said.

"Okay."

"I don't know, Sean," Patrick said. "You want gay guys to check you out…sometimes I wonder."

"I dunno. It just seems like a compliment." I pointed at Patrick and Grayson and said, "I know how critical you guys are."

They laughed and Grayson said, "That's true. That's definitely true."

The waiter came back with a tray full of waters. "Here are some waters for you, gentlemen," he said. "I'll have your drinks in a minute."

He placed the glasses of ice water in front of Patrick and Grayson, and just as he was about to put the last one in front of me, the glass slipped off his tray and spilled onto my lap. I jumped up from my seat as the waiter said, "Oh, God, I'm so sorry, sir." I grabbed a cloth napkin from the table and began dabbing my crotch.

I said, "It's okay. It's not that bad."

I sat back down. The waiter said, "My God, I am so sorry, sir." Then he grabbed another napkin from the table and started dabbing my crotch.

"Whoa, whoa," I said, holding up my hand. "I've got it, I've got it."

Patrick and Grayson hissed with laughter and turned their heads away. The waiter put the napkin back on the table and said, "Again, so sorry."

I waved my hand and said, "Listen, no problem. I've got it."

The waiter nodded and said, "I'll be right back with your drinks."

Once he was gone, Patrick and Grayson let their laughter loose.

"Of course that just happened," Patrick said.

I shook my head and smiled. "Right. My first time in a gay bar and some dude goes for my junk."

Grayson looked at me indignantly and said, "He wasn't going for your junk, Sean. He was just trying to help."

I looked up from my dabbing and said, "Yeah, Grayson, I know. I was kidding."

Grayson was always ready to call everyone out on some perceived offense. He was in a perpetual state of victimhood, whether real or imagined. I certainly understood why he might be this way, but he seemed to take a little too much delight in correcting people's words or actions. He always seemed less interested in alleviating a societal ill, and more interested in making sure everyone knew he had the moral high ground.

As we waited for our drinks, I recalled one morning at the office when a bunch of us were standing around talking before the phones started ringing. Everyone was in good spirits, despite the early hour and the fact that we were at work. I began to tell a story about my commute.

I said, "So this black guy comes up to me on Brookline Avenue and—"

"Wait a minute," Grayson interrupted. "What does his race have to do with anything?"

"What?"

Grayson said, "Why would you mention his race? What's that got to do with anything?"

Smiles left the faces of our coworkers. They were suddenly quiet and shuffling papers.

I said, "I don't know. Because I'm telling a story and I'm trying to paint a picture and in this picture the guy is black."

"Okay," Grayson said. "*And?*"

"And what?"

"And why would you use his race to describe him?"

"Why wouldn't I?" I said. "What the hell?"

Grayson shook his head and said, "Never mind. Go on."

"Jesus Christ."

"Go ahead," Grayson said. "And what happened?"

"So," I said, "this guy IN A BLUE SHIRT comes up to me and asks me if I know how to get to Fenway Park."

I looked at Grayson for his approval. He just glared at me with folded arms. I went on with my story. "So I pointed over his shoulder and said, 'It's right there.' The guy turned around and saw this huge stadium directly behind him and laughed at himself. I guess he's from Chicago and had always wanted to see Fenway. He was just facing the wrong way and didn't know it was right there. Anyway, he apologized and thanked me and we shook hands. I laughed and told him not to worry about it."

I paused.

"*And?*" Grayson said.

"That's it," I said. "End of story."

"Oh," Grayson said, "well I'm glad I just sat through that."

He unfolded his arms, walked into his office, and shut the door.

I gave the finger to the door.

I thought about that morning after getting my lap relatively dry. Grayson was a politically correct tyrant, which was hard for me to take because I came from a world that was overtly (and somewhat proudly) un-PC. As a kid, offensive was given to test your mettle—to see whether you could take it and give it back. And recess was the place where scores were settled—where sometimes two boys who slugged it out on the playground in the second grade would become best friends by the third. I often wondered whether an open burst of physical aggression between two males might be better than the sort of tepid anger that was constantly simmering between Grayson and me.

I tossed the white napkin on the table. The waiter came back with our mojitos. He made a big display of placing my drink down carefully.

I smiled and said, "It's okay, really."

"That drink is on the house, sir," the waiter said. "My apologies again."

I thanked him and he said he would be back to take our food order. Once my drink was on the table, I picked it up and studied it.

"So," I said, "what's floating around in this? Parsley?"

Grayson looked at me with a wry smile and said, "You really are a rube, Sean."

"Okay, fine," I said. "Just tell me what it is before I drink it."

"They're mint leaves."

I studied the glass again and said, "Oh, okay." I took a sip and swallowed and said, "You know, that's actually pretty good." I held up my glass and the three of us cheered.

I was feeling good. For a moment, I forgot about my writing and how I wasn't doing what I had planned to be doing. I was momentarily content with the fact that I was finally an adult living in the city earning a (mostly) livable income. I wasn't on top of the world, but for the time being, I was happy with my place in it.

I did, however, look around the bar feeling a slight twinge of exclusion. As comfortable as I was in Club Café, I didn't feel like I totally fit in. In essence, it was a gay bar filled with office professionals. I was not a gay man and I was only pretending to be an office professional. So I was, in essence, a stranger. Though I also realized that I sometimes felt the same way in the dive bars I frequented with my straight friends— when the conversation turned to sports, or truck engines, or carpentry. My view of the world was still from the outside, looking in.

When the waiter came back and asked us whether we wanted food, Grayson opened the menu and began ordering one appetizer after another. Patrick and I grinned at each other, wondering whether Grayson was going to ask us if we wanted anything. He never did. After finishing, Grayson closed the menu and looked at us as if he had just realized that we were there.

"Does that sound good, guys?"

Patrick and I laughed. "Yup," Patrick said. "Sure."

"Good," Grayson said. He closed the menu and handed it to the waiter.

"What were you like in high school?" I asked Grayson.

He looked at me suspiciously and said, "Why?"

"I don't know," I said. "Just wondering."

Grayson thought about it for a second and said, "I don't know. Normal, I guess. Pretty shy. I kept to myself."

"Were you bullied at all?" I asked.

Grayson frowned and shook his head. "No," he said, "not really. I really just kept to myself and didn't bother anyone."

I took another sip of my mojito and nodded.

"Why?" he asked me. "What are you getting at? Were you bullied?"

I thought about it the same way Grayson had. "In grade school," I said. "A little bit in junior high, but not so much after that. I started fighting back."

"Well, that explains a lot," Grayson said.

"It does?"

"That's why you have a chip on your shoulder."

"I do?"

"You do."

"Oh," I said. I took a sip of my drink and stared up at the ceiling. A scene suddenly appeared in my mind. "I remember one time in sixth grade this kid named Cody was giving me shit. He was the textbook definition of a bully. He would spit on people and just randomly start fights. He was fat and had an upturned nose that literally made him look like a pig. Anyway, one day we decided to fight up at the baseball field on Pleasant Street. He was bigger than me, but I kicked the shit out of him. I remember he ran home crying and—"

"Sean, who cares?" Grayson said. "No one wants to hear about schoolyard fights you had in the sixth grade."

Patrick began laughing.

"You ever get into a fight, Grayson?" I asked.

"It doesn't matter," Grayson said. "I'm an adult. I'm over it."

"It sounds like you're not," I said.

"Trust me, Sean, I am. Don't tell me about myself."

Grayson shook his head, sipped his mojito, and looked away. By now, Club Café was filled with the sounds of tinkling silverware and the occasional roar of laughter from other groups of male coworkers. Patrick shifted the conversation to more relatable topics. For the next two hours, we drank and ate and chatted about work. We spent most of the time making fun of everyone else at the office. Grayson and I agreed about a lot of the people we worked with, which made me want to reconsider my opinions. I mentioned that *The Phoenix* was like a microcosm of high school. There were preppies, and stoners, and geeks, and everyone else in between. I told them that as supervisors, we were like the teachers, and the CEOs were like the principals and superintendents.

"And human resources is totally the guidance office," Patrick said.

"Oh, definitely," Grayson agreed. "Did I tell you that I had to talk to HR the other day?"

"No," I said. "About what?"

Grayson finished chewing a crab cake, wiped his mouth with his napkin, and said, "It was all about Julie Belmonte. I mean, you know how she dresses, right?"

Patrick and I smiled and nodded. Julie was a petite goth girl, except she wasn't a girl—she was a forty-something woman. Decades of sun aversion had kept her pallid skin unwrinkled and no childbirth had kept her small figure frozen in youth. Like the rest of the goths who worked at *The Phoenix*, Julie dressed in black, but unlike the others, she took it to a dramatic extreme. She wore flowing velvet gowns and sometimes even a cape. Like Grayson, I admittedly thought she occasionally looked foolish, but she was a sweet person who didn't bother anyone, so I was content to just let her dwell in her cubicle, which was decorated with pictures of her and her friends dressed in medieval garb and holding swords.

"Anyway," Grayson said, "I pulled her into my office the other day and said, 'Look, I'm all about people expressing themselves, but it's not Halloween. You need to wear something more appropriate for the office."

I said, "Well, I mean, she's not *technically* violating the dress code."

"Sean, she looks like a fucking witch. What if one of our clients comes in?"

I shrugged and sipped my drink.

"What did she say?" Patrick asked.

"Nothing to me," Grayson said. "But apparently she went and told the rest of the goth kids and they got all offended. So they ran upstairs and told HR. So Kyle came down and told me I have to be more sensitive when I talk to them about their attire, or whatever."

I said, "Maybe you need sensitivity training, Grayson."

"I'm sure I'm not the only one."

"It's not going to work on me," I told him. "I have no interest in being more sensitive."

"I've noticed."

"I just don't get it," I said.

"I've noticed."

"I mean, I don't want to sound like a cranky old man, but I just don't get this new idea of constantly walking on eggshells because you might offend someone. It's life. Your feelings are going to get hurt. Get over it."

Patrick smiled and said, "You *do* sound like a cranky old man."

I said, "If you have a problem with someone, then speak up—do something about it." I pointed to Grayson and said, "If Julie had a problem with the way you were talking to her, then say something. Don't run to HR like it's second grade."

The mojitos were starting to hit me. We were all on our fourth.

"Not everyone has a voice," Grayson said. "Not everyone is like you, Sean."

"So you agree with HR, then? You think that what you said to her was out of line?"

Grayson suddenly realized I had him in a rhetorical corner. He leaned back in his chair and said, "I could have chosen my words more carefully."

"Like I said: walking on eggshells. She dresses like it's Halloween. You told her it's not Halloween and to stop dressing like it was. Period. The end. What's the problem?"

Grayson put his hand on his chest and said, "Look, don't get me wrong, *I'm* not someone who is easily offended, but some people are. In a professional environment, you have to be aware of that. That's all I'm saying."

The waiter came over and put our fifth round of mojitos down on the table. Club Café was now packed with people and our voices were rising. I was glad we had a table.

Grayson said, "Sometimes I think you're the sensitive one, Sean—all this ranting and raving you do."

"It's not one of my better qualities," I conceded.

"Then you understand how some people can be offended. Your ranting and raving shows that some things bother you."

I thought about it for a moment and said, "I mean, I get angry about stuff, but I don't get 'offended.' As a matter of fact, I'm not even sure what 'offended' is. Is it a thought? An emotion? It's so foreign to me that I don't even know."

"I'm pretty sure I could probably offend you," Grayson said with a grin.

"How?"

"Forget it. I don't want to play this game."

"Right. Because you can't. Seriously. How could you possibly offend me?"

Grayson said, "I mean, I could probably tell a straight joke that might upset you."

"There are straight jokes?"

Patrick stopped sipping from his straw and said, "Yeah, there are?"

"There are," Grayson said. "Most are lame, but some are good."

"I'm dying to hear one of these," I said.

"Me too," Patrick said. "Go ahead, Grayson. Let's hear it."

Grayson smiled at me wanly. "Okay," he said. "How is a straight white man like tofu?"

I stared at Grayson, waiting for the punch line. Then I realized he was waiting for me to ask how.

"How?"

"White, unattractive, and no taste."

Patrick giggled, but only for a moment. Grayson sipped his mojito proudly.

"Okay," I said.

"Don't be offended, Sean."

"I'm definitely not offended. It just wasn't a very good joke. It was okay, I guess."

"It's clever," Grayson said.

"It's kind of clever," I said. "But it's not really offensive. I mean, that's sort of the whole point of those jokes."

Grayson said, "Well, you're probably not offended because you're a white male. You're the majority. It's kind of hard to offend the majority."

I pointed at Grayson and said, "*You're* a white male."

Grayson rolled his eyes dramatically and said, "Yes, but I'm not straight. I'm definitely a minority, just not by my gender or race."

"But you're still two-thirds a majority. *And* you run a corporate office. Aren't you sort of 'The Man'?"

"No, I'm not," Grayson said. "'The Man' is a straight white male."

I shook my head, sipped my drink, and said, "Yeah, okay."

"*Anyway*," Patrick interjected, "what gay jokes do you know, Sean?"

"No way," I said.

"Come on," he implored.

"No way. All the gay jokes I know are really bad."

"I want to hear them," Patrick said. He motioned to Grayson and himself and said, "Obviously we don't get to hear the good ones."

"Forget it," I said. "I'm not worried about you, but Grayson will get pissed."

"Sean, I'm an adult," Grayson said. "I can handle it. You can't offend me. Trust me, I've heard it all."

"I doubt it."

"Go ahead," Patrick said.

I looked at Grayson.

"I really don't care," he said.

I took a sip of my mojito and said, "All right, well, I can only think of one at the moment, probably because it's the worst one I know."

Patrick laughed and said, "Oh, this ought to be good."

"Are you ready?"

"Go on," Grayson said.

"What's the difference between Seattle and San Francisco?"

Patrick and Grayson gave each other looks that confirmed neither of them had ever heard it.

"What?" Grayson said.

"One has ferry terminals and other has terminal fairies."

Patrick laughed, but stopped himself by shamefully covering his face with his hand.

All the humor drained out of Grayson's face. He looked at Patrick, who was flushed red and still grinning behind his hand. Grayson gave me a disgusted look, threw his napkin on the table, stood up, and walked out.

I took a long pull from my drink and practically slammed it on the table. I said, "Well, I guess that settles it."

Time briefly stood still. My mind was soaked with alcohol and emotions. I was flooded with shame, but also with anger. There was no more gray area with Grayson. I wanted to punch him in his stupid mouth, and I didn't feel bad for wanting to punch him in his stupid mouth.

Patrick removed his hand from his face and looked at me. "*Dude*," he said.

"I guess that joke was offensive enough."

Patrick laughed and said, "Yeah, I think that did it." He looked over his shoulder at the door. "Well, I guess we should get the check now." Patrick flagged down the waiter.

I took my wallet out of my pocket and said, "What a fucking asshole he is."

"Dude," Patrick said, "where did you *hear* that joke?"

"It's from a book, actually," I said. "*Truly Tasteless Jokes*. Do you remember those?"

"No," Patrick said, polishing off his drink with a slurp from his straw.

"They were a series of little paperbacks with the most horrible jokes you could think of."

"Clearly," Patrick said.

"My friends used to steal them from the local bookstore. We would sit uptown and read them out loud and I was always the one who took them home at the end of the day. I hid them under my bed with my porno magazines."

Patrick smiled and said, "Oh, Sean."

"Anyway, that's where I heard that. Like I said, I guess you just remember the worst ones."

Patrick looked back over his shoulder and said, "I wonder how pissed he actually is."

We stood up. The table was littered with crumbs, half-eaten appetizers, and cocktail glasses half-filled with ice cubes and the mushy remnants mint leaves. It looked like civilized people had dined there. I put down a few more dollars for the waiter.

"Who really knows?" I finally said.

I didn't want to work in an office anymore. I wanted to be done with Grayson and people like him. I wanted to be done with cubicles and phones and fluorescent lights. I never wanted to hear the phrase *skill set* or *let's touch base* ever again. I wanted to walk into Grayson's office and quit by flipping over his desk. I wanted to kick open the front door of *The Phoenix* and walk into the brilliant sunshine that I had worked in before.

We opened the door and stopped. Grayson, standing on the sidewalk, was waiting for us. He was facing the door with his hands on his hips, a resentful look on his face. For a moment, I considered the possibility that I had been given the opportunity to quit *The Phoenix* in a blaze of glory. Both Grayson and I had our sleeves rolled. I figured that he and I might finally have it out right on the streets of Boston. I wanted to educate his face. All of my adolescent instincts returned. I balled a fist without knowing it. Grayson walked up to me. I watched his hands. I looked him in the eye and waited for him to throw a punch. As he stepped closer, I thought about how great it was going to feel to finally hit him.

Then Grayson took his hands from his hips and folded his arms across his chest. It was the least offensive gesture he could have made. I knew he wasn't going to do anything.

And this was probably for the best. As drunk and angry as I was, I knew that a fistfight with Grayson would be a losing proposition. I knew Grayson would run to the police. He would press charges and might even say that it was a "hate crime," which was only true in the most technical sense because in the moment I truly hated him.

My right hand was still a fist, though.

"Sean," he said, "have you ever known anyone with AIDS?"

I un-fisted my hand and said, "Look, Grayson, I—"

"Have you?"

I let out a sigh and said, "No."

"Well," Grayson said, "then you don't know how awful a disease that is and how much people suffer."

"No," I said. "But I've watched a lot of relatives die of cancer and I know how awful that is."

Grayson gave me a confused look and said, "Okaaay."

"But that wouldn't stop me from making a joke about cancer."

He just looked at me.

I said, "And that's what I was about to say. If you can't laugh at it, then what can you do? Maybe that's how I cope. I don't know. We're just different, all right?"

"Yeah, we're different," Grayson said with a snide look on his face.

"Grayson! You told me to—"

"Yeah, I know, Sean. I told you to tell the joke." He held up his hand and said, "Yeah, I know."

With that, Grayson turned and walked away. Patrick looked like a crestfallen child who had just seen his parents have a fight. The two of us watched Grayson saunter down the street with his arms folded in defiance.

"Well," Patrick said, "that went well."

I shook my head.

"Do you want to grab another drink somewhere?"

"No," I said.

"Are you sure?" Patrick asked. "Just one more?"

I considered it for a moment before I finally spoke.

"No."

"Okay," Patrick said.

"I think I'm done."

An Affair

MM

And the day came when the risk to remain tight in a bud was more painful than the risk it took to blossom.

—Anaïs Nin, "Risk"

"I like him."

Anya was pointing at me and talking about me as if I wasn't there. I had just finished giving a monologue about how great it was to be a kid in the '80s, which was a common topic for me after a few cocktails. I was explaining that while *Star Wars* action figures may have been more sentimental, I could admit that G.I. Joe figures were better in quality because they had movable knees and elbows. Then, after extolling the cinematic virtues of *The Breakfast Club,* Anya, sitting across from me at the table, pointed at me and told a co-worker that she liked me. It seemed inappropriately flirtatious, but our co-worker simply laughed and nodded and sipped his vodka. He made no mention of the fact that Anya was engaged, which was something we all knew.

It was Patrick's birthday. We were out for drinks after work and I didn't really know anyone. I was still working at *The*

Phoenix. Much as I wanted to quit in a blazing, cinematic way, I'd quickly realized that real life didn't work that way. I still had bills and two roommates who depended on my third of the rent. It was only a matter of time before I quit, though. And while I waited for callbacks from other jobs, I'd spent the past few months of my employment like Peter Gibbons in the movie *Office Space*—totally not giving a shit. It got to the point where I would sit at my desk with a box of crayons, openly scribbling in coloring books. No one said a word, least of all my boss, Grayson. After the night at Club Café where he and I spent the entire evening dragging the worst out of each other, we now both knew enough to keep a safe distance and interact only if it was absolutely, positively necessary. We were like two dogs locked in a cage—we'd initially growled and snarled at each other until finally we just got used to the other one being there.

Anya had a face that had probably launched a thousand different things. One of them was *The Phoenix*'s erotic personals section, the Erosphere. It was a small insert in the paper that featured phone sex ads, ads for escorts, and a way to connect people whose sexual appetites ran to the exotic. Most of the Erosphere was dominated by people who were into domination. Anya, clad tight in shiny black vinyl, had posed for the cover on a few occasions. From what I had heard, the Erosphere was one of the few things keeping *The Phoenix* alive. The entire world was moving online.

It was a new decade at the beginning of a new century.

Anya was stunning. Upon seeing her for the first time, I immediately wanted to know more about her. I was painfully deflated when I inquired about her and Patrick laughed and told me that she was engaged. It didn't stop me from admiring her from a distance, though. We worked in different departments and my interactions with Anya were minimal. If I had to go upstairs to talk with her, though, I always stopped in the bathroom to fix my hair and make sure I had nothing stuck in my teeth.

Whenever Anya strode into the office, every male stopped and stared. Even the gay guys took a glance. She wore dark clothes and walked like a feline with enviable posture. Her skin was pale, her hair was black, and she wore just enough makeup to make her look striking, but not overly done up. Her eyebrows were arched and pencil-thin. One of them looked perpetually cocked, as if she always knew something you didn't.

I didn't know her fiancé, but I didn't like him. Paul Rizzo was a music critic and an editor for another paper. I had never met him. I didn't even know what he looked like, but his name floated around Boston in every dive bar and rock club I frequented. It seemed like everyone either knew him or had heard of him. Everyone had an opinion about him, though. Most people said he was eccentric. Some said he was a suck-up. Some said he was a nice guy. Some said he was an asshole. A local metal band in Boston wrote an entire song about beating the shit out of him.

I knew that he had blown me off for a writing gig, which, besides having a beautiful fiancée, was enough for me to arbitrarily dislike him. A friend of mine from college, Becki, who worked at Paul's newspaper—one of *The Phoenix*'s main competitors—had informed me that the paper was devoting an entire issue to professional wrestling. Becki told Paul that not only did I have a degree in writing, but I also worked part-time in the wrestling business as a villainous, heel manager. Paul eagerly told Becki that I should contact him, which I did. After a few exchanges by e-mail and phone, he eventually ignored me.

I wrote the article anyway. It was a piece about the alarming death rate of young wrestlers from steroids and painkillers, which at the time was something totally ignored by the mainstream press. The issue on pro wrestling in Paul Rizzo's newspaper came out a few weeks later, and it had only one article with any merit. I licked my wounds and went back to trying to become a full-time writer.

We were all sitting at a long table in a jazz bar not too far from *The Phoenix* offices. Patrick was at the head of the table at the opposite end from me. Since he was the only one I really knew, it would have made more sense for me to sit near him, but when we were seated by the hostess I purposely took a chair at the other end of the table so I could sit near Anya. I tried to do this without being obvious, but it probably didn't work.

We ate and drank like it wasn't really a Tuesday night. I was drinking top-shelf whiskey and Anya was drinking martinis. All of us knew that the dot-commers would pick up the bill. Whether with their corporate card or one of their own, the website guys always paid the tab. IT people and website people were like digital shamans in corporate life. They were held to a different standard on a different pay scale. No one knew what they did or how they did it, but we all knew we couldn't live without them.

As always, a few drinks did away with my social introversion. My jokes were funnier and my wit was quicker. Anya and the dot-commers were a few years my senior, but waxing poetic about the '80s put us all in the same generation. Anya was laughing at nearly all my jokes, even the ones that weren't funny. I had her strict attention. Our eye contact was deadly.

Lots of things were going through my mind. At twenty-three, I didn't know anyone who was engaged or married. I had no idea how to act with someone who was formally attached, or what was (or wasn't) okay. As Anya laughed and the IT guys ordered more drinks, I went to the men's room, where I found myself doing some moral calculus in front of the urinal.

I decided that flirting with an engaged woman was okay, but progressing any further was not. Anya's interest was enough for me. It sufficed in my mind as a silent victory over her future husband and his harmless rebuff of my writing. Anyway, I considered a woman like Anya to be way out of my league. The fact that she was so obviously digging me was arousing in and of itself. I was content to just finish my drinks, go home, and pass out in my bed with unabashed pride.

But Anya wanted to keep the night going.

After I returned from the bathroom, she suggested that after finishing our drinks, we all head over to Boston Billiards. Everyone except me declined. Patrick, who by this time was wearing a crooked triangular birthday hat on his head, was tired and toasted. Everyone else reminded us that it was Tuesday.

We didn't care.

As expected, the dot-commers picked up the check and we all stumbled out to the busy streets of Boston. I wished Patrick a happy birthday and he asked for a hug, which I gave him. He buried his head in my chest like a child, which made everyone say "Aww."

"Okay, dude," I said. "I'm not that drunk."

Patrick pulled himself away from me and snapped his fingers in regret. We all laughed. I wished him happy birthday again, then turned to Anya and asked if she was ready to go.

"Sure," she said, reaching into her purse and taking out a lighter. "One sec."

She lit her cigarette—a clove one—and we walked back toward the office. Anya seemed more at ease away from the crowd. She wore a slender grin the entire time we walked, except when she took a drag from her cigarette and squinted her eyes, as if inhaling the smoke was hurting her and she didn't really enjoy it. Once inside Billiards, I went up to the bar and ordered drinks. Anya stuck with martinis, but I switched to beer. We found a dark corner and took seats on a maroon leather sofa. We sat in silence for a moment and looked around. Billiards was a popular after-work hangout for *Phoenix* employees, but we didn't see anyone we knew.

"Where are you from?" I asked.

Anya looked at me and smiled. Her teeth were the kind of straight perfection achieved only by long years of braces. I would know.

"Missouri," she said. "Springfield."

"Really? I wasn't expecting that."

"I moved to Boston for school just like everyone else, I suppose."

"Right."

"And you? Where are you from?"

I pointed in the general direction of Medfield and said, "About forty-five minutes that way."

"I like you Massachusetts boys. You're all so smart and sexy."

We made the deadly eye contact we had been making all night, but without anyone around, it felt deadlier. As Anya picked up her martini, I noticed a tattoo around her right wrist. It wasn't anything ornate—just a small piece of black rope.

"What's that?"

Anya sipped her martini, put it down, and rubbed her tattooed wrist.

"My wedding band," she said.

"Oh, right."

"I'm engaged."

"I've heard."

"You have?"

"I may have asked Patrick if you were single."

Anya smiled. "That's sweet," she said.

I took a sip from my beer and said, "Yeah, it figures."

Anya held my gaze. I was almost positive I could have kissed her, but I diverted our attention and asked her if she was into goth music.

"Industrial," she said.

"Ah," I said. "I had a feeling. Your vibe isn't quite goth. I knew it was in that realm, though."

Anya and I moved away from the topic of her engagement. We got to know each other, rapidly. It was as if we had been admiring each other silently forever and were now satisfying a long-standing hunger. Anya's favorite author was Anaïs Nin and her favorite band was Nine Inch Nails. I resisted my instant urge to ask her stupidly whether she just liked the letters N-I-N. We talked about where we from, and who we were, but we never discussed where we were going. We were both living hard in the present.

Anya's life was not without a sad story. I had never known a pale girl who dressed all in black who didn't have at least one. She told me that her father, a German immigrant, had been an iron worker. He'd died on the job when she was a little girl. Talking about it didn't seem to bother her, though. She recounted the story with unflinching poise. Poise, I was beginning to notice, was Anya's prime asset.

Each time one of us got up to get more drinks, we inched closer together when we sat back down. By the end of the evening, we were thigh to thigh and my filter was gone. I was thinking with my mouth. After four more drinks, I came full circle and broached the subject of her engagement.

"You're going to get married at twenty-seven?"

"I am."

"And are you doing this because you're in love, or because you feel you're at the age when you're *supposed to* get married?"

"I don't know. Both, I guess."

"You're an attractive young woman. You can get married anytime you want, most likely to anybody you want. Why do it now?"

She said, "Well, I might be young, but I've seen and done some things."

I said, "And I get the feeling that you're not quite done seeing and doing those things."

Anya gave me the sexiest grin I had ever seen in my life and said, "You're killing me here."

The two of us sipped from our drinks. With no thought at all, our hands met under the table. They dovetailed perfectly. We sat in silence. I was scanning Billiards for coworkers and was sure Anya was doing the same. My heart was racing. We were alone. We were drunk. Anya finally turned and looked at me.

"Well," she said. "Just so you know, I'm all about the open relationship."

"Is that right?"

We kissed.

As it was happening, I briefly opened my eyes just to make sure this was actually happening.

It was.

We were kissing passionately, Anya occasionally pausing to take my face in her hands and look at me before starting again. Eventually, we realized that we were kissing a little too passionately for a public place so we stopped and looked around.

"We should go," Anya said.

"Sounds good."

We walked hand in hand toward Kenmore Square to get taxis. Time had passed quickly. The subway was done for the night. As we neared the large intersection of Kenmore Square, we walked down a side street. I stopped in front of a chain-link fence set up for a construction site. Anya put both her hands under my shirt and pushed me against the fence. We kissed again, this time with my hands on the sides of *her* face. A group of drunken college kids hooted and hollered from across the street.

We went on as if they weren't there.

We went on as if nothing was.

I didn't hear from Anya the next day. Nor did I see her. A few times, I thought about making up some excuse to go upstairs and talk to her, but I never did. I didn't e-mail her either. I sat at my desk wondering whether she had sobered up that morning and realized she had made a huge mistake. If she'd decided that the night before was nothing more than a drunken indiscretion, I was fine with that. We had been at the point of intoxication when reality was a side effect—when great ideas seem terrible and terrible ideas seem great. Shit happened.

My conscience was (mostly) clear. If I hadn't heard the words *open relationship*, I wouldn't have touched her. I didn't hate Paul Rizzo enough to enact some sort of passive revenge by kissing his fiancée. And the night never went beyond the chain-link fence. After a few more sultry minutes, we finally kissed one last time, said our goodbyes, and got into different taxis that took us to opposite sides of the city.

I had no idea whether Anya was really in an open relationship. It wasn't out of the realm of possibility, though. I had known a few couples in college who were in open relationships, or at least tried to be. It seemed like open relationships worked only in favor of the girl. She was always the one who had no problem finding another guy who was perfectly willing to have casual sex, but the boyfriend would always be left in the dust. I watched a lot of young men in open relationships playing video games with their buddies on a Saturday night while their girlfriend spent the same evening fucking another dude. And there were always the added complications if feelings got involved, or jealously arose, which almost always happened. After witnessing their machinations firsthand, I decided that open relationships were like communism—far better in theory than in practice.

But we were all adults now. And I had no qualms about being on the periphery of an open relationship, especially if Anya Heinrich was involved. I had no idea what the dynamics of Anya and Paul's relationship were.

And I didn't care.

I was single. I had been single since my last year of college, when things with Danielle fell apart. At first, it was painful and awkward. A few times, we had to pass by each other at the elevators in our dorm with the new person we were either dating or fucking. No eye contact was ever made, and we didn't speak for some time, but by graduation day we were friends again and all was right with the world.

I was enjoying the single life in Boston. It was liberating to have no commitments or obligations to anyone but myself. Since working at *The Phoenix*, I had slept with only one girl in the office—a clichéd (yet fun) tension breaker after too many drinks at the company Christmas party. After putting our clothes back on, the girl and I literally high-fived, and then we went on with our lives.

I had no expectations with Anya. As I sat in the office nursing a hangover that Wednesday morning, I took phone calls and responded to e-mails like even more of an office zombie than I already was. Although several people had seen Anya and me leave the jazz bar together the night before, no one asked me anything about it, not even Patrick, whose birthday revelry made him look in even worse shape than I was. I looked around the office a few times, hoping nobody knew, but wishing like hell that I could tell them all.

Anya e-mailed me on Friday. She asked me if I wanted to get lunch. I responded immediately that I did. She told me to meet her by the front door at one o'clock. The rest of the morning moved painfully slow.

Just before one o'clock, I checked myself in the bathroom mirror. I walked through the glass doors and stepped outside. It was sunny and warm. Summer in New England wasn't quite done. Anya was leaning against the building and smoking a cigarette, holding herself by wrapping her other arm around her waist. She was wearing large, dark sunglasses and very clearly people-watching.

"Hey," I said.

"Hey."

"Where do you want to go?"

"I'm not really hungry."

"Okay."

"It's nice out. Why don't we go down to the river?"

"Sounds good."

We walked down Brookline Avenue toward the Charles River. We passed through Kenmore Square and the construction site where we had kissed.

"Remember that place?" I said, pointing to the chain-link fence.

Anya smiled at me and said, "I do."

"Looks different in the daytime."

We waited for the crosswalk in Kenmore Square, which always took forever. After passing by the Boston University bookstore, we walked down to the banks of the Charles. BU kids were playing Frisbee and young housewives were walking their dogs. Anya and I sat on the grass under the shade of a weeping willow. She took off her sunglasses and kissed me. I drew back a bit from surprise, but then followed her lead. Sober, we were gentler and less frantic.

Anya leaned back and said, "I'm sorry. I've been wanting to do that all week."

"So I take it Tuesday night wasn't just a onetime thing?"

"I'm just a little baffled," she said.

"About what?"

"First of all, finding out that you had any interest in me at all surprised the hell out of me."

"Are you serious?"

"Then I find out that you're really cool and fun to be with and I totally dig hanging out with you. I never expected to find myself making out with Sean Gorman at Boston Billiards, and it just threw me a little."

The way she said my full name made me realize that I always referred to her the same way. Whenever I talked about Anya with Patrick, she was never Anya, but always Anya Heinrich. It was like she was a celebrity, or some grand entity I would never actually be near.

"Yeah," I said, "I was definitely thrown too. I feel the exact same way."

Anya smiled, looked away, and blushed. Her fair skin made it very noticeable. Causing Anya to blush made me feel like a king, but I couldn't bask in my glory for long.

"So what's your situation?" I asked.

Anya just looked at me.

"With Paul."

Anya turned away, but only briefly. She said, "The other thing that's throwing me is that I've never cheated on Paul. I'm sure there's a small amount of guilt factor in this part of it, but obviously not much."

"So you're *not* in an open relationship?"

Anya took a moment before she spoke. Her bright-green eyes went through me. I couldn't tell whether she looked angry or stunned.

Finally she said, "We were in an open relationship when we were dating. But I never did anything with it. And I don't know, now that we're engaged, if the same rules apply. We never talked about it."

I thought back to the couples I knew in college who were in open relationships—how they were always negotiating, reexamining, and setting parameters. It wasn't the way I wanted to live my life, but I wasn't going to lecture Anya about hers. I wanted her. And I didn't care about the moral gray area we were in.

"Okay," I said.

"I'm a little overwhelmed," Anya said, with no sign of emotion. "We can talk about open relationships some other time when I'm a tad more coherent."

"Okay."

Anya said, "But if you think I make a habit out of picking up cute boys on the side, I don't."

"I believe you," I said.

"It just seems like it would be a sin not to get to know you, so here I am."

I gave Anya a slight smile, and the warmth in my cheeks made it feel like I was probably blushing as well. I couldn't remember the last time I had been so thunderstruck by a woman. I looked at the river. The BU crew team was out practicing. A group of eight guys was rowing upstream while a woman at the front urged them on with shouts and grunts. Their swaying oars moved in perfect synchronicity.

I turned back to Anya and said exactly what I was thinking.

"I think I just bought a ticket for one hell of a roller coaster ride."

Anya and I spent the next few months having lunch together and going out for drinks after work. My job search was not going well. I was not getting offers for the jobs I wanted, while I *was* getting offers for the jobs that would have paid me less than I could afford. Anya asked me whether I wanted her to talk to Paul about an opening at his newspaper.

I politely declined.

Our rendezvous became more clandestine. To avoid office gossip, Anya and I stopped meeting for lunch in front of the building and began just meeting at a bar. If we met for drinks after work, it was always far away from Kenmore Square. We frequented the nice restaurants in the Back Bay as much as the dive bars in Allston. Sometimes we'd talk over martinis and calamari, and other times over PBRs and cockroaches.

I loved it.

Any reservations I had were gone. It became clear that whatever dynamic Anya had with Paul was not my concern. It also became clear that their relationship was not good. The reason Anya was able to go out so much was because Paul was never home, which made sense. His job demanded long hours and late nights. Anya had a cell phone (a device I had yet to find a use for), and occasionally when Paul would ring, she'd take the call outside and roll her eyes at me through the restaurant window.

I'd smile and raise my pint.

She'd smile and give me the finger.

The only thing Anya ever felt guilty about was bitching about Paul to me. She never expressed any regret about our long make-out sessions on street corners, but she always felt bad when she found herself complaining about her relationship. She would stop herself mid-sentence and say, "I'm sorry. I shouldn't be saying this to you. This is my problem, not yours." I'd tell her it was okay, then she would compose herself and come back to the moment.

I liked her. Anya was smart and sardonic. Sometimes her black-cloaked facade came down, which revealed the person she might have been before the death of her father. In that way, we were one and the same. The moments when Sean Gorman and Anya Heinrich finally stood revealed were the moments I wanted to embrace her as something more. But our relationship was a constant standoff, with one of us always distancing and the other always pursuing. If the true feelings we had for each other sat in the empty space between us, we rarely ever met there.

I laughed when I told Fraser and Brown I was having an affair. It seemed ridiculous. When I thought of affairs, I thought of characters on daytime soap operas. Affairs were for people in their forties. Businessmen and lawyers had affairs. I was twenty-three years old. I listened to heavy metal and wore Chuck Taylors. Part of it may have been my denial in calling the relationship what it actually was, but part of me really felt like I was nowhere close to what society might call "the other man."

And Anya and I had not had sex. At the end of each night, after we had worked each other up to the brink of sexual frenzy, we would just stop, breathe heavily, kiss each other goodnight, and go our separate ways. We talked about sex a lot though—what we liked and what we wanted to do to the other person. We did this a lot during monotonous workdays via company e-mail, not giving a shit whether we were being monitored by "The Man." Anya always ended her e-mails with the salutation, *Whips & Kisses*.

By autumn, our situation had become untenable. Anya and I were kissing more ravenously and our hands were straying more waywardly. On two different occasions, I asked her, between breaths, to come back to my apartment. This made her stop, put her hands on my face, and bury her head in my chest. She would stay silent and listen to my heartbeat, letting her own breathing calm.

"I can't," she'd finally say. "I just can't tonight."

I always let it go.

She did this twice, but after the second time, Anya sent me an e-mail the next day with the lyrics from a Nine Inch Nails song called "Kinda I Want to," which was a grindingly sexy song whose lyrics needed no interpretation.

Anya's wedding date was fast approaching. One afternoon I e-mailed her, asking whether she wanted to get together after work. She replied by writing: *Ok, here's my thing about tonight— as soon as i leave here, i've got to go to the art store across the street & buy stationery (shut the fuck up, alright?). Plus, i have a date tonight with that guy i live with, to pick out music & design invites (no, really, shut the fuck up). And while we're on the subject, let me just tell you that i always feel like a mega-bitch when things like this happen & i'm sorry that i'm not free to go wherever, whenever with you. It sucks. Not that i regret any decisions i've made, but it still sucks.*

I told her it was no trouble at all and to just let me know when or if she was available. I ended my e-mail with two words: *No pressure.*

Anya was available the following weekend. "Paul will be at the Scissorfight show on Saturday night," she said. "So we'll have the whole night to ourselves."

"That's funny," I told her. "My buddies Fraser and Brown are going to that show too."

"Oh," Anya said, "did you want to go to the show with them instead?"

"No," I said. "Not at all."

I actually *had* planned on going to the show with them, but there would be plenty of other times to see Scissorfight with Fraser and Brown, but probably no other time to finally have sex with Anya Heinrich. There was something in her eyes. And the way she said "We'll have the whole night to ourselves" made me almost positive that we were finally going to do away with the one thing that had literally left us clawing at each other.

We agreed to meet downtown at the Prudential Center Mall and find a nice place to eat in the Back Bay.

"Is eight o'clock okay?" Anya asked.

"That's fine."

"Okay," she said. "I'll call you if I'm running late."

"On what?"

Anya looked at me incredulously. "Oh, that's right. You still don't have a cell phone."

"Why would I need a cell phone? I have a phone at my house."

Anya rolled her eyes. "Whatever, old man" she said. "I won't be late. Just meet me out front."

"Sounds good."

On Saturday night, I took a long shower. I meticulously shaved and styled my hair with pomade—a relatively expensive item I used only on special occasions (Patrick had recommended it). I splashed on cologne, another thing I rarely did. I dressed myself in jeans, boots, and a black button-down shirt. I wiped the fog from my bathroom mirror and was surprised at what I saw.

I was beginning to see a man, albeit a young one. The space in my head that contained a positive self-image was still closed with a rusted padlock whose key was hard to turn. Although I still saw a shy and awkward teenager, I no longer saw him all the time. I was beginning to see a relatively decent-looking guy—maybe not the best-looking guy in the bar, but maybe the third- or fourth-. And I was on my way out the door to be with the most desirable girl at *The Boston Phoenix*. I knew that the prism through which I saw myself would always be refracted with adolescent images, but as I looked in the mirror one last time, those images seemed a little less jagged.

At seven-thirty, I took the subway from Government Center to Copley Square—the heart of downtown Boston, which all the tourists called "Cope-ley Square," instead of "Cop-ley Square." As always on a Saturday night, the streets and subway cars were filled with young people dressed up, heading to bars that were too loud and dance clubs that were too full. By the end of the night, they would all be drunk, disheveled, and drenched.

I came up from the subway and walked over to the entrance of the Prudential Center Mall. I stood in front of the huge revolving doors and watched shoppers and tourists come and go. Between their bags from Lord & Taylor and Saks Fifth Avenue were also little white boxes tied with string that contained tiny pieces of overpriced fudge. It was five past eight.

I looked around for Anya, but she wasn't there. I waited another ten minutes, watching the street performers on the other side of Boylston Street. A group of young black teenagers was playing percussion on a set of overturned plastic buckets. They jammed with such infectious precision that any pedestrian who walked by had a bounce in their step without even realizing it.

Anya still wasn't there by eight-twenty. I looked around. It would have been impossible not to see me. All around me, people were coming and going. I seemed to be the only stationary thing in the entire city.

Tricycle Man rode by at eight-thirty. I could hear him coming from blocks away. Tricycle Man (as everyone in the city called him) was an old black man who rode an oversize tricycle through Boston. As he peddled, he shouted like a siren: "UP! UP! UP!" His voice echoed off the brownstones and skyscrapers. Rather than riding in the street like the bike messengers, he barreled down sidewalks, making hapless pedestrians part like the Red Sea. He rode by me, his whooping producing a Doppler effect as he came and went. I watched the two little American flags he had fastened to the tricycle's basket flutter in his wake.

Tricycle Man's siren call made me remember Anya's phone. It wasn't like her to be late, and for the first time in my life, I wished I had a cell phone so I could find out where she was. I considered the possibility that Paul's plans had changed and she wouldn't be coming. I considered the possibility that the subway was delayed, which in Boston was always a strong possibility.

Then I considered what was probably happening.

"Shit."

I ran toward the mall and pushed myself through the revolving doors. Rather than taking the crowded escalator, I bounded up the empty marble stairs and started power walking past the stores and kiosks.

Anya and I had made plans to meet at the mall's entrance. What had suddenly occurred to me was that the mall had two entrances. We never specified which one. I had simply gone to the entrance that I always went to—the one on Boylston Street. There was another entrance on Huntington Avenue—literally about half a mile's length of commerce from where I had been waiting.

I did my best to not openly run. I kept a quick and steady pace as I weaved around women in fur coats and yuppies pushing baby strollers. All the while, I was scanning the faces for Anya's. I probably looked like a villain in a spy movie.

When I reached the other end of the mall, I sprinted down another set of marble stairs toward another set of revolving doors. As I pushed my way onto Huntington Avenue, I looked for Anya. I was out of breath and smiling. I was going to laugh and tell her what had happened.

But she wasn't there.

"Shit."

I took another look.

She definitely wasn't there.

I figured we must have passed each other inside the mall, hidden behind all the perfume kiosks in the middle of the promenade. Time was lapsing. I caught my breath and doubled back.

Back on Boylston Street.

Nothing.

Anya wasn't there.

"Fuck."

The curse came out louder than expected. A few people looked at me, but quickly looked away. I paced around with my hands on my hips, catching my breath. I figured that Anya might retrace her steps again, so I decided to stay put.

I waited.

And waited.

By nine o'clock, I accepted defeat.

I shook my head and walked back to the Copley subway station. I clinked a token into the turnstile and got on a Green Line train bound for Kenmore. I knew Fraser and Brown would just be getting to the Scissorfight show. I decided to meet up with them and salvage what was left of the night. As I sat on a bench swaying with the clacking train, I thought about everything. Kissing Anya for the first time brought a smile to my face. Remembering our lunches and our time by the Charles River made me nostalgic for things that had happened only a few weeks earlier. I knew tonight would have been our last hurrah—a grand send-off that would have finished our not-quite-so-youthful indiscretions. I couldn't deny what I was feeling.

I was going to miss it.

I was going to miss her.

After getting off the subway at Kenmore Square, I walked the same path I always took to work, but instead made a left. Lansdowne Street, which bordered the outfield of Fenway Park, was a long street of rock clubs and dance clubs. Home runs belted out of Fenway landed on its asphalt while the fans inside either booed or cheered, depending on who was hitting them. The night was loud and the air was thick with white smoke from the sausage and pepper vendors, who were there even though it wasn't a game night. They still made a killing on the drunk club kids who stumbled out to the streets with beer munchies after last call.

I made my way to Axis, one of the smaller rock clubs on Lansdowne. Thankfully, the show wasn't sold out, and after the bouncer checked my ID and fastened a pink band around my wrist, I walked inside.

"Sean Gorman, I am going to kick your fucking ass!"

I looked up.

Anya was standing on a roped-off balcony for VIPs. She was holding a martini. I held up my hands in surrender. Anya held up her index finger telling to me wait a second and began nudging her way past some people. She came down a staircase and walked up to me.

"What happened?" she said.

"I was about to ask you the same thing."

"I was waiting for you."

"Where?"

"By the entrance."

"On Huntington?"

"Yes!"

I said, "I was on Boylston."

Anya inhaled deeply and looked up at the ceiling. "I knew it," she said.

I pointed to the door and said, "We can still get out of here."

Anya said, "I can't now."

"Why not?"

"Paul's here."

"Oh."

We stared at each other for a moment. Once again, the whole world was moving around us.

I said, "I was really looking forward to—"

"I know," she said. "I know."

Fraser and Brown walked up behind Anya. I finally looked away from her. Fraser said, "Hey, I thought you couldn't make it."

I pointed and said, "This is Anya."

"Oh," Fraser said. "What's up?"

Anya introduced herself to Fraser and Brown and shook their hands while I tried to think of a last-ditch effort to get us out of there.

"Well," Anya said, "I'm going back up to the balcony. Why don't we all meet for drinks after the show?"

I looked into Anya's eyes and tried to figure out what she was thinking. Coming up with nothing, I finally said, "Okay."

"The Cask?"

"Sounds good."

Anya made her way through a throng of people while keeping her martini hoisted in the air. We smiled at each other as she walked up to the VIP section.

"You were right," Fraser said. "That girl is hot."

"That's Paul Rizzo's girlfriend?" Brown asked.

"Fiancée."

"Damn," Brown said. "I guess being a shitty music critic has some fringe benefits."

"I need a drink."

I bought myself a beer and shot the shit with Fraser and Brown. The two of them still lived in Medfield with their parents. Fraser had just started a job at Wellesley College as a cook and Brown had just started working retail at Circuit City. I didn't look down on the two of them for still living at home. As a matter of fact, I was sometimes envious because they could still enjoy home-cooked meals and never had to budget for books or CDs...or anything, really. Still though, I wouldn't have traded my far less comfortable life in Boston for theirs, especially since they could never bring a girl home at the end of the night, even though my plans for that particular activity seemed to be over.

"I take it you're not having sex with her tonight?" Fraser said.

I explained what happened.

"That sucks," he said. "Dude, why don't you just get a cell phone?"

"Because I can't afford one," I said. "Not all of us have the luxury of living at home."

Fraser held up his hand and said, "Fair enough."

"Sorry," I said. "I'm just a little irritated right now."

"No worries."

The house lights went down and my mood lifted. Scissorfight was a metal band from New Hampshire whose songs were almost entirely about New Hampshire. The guitarist and the bass player wore flannel shirts and John Deere trucker caps. The lead singer, Iron Lung, looked like a legitimate mountain man. He had long brown hair and a huge long beard and roared like a grizzly bear through gritted white fangs. They opened the show with a song called "Granite State Destroyer."

Fraser, Brown, and I rocked out and drank. A few times, I looked up at the balcony and saw Anya standing coolly by herself with her martini held aloft. We made eye contact once. I made an angry face and threw up the devil horns—the universal hand gesture for heavy metal and all-around hell raising. Anya smiled at me, sweetly. I turned around and didn't look back, all the while wondering whether she was still looking.

After the show was over, Fraser, Brown, and I wiped the sweat from our faces and made our way to the door. I looked up at the VIP section, but Anya was gone.

Fraser said, "You still wanna head over to the Cask?"

"Might as well," I said.

The Cask N' Flagon was a bar that none of us would have normally gone to, but the Red Sox weren't playing and it was nearby, which was why I figured Anya had suggested it. It was a large, dusty sports bar right next to Fenway. Television screens were everywhere and every inch of wall space was covered with Red Sox memorabilia. If it had been a game night, the place would have been packed with people and frat boys would have been brawling outside. Without the Red Sox in town, it looked like any other Irish pub in Boston, with older people sitting around, drinking amicably. Fraser, Brown, and I ordered Budweisers and sat down in some chairs next to a foosball table.

"So what's the deal with you and this girl?" Fraser asked.

I gave him a brief synopsis of the past month of my life.

Fraser said, "So have you met Paul Rizzo?"

"I don't even know what he looks like," I said.

Brown let out a chuckle and said, "Speak of the devil."

224

We looked over and saw Anya walking in with Paul. The three of us stood up. Anya pointed at me and said, "Paul, this is Sean. We work together."

We shook hands.

"How's it going?"

"Good," I said.

Fraser and Brown introduced themselves.

Anya said, "I'll go get drinks."

She walked over to the bar. The four of us sat down. I couldn't get over how nondescript Paul Rizzo was. He was average in height and build. His dark hair was short with no style at all. He was dressed in a black T-shirt, black jeans, and black Doc Martens. I didn't know what I was expecting, but I wasn't expecting someone I had probably stood next to in a bar or walked by on the street a million times.

"So what did you guys think of the show?" he asked.

"Awesome," Brown said. "I mean, Scissorfight is always awesome."

"They are," Paul said. "They're good guys, too. They're friends."

Fraser and I shot each other a look. Having known each other since kindergarten, the two of us could often communicate without speaking. The way Paul Rizzo had said "They're friends" made him sound totally douchey. Since graduating high school, Fraser, Brown, and I had gotten more into the local music culture in Boston. As much as we enjoyed the bands, we hated the scenesters from Allston and Brighton who only went to shows just to be seen by other people who were there to be seen. All of them were "friends with the band." We never got involved with any of that. We just went to the shows, watched the band, bought a CD, and went home.

But of course, Paul Rizzo might have been different. He was a fairly well-known music critic and I was sure he had a lot of people kissing his ass, especially local bands wanting a good review. As I sat across the table listening to him, I wondered what sort of life he lived—a life where he was always schmoozing with people to get a story and where people were always schmoozing with him to get their story told, a life where his fiancée was screwing around with the guy sitting right across the table from him.

I sat feeling a uniquely male combination of both pride and guilt. Anya came back with two bottles of beer. She sat down next to Paul and smiled at me as Paul talked with Fraser and Brown about an alternative hardcore band called Sam Black Church. The three of them were way more into that sort of music than I was, so I just sat back and listened. Anya and I were gazing at each, occasionally looking away when it became too obvious.

"So what are you into, man?" Paul asked me.

I quickly took my eyes off Anya. "I'm not really into punk or hardcore," I said. "I'm just kind of a dyed-in-the-wool metalhead."

"Right on."

Paul then rattled off eight local metal bands, asking me whether I had heard of them. I said no every time, which was followed by an elaborate description of how each one sounded. I just kept saying "Cool" between sips of Budweiser.

We ordered one more round of beers. Paul spent most of the evening talking with Fraser and Brown because they were far more tuned into the music he liked. Anya and I continued to look at each other, but eventually the two of us faded off into boredom and began staring at the TV screens by the bar. *Saturday Night Live* was on.

After finishing his beer, Paul looked at Anya and said, "Ready to go?"

Anya snapped out of her trance and said, "Umm, yeah."

Paul shook Fraser and Brown's hand and said, "Nice meeting you guys." He turned to me and said, "Sean, nice meeting you." I shook his hand and said, "Thanks, you too." Anya looked at me and smiled.

"See you Monday," she said.

They left.

"Well, that was weird," Fraser said, taking a pull from his beer.

"He seems all right," Brown said. "I can see why bands write songs about punching him in the face, though."

I looked back at the TV and thought about how seeing *SNL* at midnight was always proof that the weekend had not gone well.

Anya got married and came back to work a week later, after her honeymoon. We saw each other all the time, but never in the same way. Everything between us stopped. Even if we had had the chance to be alone, I don't think we would have ever spoken about anything anyhow. We passed each other in the hallway once, just the two of us, and we each said hello as if we were acquaintances and nothing more.

For a while after she was married, Anya was cold—not just to me, but to everyone. She never smiled and didn't really speak unless she was spoken to. I considered asking her about it, but I didn't, mostly because I was so focused on the future, instead of the past or even the present. My job search had finally turned around and I was just waiting for one more phone call before I could give my two weeks' notice. I was nearly checked out of *The Phoenix* in every possible way. Unfortunately, I still had to deal with my boss, Grayson. One Thursday afternoon, he called me into his office.

"We have an issue with our section and the website," Grayson said to me after I came in and took a seat. "Anya will be down in a minute."

I straightened up in my chair. Grayson picked up his phone and dialed someone. He cradled the receiver with his shoulder and chin while he looked at his monitor and clacked away on his keyboard. I had no idea what the problem was or what he was talking about.

The door to Grayson's office opened and Anya walked in. I looked up at her and smiled. She just glanced at me, but her green eyes shot through my entire being. My instinct was to ask her what was wrong, but I didn't. She sat down next to me and angrily stared at Grayson. Grayson, not looking at her, kept talking on the phone and clicking his mouse. After about a minute, he finally hung up and turned to us.

"Okay," he said. "So, this morning…"

Grayson saw Anya's glare.

"Are you okay?"

Anya stared at him for a moment before she answered.
"I'm getting a divorce."
I said nothing.
"Oh," Grayson said.
"But I'll be fine."

Shattered Glass

MMI

It is hard to contend against one's heart's desire; for whatever it wishes to have it buys at the cost of the soul.

—HERACLITUS

Innocence is like polished armor; it adorns and defends.

—ROBERT SOUTH

"867-5309?"

"What?"

"Like the song."

Jenny looked at me blankly and said, "I don't know it."

"Never mind," I said. "It doesn't matter."

Twenty-five was the first year of my life I began to feel older. Although I was no longer measuring my years in academic increments of four, I had been in the real world that long, working a real job but still not making real money. A few gray hairs had sprouted. It was the first year I had begun to seriously think about health insurance and retirement plans, even though I had neither. Twenty-five was the first year I realized that I was a quarter-century old. It was also the first year I began to have an awareness that there were women younger than I was and that they were totally unfamiliar with pop songs from the 1980s.

Jenny and I started talking out of necessity. The house party in Allston was packed and she and I were cramped next to each other in the front hallway. She was short and cute and wearing a brown argyle sweater. When she spoke, she looked up at me through her pointy-rimmed granny glasses. She looked like a college student who lived in Allston because she was a college student who lived in Allston.

The term *hipster* had not yet entered my vocabulary, but I knew Jenny was a type. She was the type found only in cities. I knew this because I had grown up in the suburbs and had never seen people like Jenny until I moved to Boston. My only reference for people like her was the Weezer song "Buddy Holly" and the lyric that mentioned "Buddy Holly glasses." The only thing I knew about people like Jenny was that they were cool, and smart, and had a good record collection.

I had been a metalhead throughout all of my teenage years and still dressed like one, just without the long hair, which I had finally cut off just before graduating college. My reference point for how to dress was still Metallica—black shirts and dark-blue jeans. I also had long sideburns, so I was sometimes mistaken for a rockabilly kid, which was okay because I liked that music too. In the young social circles of Boston I ran in, I felt like I was always in a perpetual state of high school where everyone was still defined by what music they listened to.

"Do you like Slayer?" I asked Jenny.

She smiled and said, "Umm, they're okay—a little intense for me."

"Understandable."

"So where do you go to school?"

I laughed and said, "I'm in real life now."

Jenny laughed too. "Oh."

"I went to Emerson, though. I majored in creative writing—sort of useless."

Jenny said, "No, that's cool. I go to BU."

"Really? What for?"

"Photography."

I laughed and said, "Well, it sounds like you'll have a useless degree, too."

Jenny said, "Well, photojournalism, so maybe not."

"Oh."

Jenny smiled and said, "It's okay. I know it's not pre-law or anything."

"Are you a senior?"

Jenny gave me playfully indignant look and said, "Sophomore."

I covered my face in embarrassment. "I suck," I said.

"It's okay," Jenny said. She narrowed her eyes and tilted her head with curiosity. "How old are you, by the way?"

"Twenty-five."

"Cool."

"And you?"

"Nineteen."

"Cool."

Jenny and I took sips from our Pabst Blue Ribbons and looked around the party. Our respective friends were in the kitchen doing shots, and getting to them through the crowd of people seemed like more of a hassle than it was really worth.

"So who do you know here?" Jenny asked me.

"I know one of the girls who lives here."

Chloe and I had had a complicated relationship in college, which was only slightly less complicated now. The two of us met when I was a senior and she was a freshman. We had mutual friends who were juniors. We got to know each other on Monday nights, when I would go down to my buddies' room to watch wrestling. Chloe was shy and didn't say much, but I noticed that a lot of her attention was focused on me and she laughed at a lot of the jokes I made.

Except for the racy ones. She didn't like those. Chloe and I were so unalike, we might as well have come from different solar systems. She was a Christian who still styled her blond hair like an eleven-year-old girl's—long, with straight bangs cut just above her eyebrows. My friends and I referred to this type of hairstyle on girls as "homeschooled hair." Chloe loved dogs and Disney movies and, by her own admission, never got into trouble as a kid. She went to summer camp. She adored her family and talked about them a lot.

I was nothing like her and could see why she was intrigued. Chloe hadn't been homeschooled, but in the parochial high school world she came from, someone like me didn't even exist. I, on the other hand, wasn't totally unfamiliar with someone like Chloe. One of my girl friends in high school was similar, but not as chaste. That girl was not a virgin, unlike Chloe—a fact she was neither proud of nor ashamed of. For her, it simply hadn't happened yet.

Chloe was cute, but I didn't see her as sexual. She was pretty, but exuded nothing sensual. To my eyes, she was too adorable and clean to think about in some sweaty, pornographic way. When Chloe wasn't around, her friends would tell me how much of a crush she had on me, but I would just wave it off and say, "I really can't."

I did not, in any way, want to corrupt Chloe. I did not want to date her, nor did I want to take her virginity—something, as a man, I never understood the appeal of. I had already done it twice, and twice was enough to realize that it was a huge and vastly over-rated burden. I knew that four years of college life would mature Chloe, and I wanted that to happen for her organically, instead of me instigating it. I was twenty-one and she was eighteen; in collegiate years, three years was a lifetime.

But as the months went on, Chloe began to morph. She changed her hairstyle and wore new clothes. Nothing provocative—just shirts and jeans that were more form-fitting. I began to see the outline of a perfect body that had been kept under wraps. Although Chloe was still far from an extravert, she began walking around campus with a bit more stride in her step, a new ponytail bouncing behind her.

And she really wanted me to kiss her.

But I wouldn't.

One night, we were up late, chatting on her dorm room floor. I was talking and talking and suddenly noticed that Chloe had moved closer and closer.

I stopped talking.

"Why don't you kiss me?" she said.

"I can't."

She smiled, almost wickedly, and said, "And why is that?"

I was suddenly seeing her in a *very* sexual way.

She raised her eyebrows and said, "*Hmm?*"

"I really don't want a girlfriend right now," I told her.

Which was true.

Shortly into my senior year, I had broken things off with Danielle, whom I had been dating since my own freshman year. After things ended with Danielle, it was like I woke up the following day and suddenly realized I was surrounded by a thousand attractive women. I didn't tell Chloe about not wanting to corrupt her, or my total aversion to taking her virginity, but my one honest statement seemed honest enough for the time being.

Chloe said, "But we like each other, don't we?"

"I just really don't want a girlfriend right now," I repeated.

Chloe shrugged her shoulders and moved away.

I had been given the opportunity to elaborate and put the nail in the coffin, but chose to be ambiguous. Unselfishly, I didn't want to hurt Chloe's feelings. Selfishly, I wanted the door of opportunity to remain open. She looked different. She seemed different. Temptation was becoming harder to resist.

One night, my resistance nearly failed.

It was two a.m. and I had been at an Irish pub, drinking copious amounts of Jack Daniel's with my friends. I stumbled back to the dorm and when I got off the elevator, Chloe was coming out of the bathroom.

"Heeeeey!" she exclaimed, running up to me and throwing her arms around my shoulders.

"Hey," I said. "Are you drunk?"

"Yup!"

"Really? When did you start drinking?"

"About a month ago."

"Oh."

"What are you doing?"

"Going to bed," I told her.

"No, you're not," she said. "Let's hang out."

I said, "Okay," and the two of us walked to her room. Once inside, Chloe flicked on the light and flopped herself down on a large beanbag chair. I sat near her on the floor.

"Do you have any more booze?" I asked.

"No," she said. "We drank it all."

"Okay."

"What did you do tonight?" Chloe asked.

"Got drunk at Flynn's and yelled about wrestling."

"Don't you do that *every* Friday night?"

"Yup."

"You're ridiculous," she said.

Just then, the fire alarm went off. The two of us groaned. The fire alarm in our dorm went off at least once a week. I had been dealing with it for nearly four years, but Chloe was still new to it.

I got up first. Chloe stood, but I put my hand up and said, "Fuck that. We're not going anywhere." She flopped herself back down in the beanbag and languidly said, "Okay."

I walked over to the door and turned off the lights. Then I went over to the windows and pulled down the shades. Not leaving during a fire alarm was something a lot of students did, but getting caught meant a fine from the RAs. I had done it many times. Chloe had not.

"What if there's a fire?" she asked.

"Is there ever a fire?"

"Good point."

The dark room was now intermittently lit by a flashing strobe light. It was like Chloe and I were in a dance club, but instead of hearing techno music, we heard the blaring whoop of a fire alarm.

I said, "That will shut off in a few minutes, but the strobe will still flash for a while."

"Okay."

Chloe was sitting lazily in the beanbag. She had a smile on her face and her arms were folded across her lap.

"What a pain in the ass," I said while I paced around the room with my hands on my hips.

"Come sit with me, grumpy," Chloe said, moving over to make space.

I sat down. Chloe cuddled up next to me and put her head on my shoulder. We sat in silence, listening to the other students outside the door. Some were laughing and some were complaining. Eventually, everything got quiet and the alarm shut off.

The strobe continued to flash. Chloe and I sat in (almost) total darkness.

"Are you sure you don't want to make out?" Chloe finally said.

"I hate you."

Chloe laughed and teasingly said, "No you don't."

"I do right now."

"No you don't."

"Yes I do."

"No you don't."

I inhaled deeply and stared at the ceiling. I closed my eyes and thought, but only for a moment.

I got up and straddled Chloe.

My blood was pulsing with Jack Daniel's. Chloe put her hands on my hips and smiled. I looked down at her, watching her face appear and disappear with each flash of the strobe. After a few minutes, it stopped. I reached over and pulled up a shade, letting the dim glow from the streetlights fill the room.

I said the first thing that came to my drunken mind: "Why don't you show me your boobs?"

Chloe said, "Okay," and pulled down her top, revealing a gorgeous pair of breasts. I threw my head back and climbed off her. Chloe covered herself and laughed.

"What?" she said, looking down at me from the beanbag.

I covered my face and said, "Those are beautiful."

"Thank you."

I writhed on the floor while Chloe sat back and waited for me to return. She lifted her shirt back over her breasts, but leaned back and arched herself in a way that looked sweetly inviting. I lay on the floor and thought.

Finally I stood up and said, "I have to go."

"You do?"

I walked over, leaned down, and kissed her on the cheek.

"I do," I said.

I left without looking back, closing the door gently behind me.

Chloe passed Jenny on her way to the kitchen.

"Do you know Chloe?" I asked.

"I don't think so."

"Chloe, this is Jenny. Jenny, Chloe."

"Hi."

"Hi."

"What are you doing out here in the hallway?" Chloe asked me.

"Avoiding people," I said.

"That's good, Sean. I'm glad you came to my party to avoid people."

"Actually," I said, "I have to go to the kitchen to get another beer." I turned to Jenny and said, "Do you want one?"

Jenny shook her empty can and said, "Sure."

"I'll be right back."

Chloe and I squeezed our way into the kitchen. I opened the refrigerator and reached in for two more cans of Pabst. As soon as we were far enough away, Chloe said, "Still going after freshmen, huh, Sean?"

"Don't start," I said, keeping my gaze inside the fridge. I grabbed two cans with one hand and closed the door. "Besides," I said, "she's a sophomore."

Chloe shook her head slowly and gave me a disapproving look.

"*What?*"

"You're unbelievable."

I cracked one of the beers and gave Chloe a look of my own. I said, "You knew what you were doing."

I finally gave into temptation at the turn of century. Chloe and I went out for New Year's Eve with every intention of partying like it was 1999. We had gone to see a rockabilly band with Fraser and Brown and gotten drunk beyond comprehension. We were far away from Boston and had booked hotel rooms near the club. Though it was never discussed who was going to be rooming with whom, it was obvious where bodies were going to crash. At the end of the evening, Chloe and I said goodnight to Fraser and Brown and stumbled back to our room, which was spinning for both of us.

As soon as the door closed, we kissed, undressed, and threw each other onto the bed.

I didn't take her virginity.

After I graduated, Chloe travelled to Europe where, one night, she'd had sex with a friend of hers. She'd told me about it after coming back to Boston. I had always taken her as the type that would fall in love with whoever took her virginity, but I was totally wrong. Chloe shrugged it off as no big deal and remained friends with the guy after she got back. As best I could tell, she had finally had sex simply because she was getting to the age where virginity was less of a virtue and more of a liability.

After New Year's, Chloe and I continued having sex as friends with benefits—a new phrase and arrangement I was very comfortable with. I told her that I didn't regret what we had done in January, but that I still didn't want a girlfriend, which was still true. She seemed fine with that, and after seeing her nonchalant attitude about the guy she had lost her virginity to, part of me figured I was in the clear.

But part of me also didn't.

My conscience wasn't entirely clear. On the one hand, I knew that I was being honest with Chloe. I had expressed, in no uncertain terms, that I did not want to be in a relationship with her. On the other hand, I was old enough to know that meant nothing.

And by the end of the summer, Chloe and I were lost in familiar territory. We were right back to where we had been while I was still in college—her pursuing and me distancing. No amount of conversation seemed to remedy our situation, and I finally reached a point of anxious frustration.

I stopped taking Chloe's calls, hoping both her and the situation would just go away. But one day I hopped aboard a subway car and Chloe was standing right there in front of me. She was with a group of mutual friends. I grabbed hold of the safety rail and said hello to all of them, except her. As the train began to move, Chloe kept straining to get my attention—at one point even tugging at my sleeve—but I just turned my back on her. After three excruciatingly long subway stops, I finally said good-bye to our friends and walked off without saying a word to her.

It was the cruelest thing I had ever done to the sweetest person. I thought that getting Chloe to hate me would solve everything, but after several days, I realized how stupid that was. It also occurred to me that since knowing her, there were so many times that being around Chloe had reduced me to feeling like just a relatively human being. I truly hated myself and tormented myself for over a week. Even though I thought that initiating contact with her was a bad idea, I eventually called to apologize.

I let her scream at me, holding the phone away from my ear as she cried and accused. I tried to explain myself, but the words sounded ridiculous even as I said them. I apologized again, which was met with a click and a dial tone.

"I might have known what I was doing then," Chloe said, her arms folded across her chest. "But I definitely know what I'm *not* doing now."

"And what's that?" I asked.

"I'm *not* being obsessed with you."

I smiled, embarrassed, and said, "Fair enough."

"Jerk."

"I'll give you credit," I said. "The fact that I'm here right now is a testament to your kindness. I'm glad you reached out. I'm glad we're friends."

Chloe narrowed her eyes dramatically and said, "Hmm."

"All right, well anyway, I'm going to go back to the hallway now."

"You do that."

Chloe followed me with her eyes as I made my way through the crowd. Jenny was exactly where I had left her, not talking to anyone. I handed her the unopened beer, which she cracked and held up.

"Cheers."

I tapped my can to hers and said, "Are you not the social type either?"

Jenny shrugged and said, "Eh. Maybe I'm just not feeling it tonight."

"Why's that?"

Jenny looked up at me and said, "Well, I might as well be honest—I just broke up with someone."

"That sucks," I said. "Recently?"

"A few weeks ago, but, you know, it's an ongoing thing."

"It always is."

"Yeah."

"Are you over it?" I asked.

"Pretty much."

I said, "Girls seem to initially take it harder, but get over it pretty quickly in the long run. Guys are the opposite. They initially party and don't care, but then two months later they totally collapse and realize they want the girl back." I studied Jenny's face in the hopes that my philosophical yammering had somehow impressed her.

"Well," she said with a wry grin, "I wouldn't know anything about that."

We smiled and drank from our cans. Jenny and I talked until eleven o'clock in the evening became one o'clock in the morning. I told Jenny about growing up and listening to Megadeth. She told me about growing up and listening to Ani DiFranco. The two of us found some common ground in books. She liked Bukowski and I liked Kerouac.

"Although," she said, "I understand that Bukowski wasn't technically a Beat writer."

I sipped my beer and smiled. "I like that you know that," I said.

Jenny smiled and said, "I like that you *like* that I know that."

We gave each other flirtatious glances that lingered just long enough.

"So you live here in Allston?" I asked.

Jenny pointed to the door and said, "Right down the street, actually."

"Oh really? Did you crash this party? Did you just walk by and say, 'I'll check out this party?'"

She laughed and said, "No, my friend knows Brooks."

I said, "Oh, right. Yeah, Chloe lives here too."

"Right," Jenny said. "You mentioned that earlier."

"Oh," I said, "I didn't know if I had."

"You did. Did you date her?"

"Who? Chloe? No, we never dated."

"Oh."

There was a pause. Whether it was a natural pause or Jenny suspected something, I didn't know. Regardless, the alcohol made me elaborate.

"I mean, like, we never *technically* dated."

Jenny smirked and said, "So you've fucked?"

I laughed into the top of my can, which made a whoosh sound. "I mean, well, yeah."

"I thought so. Is it over?"

"Yes," I said.

"That's cool," Jenny said. "I mean, it's cool that you can still be friends."

"It is."

A guy wearing a green Lacoste shirt with a popped collar barreled his way past us and knocked into Jenny's beer. Her can didn't drop, but frothy liquid spilled onto the floor. I tensed up, but the guy immediately turned to Jenny and apologized. He even came back to the hallway with a new beer for Jenny and paper towels to clean up the mess. My chest deflated.

"Sorry again," he said, getting up off his hands and knees with the soaked paper towel.

Jenny told him not to worry about it and he left.

"That was nice," I said.

"Do you want to go to my place?" Jenny asked. "It's quieter there…obviously."

I wasn't positive I had successfully concealed the surprise on my face, but when I said "Sure," it sounded composed.

"Cool."

"Let me just tell my friends I'm leaving," I said.

Jenny nodded and I made my way back down the hall to find Fraser and Brown. In the kitchen, three hipsters—a girl and two guys—were sitting around a table. They were writing cryptic fan letters to Nicholas Cage on the back of Budweiser labels, swearing that they would send them in the morning. They were giggling and stoned, but intensely focused on what they were doing. Brown had miraculously found a girl who also liked Norwegian death metal, so his attention was very occupied. Fraser was drinking Pabst with a skinny guy whose arms were covered by colorful sleeve tattoos. They were discussing the first three Black Flag albums. It was late and the party was past its apex—the point where the prospect of a quiet, empty apartment was awkward, so people were calling it a night.

"I'm leaving with this girl," I told Fraser.

"Who?" Fraser asked, running his palm over his freshly shaved head. Fraser had begun losing some follicular real estate and had recently decided to just beat it to the punch. Coupled with his long goatee and smart eyeglasses, this made him look like a maniacal intellectual, which was maybe what he was going for. Either way, it suited him.

"This girl I've been talking to," I said.

Brown paused his own conversation for a moment and said, "Hmm. Is that the girl who stole her grandmother's glasses?"

I let out a small laugh and said, "Yeah."

"Cool," Fraser said. "Are you coming back?"

"That's the thing—I don't know."

"So what should I do? I'm your ride."

I thought about it for a second and said, "I'll figure it out."

Fraser raised his beer can and nodded affirmatively. Brown went back to discussing an epidemic of satanic church burning in Oslo. Chloe, who had come in and overheard the last part of my conversation, stepped forward. She gave me the same look she had been giving me earlier.

"I'm leaving," I told her.

"I heard."

"Thank you for having me."

"Hmm."

I opened my arms and we embraced. Chloe walked into the other room, but not before giving me one last look that I interpreted as *You're ridiculous*. I met Jenny back in the same spot we had been all night. I walked up to her and said, "Okay, let's go."

"Everything okay?"

I said, "Yeah. Why?"

"With your friend?"

"Chloe? Yup."

"No, I meant your guy friend. Isn't he your ride home?"

"Oh, Fraser? Yeah. It's all set."

"It is?"

"Yeah. Why?"

"So how are you getting home?"

"I don't know," I said. "I'll figure it out."

Jenny gave me another flirtatious grin. She turned and led me out the door.

I had never had a one-night stand, but I was pretty sure I was finally about to have one. I had slept with eight women in my life and they had all been a girlfriend, a friend, or an acquaintance. I had never, in the span of one evening, met a girl, had sex, and left knowing I wouldn't see her again.

And I was always suspicious of guys who claimed they had. Although I wasn't opposed to the idea of having a one-night stand (quite the opposite, actually), the chances of pulling one off seemed very slim. At the time, it seemed inconceivable that I could convince a woman I had just met to have sexual intercourse with me. I always assumed that all women viewed strange men they didn't know as ax murderers.

When Jenny and I reached the end of the block, she started walking up the front stoop of a brownstone. I looked back down the street. I could still see Chloe's apartment.

"Wow," I said. "You weren't kidding when you said you lived right down the street."

Jenny laughed as she inserted the key into her front door. "Come on in," she said. The hardwood floors in the hallway smelled like the gymnasium in my old elementary school—old and musty, yet freshly varnished. The first thing I noticed about Jenny's apartment was its spaciousness. Students in Allston were lucky to have a small studio, but Jenny's apartment had a large living room with what appeared to be two bedrooms. One of the doors was closed.

"Do you have a roommate?" I asked.

"Hello!?" a female voice called out from behind a closed door.

Jenny's eyes became as large as hen's eggs.

"Apparently so," I said.

Jenny turned to me and put her index finger to her lips. There was an awkward silence. I looked around the apartment, waiting for something to happen.

"Hi," Jenny called out, apprehensively.

"Hi," the voice responded.

"I thought you went to your mom's," Jenny said.

"I did. She was being a bitch, so I left."

"Oh."

"Who is here?" the voice asked.

"A friend," Jenny said.

Silence.

I had been standing with my hands in my pockets, shifting my eyes from Jenny to the closed door and back. After the conversation between Jenny and the phantom behind the door seemed over, I pointed to the hallway and said, "Listen, I can…"

Jenny shook her head. "No," she whispered. "Let's just go sit down."

We walked over to a couch that was covered with zebra print. Jenny sat down, but then stood up.

"Do you want a beer?" she asked, still somewhat whispering.

"Sure."

Jenny went to the fridge and took out two bottles of Miller High Life. She handed me the beer and we twisted off the caps. I hadn't seen a Miller High Life since I was a kid. The bottle looked exactly the same.

We talked for almost an hour before a loud bang came from the bedroom. The two of us looked over at the closed door, then back at each other.

I leaned into Jenny and quietly said, "I don't think your roommate wants company right now."

"It's not that."

"It's not? She doesn't seem happy that I'm here."

Jenny closed her eyes and shook her head. "She's not happy because I'm here with a guy."

I gave Jenny a puzzled look. "She's, like, protective of you?"

Jenny looked down at the floor, guiltily. "No," she said. "She's the ex I was telling you about."

"Oh."

"I'm sorry. She wasn't supposed to be here."

I placed my beer down on the coffee table and said, "So wait, what am *I* doing here?"

Jenny placed her beer down next to mine. She took the sides of my face in her hands and kissed me. Her kisses were soft and she used her tongue sparingly. I followed suit, thinking she was probably used to kissing women. Alcohol and eagerness were in full control of me. As we kissed, I became totally unaware that there was a jilted lover in the next room. I was completely focused on the pretty girl in my hands, and the new idea of being sexually intimate with a perfect stranger was exhilarating.

Suddenly, the bedroom door flew open with a bang. I heard footsteps, followed by the slamming of another door. Jenny and I retracted from each other. I opened my eyes and looked, but Jenny's ex had flown into the bathroom so quickly, I saw nothing but a blur. Jenny and I sat back and looked at each other. A few moments of quiet passed.

Finally, Jenny called out, "Marcy, is everything okay?"

"I'M FINE."

Jenny took off her glasses and pinched between her eyes.

"Is it always like this?" I whispered.

Jenny's expression turned from frustration to resentment. She whispered, but whispered forcefully: "She's moving out next week. I *told her* that I was going to start seeing other people. She *knows* this."

"I don't know what to do," I said.

"I don't either."

We sat quietly and looked toward the bathroom. I stared at the crack of light underneath the door, expecting shadowy movement, but there wasn't any. I waited to hear sobbing or crying, but there was nothing but dead silence everywhere. After a few minutes, I realized that the three people in the apartment were all having three intense thoughts and those three intense thoughts were all vastly different. Jenny placed her hand on my knee. I put mine on top of hers. The two of us sat for another few minutes, hand in hand in silence, waiting for the door to open.

But it never did.

When things seemed calm, Jenny and I pulled in to each other again and started kissing. I moved my hand to her hips and she moved hers toward the bulge in my jeans.

An explosion of glass shattering.

Jenny and I jumped back from each other again, but this time Jenny stood up and ran toward the bathroom door.

"Marcy, are you okay!?"

Silence.

"Marcy?"

Silence.

"Marcy, are you okay?"

"I'M FINE."

"What happened?"

"I'M FINE."

"What broke?"

Silence.

Exasperated, Jenny finally walked away from the door and sat down next to me.

"I'm gonna go," I told her.

"I'm sorry," she said.

I held up my hand and said, "Forget about it."

Jenny led me out of her apartment and into the front hallway. She closed the door behind her and we kissed again.

"I have to go," I finally said.

"One sec."

Jenny scampered back inside and came back with a small piece of paper.

"Here's my phone number," she said.

"Thanks," I said, placing the number in my pocket, guiltily assured I would never call it.

We kissed one last time and I walked back toward Chloe's apartment. As soon as I got to the front door, I knew the party was over. The house was dead quiet and all the lights were off. I cursed under my breath and walked up to the porch. I turned the doorknob slowly, figuring it would be locked.

To my surprise, it wasn't. I entered and tiptoed through the darkened apartment until I found Chloe's bedroom. I opened the door slowly, but it creaked. I winced. Chloe sat up in bed.

"Hello?" she said, sleepily.

"It's me," I whispered.

"What are you doing?"

"I need to stay here tonight."

Chloe laid back down and pulled up the covers. "Okay," she said.

I took off my coat and said, "Don't worry, I'll sleep on the floor."

Chloe turned on her side so her back was facing me.

"Oh, you're definitely sleeping on the floor."

Until We're Strangers Again

MMXIV

*In cartoons, in movies, time passes differently.
There are flashbacks and flashforwards.*

—Warren Spector

From 1999 to 2014, I worked as a villain in the professional wrestling business.

I wrote a book about it.

The Books

MMXIV

I learned a long time ago that reality was much weirder than anyone's imagination.

—Hunter S. Thompson

I've never contended that I had a really horrible life.

—Mary Karr

"Do you know who this guy is? He wrote a book."

"You wrote a book?"

"I did."

I looked down, somewhat embarrassed. I always felt there was something hideously obnoxious about going around and saying, "I'm a writer." Though I was certainly proud of the fact that I had finally written a book—a book that sold moderately well and received mostly positive reviews—I was still not comfortable calling myself "a writer." For one thing, it wasn't my full-time occupation. As for most people—even authors who had made it onto the *New York Times*'s Best Sellers list—scribbling prose did not pay my mortgage. For another thing, I was not "a writer" in any cultural sense of the word. At thirty-six years old, I still held on to my teenage stereotypes about writers. Writers were socially awkward people who had bad posture and smoked unfiltered cigarettes. I listened to loud music and drove a red muscle car—all symptoms of a midlife crisis I was just sort of going along with.

I had known Olivia for all of about fifteen minutes. It was a summer night—one month after my first book was published—and I was at Victory Lane, a bar in the suburbs I had a love/hate relationship with. It had a NASCAR theme, and as far as style was concerned, every expense was spared. Pictures of Dale Earnhardt hung on the walls and checkered flags hung from the ceiling. One night, I dubbed it the "Racecar Bar," which was made even funnier when my friends with Boston accents started calling it the "Racecah Bah." The place was literally divided down the middle between townies playing Keno and drinking Budweiser, and younger people texting on their cell phones and drinking Narragansett. As much as I hated the NASCAR theme, the beer was cheap, the jukebox was good, and I always had a good time whenever I went.

Olivia and a friend of hers from high school had taken seats at the table behind me. It was karaoke night. We began talking after she asked me for the large binder that listed the songs available to sing. I picked up the three-ring notebook, placed it on her table, and asked, "What are you singing tonight?"

"Umm, probably nothing," she said. "I just like to look. Will you be singing tonight?"

I held up my pint of beer and said, "It depends. If I am sober enough to drive, then I am too sober to sing."

"Good rule," she said with a laugh.

We started making small talk. Olivia was from a nearby town. When I told her I was from Medfield, Olivia turned up her nose and put on a bourgeoisie accent. "Medfield?" she said. "Oh *really*?" I laughed and told her the thing I often found myself saying to people with regards to my hometown: "I'm from *old* Medfield."

I was about to ask what year she graduated high school, but I stopped myself. She was obviously a lot younger than I was, and I suddenly didn't want to know. I didn't want to know because it would have reinforced what I painfully knew—I was getting older. Too old, probably, to be flirting with a girl Olivia's age. I also didn't want to know because I figured as soon Olivia asked my age and "thirty-six" came out of my mouth; she would have stopped talking to me, which I legitimately didn't want to happen.

There was an immediate spark. Within minutes of talking, we were cracking each other up and having a good time. She was easy to talk to, and when she told me that her majors in college were psychology and theology, she had my undivided attention.

She was my type: tall, brunette, and smart, with a friendly, automatic smile. She had athletic muscles even though she told me she didn't work out, and she had a quick wit to match her natural beauty. Although I had dated women who didn't fit my type, I occasionally found myself falling back into it like a safety net. This was something I was very much thinking about as we ordered more drinks.

Just as Olivia and I were getting into a more serious conversation about religion, a young guy who looked like Jesus walked into the bar. He was wearing a Chaotic Wrestling T-shirt. We pointed at each other.

"Whoa," he said. "Sean Görman."

"Where did you get that shirt?" I asked.

"We've actually met."

"We have?"

We shook hands (again, apparently). "I'm Rob," he said. "I started working as a referee for Chaotic just before you left."

"Oh, okay. I'm sorry I don't remember."

"That's cool," he said. "What are you doing here?"

I pointed at Olivia and said, "Talking to this girl. We just met."

Rob looked at Olivia and said, "Do you know who this guy is? He wrote a book."

I now had *Olivia's* undivided attention. I tried to explain what I did in wrestling. She just sort of nodded as I talked and I finally said, "I used to get paid to make people mad."

"Are you done with wrestling?" Rob asked, hearing my use of the past tense.

"Probably," I said. "I think I've had my fill."

"That's too bad." Rob looked at Olivia and said, "This guy was great. The fans *hated* him."

Olivia laughed. Then she looked at me and said, "Really?"

"They did," I said.

Rob looked at me and extended his hand. "Well," he said, "good to see you, man. I hope you come back."

I shook his hand and told him "thank you," which he probably didn't realize I meant in two different ways. He walked over to the other side of the bar and sat with his friends.

I wasn't planning on mentioning either my book or wrestling to Olivia. Although the two things were integral parts of my life, I was interested to see whether I could get Olivia's interest without them. The main theme of my book centered around the clash between my onstage persona and my real-life persona. Having been out of wrestling for well over a year, I had decided that when it came to dating women, I wanted my real-life persona to be the first foot forward.

But fate had other plans, and Olivia seemed to be okay with it. As we were talking, a British rugby player moseyed up to Olivia's unattended high school friend, Beth. The guy was redheaded, sunburnt, and spotted with freckles. He was also completely shit-faced, and within minutes he had his limp arm around Beth's shoulder. Between the slurred speech and his Cockney accent, none of us could understand a word he was saying. However, when he took out his cell phone during last call, we all knew what was happening. Beth looked slightly panicked.

"Oh, boy," Olivia said to me. "I think we'd better go."

"Well," I said. "I don't want you to feel left out."

"What do you mean?"

I said, "I can give you my phone number too if you'd like."

Olivia laughed and said, "Oh, I don't know."

I shrugged one shoulder and said, "All right, then. It was nice talking to you anyway."

As I was about to walk away, Olivia reached into her purse and took out her phone. She looked at me and smiled. She said, "I was just kidding. You can definitely give it to me."

For the next three weeks, Olivia and I got to know each other through texts, which I had begrudgingly accepted as a regular form of communication. Friends my age used texts to answer short, practical questions like *What time do you want to leave?* Younger people, I noticed, were content to have an entire conversation through texts, which struck me as odd. Anytime a twenty-something started sending me a mass of text messages that amounted to whole paragraphs, I would finally stop them and type, *You know you can just call me, right? Keystrokes don't have to be involved here.* It was something that clearly showed my age.

But Olivia couldn't physically talk. Just days after we met, she went in for a tonsillectomy. She was texting me from her sofa in between daytime television and vanilla ice cream. I was informed of this when I finally asked her on a date and she told me it might be a while before she could eat or drink.

Don't worry, I texted her, *I had my tonsils out when I was in kindergarten. It wasn't that bad.*

Oh yeah? she replied. *When was that by the way?*

I smiled as I typed, *You want to get into the age thing now?*

Might as well hahaha, she responded.

Sitting in my living room, I typed the truth into my phone. Lying wasn't even a momentary consideration.

My birthday is on June 27th and on that day I will be 37 years old. I added, *So, what do you think about that?*

There was a pause. Olivia wrote back, *Hahaha. I thought you were 30 but that's not bad!*

And you? I responded.

I'm 22.

My eyes probably widened. I'd thought she was older, less because of her appearance and more because of how she carried herself. She walked with confidence and dressed well. She spoke like an adult, which I supposed she technically was. There was something innate, yet undoubtedly mature about her.

More than a decade in professional wrestling had suspended me in a state of perpetual adolescence. I partied like I was still in my twenties long into my thirties. I never got married or had kids. I stayed mostly single, and by the time I was staring down forty, I was beginning to realize that I was living like an eighteen-year-old with a mortgage, a fast car, and a fair amount of disposable income. Some of my friends were more than happy to call me on my bullshit. Each time my friend Katherine visited Boston, she affectionately called me a loser. We'd gone to college together. She had become a mother, and a wife, and a New York attorney. I had become a thirty-something who spent his weekends wearing purple suits and playing pretend. "I'm doing what I want to do," I would tell her whenever she busted my chops. "I'm happy and wouldn't trade it for anything." Not even Katherine, with all her rhetorical skill, could argue with bliss.

Olivia sent another text: *What do you think about that?*

I smiled and wrote, *If you're okay with it, then so am I.*

Okay good, she replied.

My success in pro wrestling had only been regional. I never made it to "the big time" and I was only ever "famous" within fifty feet of whatever building I was performing in. Still, though, being up onstage elevated me both literally and figuratively. It allowed me to be with women who, under normal circumstances, would have been far out of my league, some of whom were much younger. Just prior to leaving wrestling, I found myself in a parking lot just outside of New York, making out with a nineteen-year-old girl in the front seat of her Toyota. Her 2011 graduation tassel hung in my face from her rearview mirror like a judgmental albatross. Though the grinding was hard and the windows were steamed, I ended up just going home out of fear that things would get complicated between us—plus the fact that I was in another state and would have had to take her back to a hotel room, which, even for me, felt way too sleazy.

Contrary to what my history indicated, I didn't really have a penchant for young women. As a matter of fact, most Millennials annoyed me. I was irritated by their lifeless pop music, their obsession with their cell phones, and their insistence on finding everything offensive. This also showed my age. As a young man, I had been endearingly angry, but now I was just old and curmudgeonly. While Olivia and I finished up our text conversation for the night, I wondered why a woman fifteen years my junior would be interested in me. I figured that since women matured faster than men and pro wrestling had arrested my development, Olivia and I were meeting somewhere in the middle.

Or something like that.

I was clueless. I had no idea why I would have any appeal to a woman Olivia's age. I tried to stay current, but made no effort to be hip. And as much as I enjoyed new music and movies, I always found myself pulled down by the heavy anchor of nostalgia, still locked in my love for the music and films of my youth. Being around the rookies in wrestling probably made me sound younger than I actually was. Sometimes I noticed their youthful vernacular seeping into mine. Other than that, I felt just about as old as I was.

But the punk attitude from my youth had only gotten more punk with age. The more rings I acquired around the trunk of my tree, the less of a fuck I actually gave. Though I never liked punk music, I always liked its spirit. I liked the idea of questioning authority, looking for truth, and cutting through the bullshit to get to the essence of *it*. I had never really put on an act to get laid, and I put on even less of one as I neared forty. I wondered if part of my appeal for Olivia was the fact that I wasn't bullshitting her, as so many of the guys her own age probably were.

After Olivia's convalescence, we had our first date at a restaurant a few towns over, in Franklin. I chose the place because it was nice but not too nice. We sat at the granite-topped bar in the warm lighting coming from behind the backlit vodka bottles. It was a Thursday night and the place was filled with older people in business attire drinking martinis from chilled glasses. I ordered a mojito and Olivia asked me what it was. After I told her, she said it sounded good and ordered one too. "I've been drinking them for a while," I told her. After we got our drinks, we clinked our glasses together and began talking.

"So you have the night off from work tonight?" I asked.

Olivia sipped her mojito and said, "Wow, that's really good. Anyway, yeah. I have to work all weekend, which totally sucks."

"Where do you work again? I don't think I ever asked."

"I work at the mall, at a clothing store. It's okay. I like the people and I actually like the clothes, but obviously it's not a permanent job for me."

"Right," I said. "It sounds like you're in the same boat as most college grads. You'll find something, though."

Olivia looked at me and smiled. She said, "Umm, yeah, I haven't graduated yet."

"You haven't?"

"No, this is my last year coming up."

"Wait," I said, "aren't you twenty-two? Did you take a year off?"

Olivia sipped her drink and laughed. "Oh, yeah. I guess I never told you that I was still in school."

I smiled, shook my head, and put my drink down on the bar. "No," I said. "You definitely didn't."

Olivia told me about repeating the first grade. She had to have eye surgery when she was a little girl, which made her miss three months of school. Apparently she'd had a rare condition that could have been permanent if it wasn't operated on quickly. Hearing her describe wearing a huge eye patch and missing all her friends tugged at my heartstrings more than I expected, and I wasn't even drunk.

"So, yeah," she said, "I stayed back in the first grade."

"That sucks," I said. "But your eye seems fine now."

"Oh, it's totally fine now, but it was really messed up. That's why it needed to be done right away. It couldn't wait."

I nodded and sipped my drink. Olivia was sort of studying me.

"So, yeah," she said, "that's why I'm still in college at twenty-two." She smiled and said, "Is that okay?"

I was taken aback just a little. "'Is that okay?'? What do you mean?"

Olivia said, "Well, you know, is that weird for you?"

"Not gonna lie," I said. "It kind of is."

"But I'll be done next summer. I'm looking forward to it."

"Do you live in a dorm?" I asked.

"No, I live in an apartment off campus."

"Good," I said. "All right, that's good."

We laughed faintly, picked up our menus, and ordered a small pizza to share.

A lot was going through my mind as we sat at the bar getting to know each other. After Olivia told me she was twenty-two, it had never occurred to me that she might still be in school. I just thought she was living with her parents after graduation. I figured Olivia had avoided telling me she was still in school for the same reason I had avoided telling her my age. But I was going to be thirty-seven years old in a month and the thought of visiting my girlfriend at a college dormitory was insane. Like taking a nineteen-year-old to a hotel room, it was a moral Rubicon I just wasn't going to cross.

But I liked the girl. Regardless of her age, I genuinely liked her. She loved children and dogs, but not in the insipid way that some women liked children and dogs—I could tell by the way she spoke. She was sincerely nurturing and wanted to help those who couldn't help themselves. That was why she was majoring in psychology and it wasn't an act. And she was definitely mature for her age, which was something she both knew and prided herself on. As she explained it: "I was an only child, so I spent more time around adults than children. So I think that just sort of rubbed off."

Olivia was like a young fusion of my three previous girlfriends. I always tried not to compare a new woman to my exes, but like everyone, I often failed. Whether I liked it or not, the women I had loved in my past had become the archetypes for the ones I might love in the future.

And I couldn't help but wonder which people in Olivia's own past I was being compared with. Halfway through our date, Olivia and I broke one of the rules of first dates by talking about our exes. I gave Olivia a succinct overview of my ex-girlfriends and why things ended and Olivia followed suit, but she had just one story to tell. The only boyfriend she ever had was her boyfriend from high school. When I talked about my high school girlfriend, it felt like a century ago. Olivia talked about it like it was last week.

I began to see all the potential disasters. I had fifteen years' worth of life on Olivia. And I had packed no small amount of living into those fifteen years. As mature as Olivia was, I knew that nothing could compare with real-world heartbreak and what it taught you. Inside my head, I was seeing myself in the third person. I scanned the restaurant and wondered what I was doing there. Why was I on a date with a college student? Why was I on a date with a girl who had been a zygote when I was a freshman in high school? What purpose did it serve? How could the outcome be anything but terrible? I was past the point in my life when I would willfully engage in romantic self-destruction (or so I thought). Throughout my entire adulthood, I struggled hard with pessimism. I tried desperately not to always see the end of things at the beginning of them. Still though, I liked Olivia. And as we sat there at the bar, I thought that the best thing for her was to live her young life without me. We were only thirty minutes into our first date and part of me already wanted to let her go.

The rest of the evening went by quickly. We never stopped talking or laughing, and surprisingly, our age gap was never brought up, nor did it seem to matter. A few times, I looked around to see whether any of the other patrons were looking at us strangely. None of them appeared to be. In my eyes, Olivia's age changed with each moment. She appeared to be older or younger, depending on what she was saying, or how the light fell on her face. Later, though, when I looked behind the bar and caught a glimpse of us in the mirror, we looked like any other two adults on a date. Nothing about it seemed strange, but the feeling that I should end things before they even began was still tugging at the back of my brain stem.

"How far away is your college?" I asked.

"It's a little over an hour," Olivia said. "It depends on the traffic and how you go. Why?"

"Just wondering."

"Yeah, it's not too bad."

I nodded. We sat in silence for a few moments, but it wasn't uncomfortable silence. We were actually smiling at each other.

"Well, this has been really nice," Olivia said.

"It has," I said.

"Talking to you is really easy."

"It's really easy talking to you too."

I signed the check and slid it to the bartender. Olivia put her hand on her chest and gently laughed to herself.

"What is it?" I asked.

"Actually," Olivia said, "this is probably the best date I've ever been on." She composed herself and said, "So thank you."

I couldn't let her go.

"So I read your book."

"Oh God. Are you serious?"

"Yeah."

I said, "Well, you didn't have to buy it. Why didn't you tell me? I would have given you a copy."

"That's okay," Olivia said. "I don't mind. I actually ordered it the day after we met. It gave me something to do while I couldn't talk. It was really good."

"Thank you."

Olivia reached into her purse and took out a small notepad. "So," she said, "I have a bunch of questions."

"Oh God."

We were in my kitchen and on our third official date. I was cooking tacos while Olivia looked through her notepad and began asking questions. I was glad to have my hands busy slicing tomatoes, because I was in a minor state of panic.

There was never a doubt in my mind that I would write a memoir. And there was never a doubt in mind that I would write a memoir about wrestling. What I never considered, however, was how writing a memoir might affect any of my potential relationships after the book was published. While I agonized over how my friends and family were going to take the book, I never once thought about how a woman who was interested in me might take the book.

And yet there she was in front of me, flipping through a notepad.

Olivia asked me about the people in the book—what their real names were and what they were doing now. I was giving her the sequel that no one, except the characters in the book, would ever know. She asked me how I felt about them now and whether I still saw any of them. "Almost all of them," I told her. It seemed like Olivia was excited to have read a book and finally had the opportunity to ask the author about all the unwritten details.

I answered everything easily and honestly, but it was an incredibly weird feeling. It occurred to me that people I didn't know were reading my memoir. I had *readers*. Listening to Olivia recount scenes in my book made the abstract a reality. Before, the notion of a reader was just a faceless entity. Now one of them was standing in my kitchen.

Emotionally, it also put me at a huge disadvantage and made me feel extremely vulnerable. As much as Olivia and I were getting to know each other, she now had a massive chuck of my past sitting on her bookshelf. She now knew way more about me than I knew about her. Like the concept of a reader, the idea of putting intimate details about my life between the covers of a book was only an abstraction until the intimate details about my life were actually in the mind of a physical person standing right in front of me.

After I answered Olivia's last question, she scanned her notes and said, "I think that's it. Anyway, I thought it was really good. I really liked it." She put the notepad back in her purse.

"That's it?"

Olivia gave me a quizzical look and said, "Yeah, why?"

"So, you're not going to ask me about all the crazy shit in there?"

"Like what?"

"The sex, the drugs—all the stuff that everyone else asks me about."

Olivia shrugged her shoulders and said, "Oh, yeah. That stuff didn't really bother me."

"Really?"

"No," Olivia said. She walked over to my refrigerator and said, "Can I have a beer?"

"Sure, I'll get it."

Olivia said, "No, that's okay."

Olivia opened the fridge and took out a Corona. She walked over to where I was standing and opened the bottle with a bottle opener. Then she walked around me and took one of the lime wedges off my cutting board and squeezed it into the bottleneck. She orbited around me while I stood motionless holding a spatula.

"Thanks," she said.

"No problem."

Olivia took a sip of her beer and said, "Anyway, yeah, that stuff doesn't bother me."

"You don't look at me differently now?"

"No," she said. "Not at all. I mean, is your life still like that?"

I thought for a second. "No, I guess not," I said.

"So who cares? Everyone has a past."

"Do you?" I asked.

"I guess," Olivia said. She took another sip of her beer and smiled at me. "It's just not as crazy as yours."

"Or as long," I said.

"No," she said with a laugh. "Definitely not."

I smiled and sliced onions without tears.

I was hoping we were finally going to kiss.

My first book reading—the first book reading I had ever done in my life—was held at an art gallery in Medfield. The local newspaper had run a story about my book, and a woman who worked for the gallery contacted me about doing a reading. I was ecstatic.

I quickly wrote down an outline of everything I wanted to say. Although I had years of public speaking experience, my anxiety was high. I wasn't going to be performing as a "character," and everything depended on me. In wrestling, I was only *part* of the show. If I was unable to make an event due to illness, the show could go on. The pressure of flying solo with everything on my shoulders made me neurotically crazy. Weeks before the reading, I told my friends that I didn't want to go out to bars for fear of catching a cold. They said I was insane as I doused my hands with another heaping load of hand sanitizer.

They were probably right.

The Zullo Gallery wasn't far from my friend Colin's apartment in downtown Medfield. The night of the reading, a few other close friends and I sat in his living room, casually drinking beer. I had only two hours to go before the event, and being so close to the finish line eased my worry. Olivia wasn't able to come, which was fine. Having her there would have just been added pressure. Though not totally relaxed, I was still in the best of moods.

Just before seven o'clock, we all walked to the center of town, and I couldn't help but look back. All around me were the landmarks of my youth—the convenience store we used to buy sodas from and the park we used to loiter in. It would have been typical for me to feel that my past was a million years ago, but when the center of a small town never really changes, it can make a million years seem like just a moment ago. As a kid, the only two things I ever wanted to be was a manager in pro wrestling and a writer. And while I hadn't achieved the worldwide success I had hoped for, I had still done it. It wasn't hard for me to look at Baker's Pond and see my fifteen-year-old self. He was gangly, nervous, and insecure. He was mad at the world. He was dreaming about getting out of Medfield. He had little hope for the future. And as we walked the final steps to the downtown area, I couldn't help but look at the empty park bench where I used to sit and wish I could go back in time. I wanted to hand that fifteen-year-old ten dollars and tell him that everything was going to be okay.

As I climbed the steps to the gallery, I could hear the murmur of a large crowd. Colin looked back at me and said, "It sounds like there's a lot of people here." And as I made my way up and turned the corner, my heart almost seized like a piston in an engine.

Standing in front of me were a dozen of my high school classmates. I had heard that a few might be coming, but I was bowled over when I saw how many were actually there. I immediately started shaking hands and giving long, affectionate hugs. Very few of them still lived in Medfield, and some had come from as far away as New Hampshire. It was like walking into a surprise birthday party and actually being surprised. I couldn't believe that I was standing in a room with some of these people almost twenty years after last seeing them, let alone at a book reading for a book I had written. I had reached a new horizon of humility. I felt like I needed to spend the rest of my life saying "thank you" with every other breath.

Something I had never told anyone was that during my time in wrestling, I would often imagine the people I went to high school with sitting out in the audience. Although I felt a great deal of pride and excitement each time I walked into the ring in front of a huge crowd of a thousand people or more, it was never fully satisfying just being in front of a mass of strangers. There was always a part of me that needed to envision my classmates sitting in the seats, like I was performing at an assembly back in high school. I never asked any of the wrestlers whether they also did this, but I was always curious. In many ways, all of us in wrestling were a bunch of insecure extroverts. Why I did this mental

exercise before going into the ring was never lost on me—I needed to say, even just internally, "Look at me now." I had done this
a hundred times as a performer and figured that seeing my high
school classmates out in an audience would always just be some
unattainable goal I would never really achieve—a surreal fantasy
that I would never actually see.

Until I was actually seeing it.

Seldom were moments in my life ever "like a dream," but in
the Zullo Gallery that night I was very clearly standing right in
the middle of one. After walking up the stairs, I felt so euphori-
cally drunk I thought I might actually faint.

Fraser was there with his parents, but Brown wasn't. Unlike
a character in a book or a movie, he had just sort of vanished
from my narrative without much explanation. A few years earlier,
Brown had decided to follow his parents out to the rural parts
of western Massachusetts, where he essentially became a recluse.
He ditched his cell phone and his car. Even though I still saw
him a few times a year—usually on his birthday—I really missed
the days when I could just stop by his apartment on a random
Saturday night, drink beers with him, and listen to old Metallica
albums until four o'clock in the morning. I missed that, and I
missed him as a friend. While Fraser and I often bitched about
society and talked about leaving it, Brown actually did it. Like his
decision not to graduate high school, it was something I understood and respected, but wouldn't have done myself. I could be
as misanthropic as anyone, but the egocentric glory of the room
I was presently standing in was always enough to pull me away
from a solitary life in the woods.

The gallery was packed with people. After greeting as many of my old classmates as I could, I was pulled away and introduced to some men and women in business attire. They were the executives from Needham Bank—a local bank that had sponsored the event and provided the hors d'oeuvres that everyone was snacking on.

In the background, the PA was playing "It's a Long Way to the Top (If You Wanna Rock 'n' Roll)," which was something I had planned beforehand. I used to listen to the song while driving to wrestling shows to get pumped up. I stood off to the side while the gallery director took the microphone and everyone sat down in white folding chairs. AC/DC was switched off and the director introduced one of the reps from Needham Bank, who talked about the bank and all the different events they sponsored throughout the year.

As I waited, I looked out over the crowd. My mom was sitting in the middle with a few of her friends. She looked proud and happy, which warmed me like a good shot of bourbon or, I thought, her beef stew. The seats up front were filled with older people drinking chardonnay. My high school classmates lined the back wall. As the rep from the bank spoke, I noticed that some of the girls (now married women) were among the prettiest and most popular girls from my class. Though they probably would have bashfully denied that fact in the present, my memory of the past knew it was true. I looked at a few I had had quiet crushes on, still amazed they were there, still quietly crushing on them.

In front of the crowd, my mind was focused, yet still occasionally wandering. I was thinking about how childhood was the time when everyone was sculpted from earthly clay. Adulthood put some finishing touches on the different shapes we all became, but childhood was the time our real form was molded. My ex-girlfriend Maxine once said that I was "obsessed with school." I knew what she meant. She didn't mean that I was obsessed with actual school, just that I was obsessed with the past.

She was right.

I was born with a Proustian ability to remember things past. My memory switched on in my grandmother's house when I was three years old and had revved in high gear ever since. I never really understood what a photographic memory was, but when I read about something called hyperthymesia—a condition where people can literally recall every single day of their life—I figured that I was somewhere on that spectrum. I couldn't remember every day of my life, but I could remember a large amount of detail from long-past events. Sometimes if I offhandedly mentioned something that had happened when I was a toddler, my mother would look at me with astonishment and say, "My God, how do you remember that?" And I would always reply with, "I dunno…I just do."

Why I was drawn to memoir writing was never a mystery to me. It was something I could always *just do*. And as the rep from Needham Bank finished his introduction, I took one last look at my high school classmates. Part of me thought that I had won life. Another part of me thought that my friend Katherine was right—I was a loser. I was thirty-seven years old and I still wanted to impress the people I went to high school with. Even though I had rejected them in some ways, in one large way, I still desperately wanted their attention and approval.

And it seemed like I finally had it.

As I took the mic and stepped in front of the audience, the room filled up with applause. I smiled graciously and waited for it to settle. Once I began to speak, I spoke about the past. And even though I was standing in the place where it all began, I knew I was somewhere very far from where my feet had once stood.

Olivia and I kept on all summer. We ate dinners and watched movies and took weekend trips to Cape Cod. We did all the things that couples do, but never discussed whether or not we were really a couple. The only time we ever got near the topic was just before the Fourth of July. Olivia asked me to come with her to the lakefront cabin in New Hampshire where her parents stayed each year.

"Your parents will be there?" I asked.

"Yeah," she said. "Why?"

"You want me to meet your parents?"

"Sure. Why not?"

We were sitting in my living room, drinking margaritas. I took a small sip from my icy glass and placed it down on my coffee table. "Well, do you think we're at that stage yet?"

Olivia smiled at me and said, "I don't know. Are we?"

"I don't know," I said. "That's my point."

"I see what you mean."

She looked disappointed, but tried to conceal it. I felt bad, but I told Olivia that I didn't believe in any set rules for dating; it just felt a little early to be meeting her parents. We had been seeing each other for a little over a month, and because of our conflicting work schedules, that time was limited to one night during the week and one night during the weekend. Finally, I said, "I'm sorry. I'm just not comfortable with that right now."

Olivia shrugged her shoulders and picked up her margarita. "That's okay," she said. "It's just always a fun time and I thought you might like it. Maybe next time."

We moved on.

All summer long I debated how I felt about Olivia, and my feelings were never consistent. On Tuesday, I would resolve to get more serious with Olivia and make things work. On Wednesday, I would resolve to break it off before things got too complicated. On Thursday, I would fail to do either.

My affections for Olivia were pure. She was strong, sweet, and quirky. I liked her optimism and the way she lost her breath when she laughed. The only time our age gap felt strange was when we talked about where we were during 9/11. I was at work after college. Olivia was in the second grade. Beyond that, I began to see our age difference as less of a problem and more of an asset. I enjoyed listening to her talk about her childhood because it was so remarkably different than mine. She seemed to like hearing about my childhood because I was living history. We introduced each other to new music, which I loved.

Number-wise, our ages were never a problem, but where we were in our lives was. I knew that Olivia's still being in college was either going to be a fork in the road or a roadblock that couldn't be negotiated. I didn't want to fall for someone I was never going to see, or was just going to leave. And I didn't want to hold Olivia back from doing what she needed to do after she graduated. As September approached, I knew that one of us was going to have to decide.

I gathered the courage just before Olivia left for school. It was a Sunday afternoon and we were sitting on a park bench at Baker's Pond. It was the place that, for reasons I didn't know (yet there were probably a lot of them), I had decided to take us. I was nervous and trying not to show it. Before I spoke, I looked around and saw that Olivia and I were the only ones in the park. It was a beautiful, sunny day. I wondered where all the teenagers were and why they weren't hanging out like my friends and I used to. I grumpily figured they were probably sitting in their finished basements playing Xbox and talking to people online with those ridiculous headsets. I shook away my distractions and got down to it.

"So I've given this a lot of thought," I said during a conversational lull.

Olivia looked at me, a bit surprised. "Okay," she said.

"*A lot* of thought," I emphasized. "I've actually been sort of agonizing about it."

Olivia nodded as if she knew exactly what was coming.

I said, "Do you think things are going to work out between you and me after you go back to school?"

Olivia said, "It doesn't sound like you do."

I nodded and looked at the ground. "I don't," I said.

"Why?"

"A few reasons." I looked back up. A police cruiser passed by on North Street, the officer inside casually riding with his elbow out the window. "I mean, you're over an hour away. I know that seems like nothing sitting here talking, but in day-to-day life, that's a huge problem—at least for me, anyway."

"Well, yeah," Olivia said. "We would see each other less than we do now."

"A lot less."

"Right."

I said, "I mean, I'm just being honest here, but when I get home at five o'clock on a Tuesday I'm just not going to want to drive over an hour to see you, then see you for a few hours and drive over an hour to come home late at night. And I wouldn't expect you to do that either. So the only time we'll ever see each other is on the weekends, which is fine until one of us maybe wants to do something else, like, with our friends, so then it's pressure and the other person gets resentful...." I knew I was sounding neurotic. I said, "I know I sound neurotic."

"So you don't want to just see how it goes?"

"That's the thing." I stopped and thought for a moment. "That's what I've been agonizing about. Because part of me thinks you're right—I should just chill out and see how it goes and stop being so nuts."

"O-*kay*."

I paused again, trying to think of the best way to say what I was about to say and realizing there was no best way or good way. Finally I said, "This is one of those times where I hate to sound all wizened because I'm older than you, but there's no other way to put it."

"What do you mean?"

"I've been through this before," I said. "The long distance thing. Twice, actually. Not only that, but I've seen tons of other people go through it. It just doesn't work. It never does. I mean, didn't you see a bunch of people break up with their significant others from back home during your freshman year?"

Olivia thought about it and said, "I guess, yeah. Some."

"Plus," I said, "what about after you graduate? Aren't you going to California?"

"I'm still not sure I want to do that."

"That's what I mean," I said. "I don't want you to hold back on going because of me. If you have something lined up out there, then you should go do it. Don't stay here because of me."

"Oh, I wouldn't," Olivia said. She looked at me and smiled apologetically. "I mean, no offense. But, if that turns out to be the best thing for me, then I would go."

"Good," I said.

Olivia looked out over the park while I looked at her. We sat in silence for a few moments. She turned back to me and said, "Well, this is sad."

"It is."

I looked down.

A ground nest of yellow jackets was right in front of us. I hadn't noticed it. They were coming and going from beneath a small root sticking up from the dirt. I pointed and said, "Look at that."

Olivia recoiled and kicked her foot away. "I can't believe we didn't see that."

I waved it off and said, "They're fine as long as you don't bother them."

We turned back toward each other. We smiled sadly. Olivia said, "Well, you've been the nicest guy I've ever dated."

"Thank you," I said. "This has been the easiest breakup I've ever had."

We laughed a little, then sat quietly. A few cars drove past. The wind stirred the leaves. A bobwhite chirped out its mating call from the east, which was returned by another from the west.

Finally Olivia said, "I'm hungry."

"So am I."

"Can we still go to lunch?"

"Absolutely."

We stood up and hugged. We held one another for a while, each of us looking at something different over the other's shoulders. Olivia was probably seeing her future—leaving college and moving to the West Coast. I was seeing my past. I had been single for eight years, and in that whole time I had never really been struck by any of the women I dated. For a long time, I thought that I might be done with coupled life. A solitary life was fine, but Olivia showed me that another life was fine, too. I still had the capacity to love someone and accept her love in return. She showed me that I wasn't as curmudgeonly as I sometimes thought I was. I felt bad about keeping Olivia at arm's length the whole summer, but it was self-preservation. I knew there was something there, but I knew the logistics of that thing were untenable. I also found the old cliché to be true. As much as I didn't want Olivia to leave, the truth was that I loved her and so I needed to let her go.

We left the park and drove to a seafood restaurant in Dedham. Even though Olivia and I had just ended our relationship, nothing really felt awkward. We drove in my car with the windows down just like always. We chatted while Olivia scanned the dial on the radio just like always. In some ways, it seemed like we were happier now that the huge rock on our shoulders was finally gone.

We went to a place called the Summer Shack, which was owned by a local seafood chef who was fairly well known in New England. Although the food was upscale, the Shack itself wasn't— oyster specials were written on chalkboards, and a wooden statue of a fisherman in a yellow raincoat greeted us at the door. Olivia and I walked in and took seats at the bar. It was mid-afternoon, just between lunch and dinner. The Red Sox game was on the TVs and the only other people there were another couple sitting at the far end of the long bar.

Olivia and I both ordered pints of beer. I thought about sardonically toasting to our smooth breakup, but didn't. Everything between us was as easy as it had ever been, and I didn't want to tempt fate. The bartender—a stocky man with a shiny shaved head and a dark goatee—took our orders. Olivia looked up at the rafters of pinewood and said, "I like this place. It's cozy."

"The food's really good, too," I said.

I leaned back in my chair and folded my arms. Olivia and I looked up at the Red Sox game, but without interest. Neither of us was a sports fan. The bartender placed a basket of cornbread in front of us and walked over to the other end of the bar. He pointed at the couple sitting by the cash register and said, "Can I get you guys another drink?"

I glanced over at the couple. The man was thin with rectangular eyeglasses and smooth facial features. He was blocking my view of the woman, but I could see that she was wearing a Red Sox cap with a tattered brim. I turned back to my beer and took a sip. Olivia was smoothing butter over a piece of cornbread. "This is amazing," she said. "I'm so hungry."

I took a piece of cornbread and put it on my plate. The Sox game went to commercial. An ad for Sam Adams beer came on. It showed the large metal tanks inside the Sam Adams brewery in downtown Boston. The bartender was still at the other end of the bar, leaning over his knee with one foot on a crate. He was looking up at the television along with the other couple.

"Have you ever been to the Sam Adams brewery?" he asked them.

I looked over.

The woman shook her head and said, "No, but we've been to a brewery in Europe."

Her voice.

I narrowed my eyes and leaned forward so I could see her. I wasn't aware of my jaw dropping, but it probably did. I looked at Olivia, merrily eating a piece of cornbread. I looked back at the woman. For a minute, I wasn't completely sure I was seeing who I was seeing.

It was Maxine.

It was my ex-girlfriend—my last girlfriend, from eight years ago. I hadn't seen her in years, since one final meeting at a different bar in Dedham that ended with the both of us in angry tears.

"Holy shit," I said quietly.

"What?" Olivia asked, taking a sip of her pint.

I pointed behind me and whispered, "That's my ex-girlfriend."

Olivia looked over my shoulder with both curiosity and surprise. "Which one?" she asked.

"Maxine," I said.

"The one from your book?"

"*Yes.*"

Olivia looked over my shoulder again. Then she looked at me. "What are you going to do?"

I took a long pull from my beer.

There had always been a real possibility that I was going to see Maxine again. People ran into people. It was just how the Boston area and, it seemed, my life, had always been. Theoretically, I had prepared myself for the moment. But I could not have prepared myself for the *actual* moment—Maxine sitting there with her (I assumed) boyfriend and me sitting there with the twenty-two-year-old I had just broken up with thirty minutes earlier. I also couldn't have prepared myself for her reaction if she had read my book. Although Maxine and I had not spoken in nearly a decade, finding out that I had written a memoir was only one Google search away. Finding out that she was in it (under an alias) was only a matter of getting through the first fifty pages. The *actual* moment was a perfect storm of chance, discomfort, and worry.

After reading my first book, Fraser and Brown had both said that I was extremely fair to Maxine, and they placed great emphasis on the word *extremely.* Putting Maxine in my memoir was crucial, as she was a crucial part of my life during the time I wrote about. But as I was writing it, I knew that I was walking a delicate line between telling the truth and not seeking revenge. Maxine had ended our relationship, for what I felt were unfair reasons at a very difficult time in my life.

That was my truth.

But I made a great effort to tell her truth as well. I even went so far as digging up some old e-mails she had sent me just so I could convey to the reader exactly what she was thinking and exactly why she made the decisions she made. Fraser and Brown pointed out a number of things I omitted that would have put Maxine in an unfavorable light, but I just waved it off by saying, "Settling scores in memoirs is cheap and makes for bad memoirs."

It was true. Maxine had shattered my heart. It wasn't my first breakup, but it was the first time in my life that I experienced the sudden absence of a constant presence. I had deeply loved her. For a long time, instead of getting over it, I got more into it. It took me a while to get over Maxine—longer than it took me to get over anyone else—but by the time I was sitting at the bar with Olivia, I was, in fact, over it. In many ways, writing about her had been therapy, as writing for me so often was.

"Are you going to talk to her?" Olivia asked me.

I shook my head and took another long sip from my beer. I finally looked over. "Maxine!" I called out.

Maxine, her boyfriend, and the bartender all looked over. Maxine's eyes went wide, but she quickly composed her face. She put down her half-eaten onion ring and said, "Oh, hey, Sean. How are you?"

"Good," I said. "Do you still live in Dedham?"

Maxine swallowed her food and shook her head. "No, we're helping my brother renovate."

"How's it going?"

Maxine said, "Remember how the light in the bathroom was right over the shower?"

I didn't.

"Yeah," I said.

"Well, he's fixing that right now. So, we're taking a break and then we're going back."

"Oh, okay," I said.

From across the bar, the two of us nodded at each other in silence, waiting for someone to say something. Since I had initiated the conversation, I figured it was Maxine's turn to speak, but she didn't. Instead, we just bobbed our heads for a moment and then went back to our food. Her boyfriend and I glanced at each other, but I couldn't read his look. It seemed like a strange combination of contempt and confusion, or maybe something else. Maxine, on the other hand, looked like she wanted to crawl under a rock. That, I was certain of. I turned back to Olivia and raised my eyebrows.

"Okay," she said quietly. "Awkward."

"I wasn't going to just ignore her." I glanced over my shoulder and said, "Although it seems like she was just going to ignore me. I wonder if she saw me when we first came in."

"I don't know."

I looked around the empty restaurant. "She must have," I said. The bartender came over and placed our food in front of us. "Whatever."

Olivia and I ate in relative silence. Occasionally we mentioned how good the food was, but beyond that, we just quietly watched the Red Sox game neither of us cared about. I ordered another beer. I was in a state of silent anxiety. I never looked to my left, even though it was the only thing I wanted to do. It was like eating lunch in my kitchen and ignoring a fire on the stovetop.

I wondered what Maxine was over there thinking about. It was odd sitting in a bar and not speaking to the one person who, besides Fraser and Brown, knew me better than anyone else on the planet. A trip to the future for our past selves would have been heartbreaking—seeing the two of us in a restaurant with other people at our side, not saying a word to each other. To the bartender, Maxine and I probably looked like acquaintances. To anyone else, we probably looked like strangers. Our past selves would have been devastated. For a few moments, I was overtaken by all the emotions I thought I had left behind. I could hear both my past self and my present self saying, *This couldn't have happened.*

But it had happened.

The reality was that Maxine was at one end of the bar eating onion rings with her boyfriend and I was at the other end eating a lobster roll with the girl I had just broken up with. It was hard not to smile at the absurdity of it all, if only to myself.

We finished our meals. I took the check and paid the tab for what I assumed would be the last time for Olivia and me. We stood up and pushed in our chairs. I looked over at Maxine. She and her boyfriend were absorbed in the ballgame.

"Well, Maxine," I called out across the bar. "Good luck over there."

"Thank you, Sean," she said. "Always a pleasure to see you."

We looked at each other with muted smiles. I heard the sarcasm in her voice and she knew it.

Maybe she had read the book.

Or maybe she was just being a bitch.

I suddenly missed her cheekiness and filled up with warm nostalgia at the thought of it.

"Tell your brother I said hello," I said.

Maxine nodded gracefully. "I will," she said. Her voice was sincere again.

We left.

Outside in the parking lot, I laughed and shook my head.

"Well, that was something," Olivia said.

I opened my car door and said, "It sure was."

We drove again with the windows rolled down, Olivia again on the radio dial. I was quiet and my eyes were narrowed pensively.

"What are you thinking about?" Olivia asked.

"A lot."

"I'll bet."

"That was crazy."

"Are you okay?"

"I'm fine."

"Do you want to talk about it?"

"About what?"

"I don't know," Olivia said. "Anything?"

I thought about it and said, "Actually, do you want to know what I was just thinking about?"

"What?"

"I was thinking about how I'm glad you were there for that."

"Because no one would ever believe it just happened?"

"Exactly."

The Movies

MMXV

Life changes fast.
Life changes in an instant.
You sit down to dinner and life as you know it ends.

—Joan Didion, *The Year of Magical Thinking*

"What?"

"Sean, you need to come to the house right away!"

"What? What happened?"

The phone dropped.

"Hello?"

A woman's voice.

"Sean?"

"Yeah?"

"Sean, something happened at your mother's house and you need to come here right away."

"Okay."

I hung up. I stood up from my chicken dinner. I put on my shoes, grabbed my car keys, and ran out the door. It had been my youngest brother, Jon. Jon never called me. Jon never texted me.

We had a very twentieth-century relationship. We saw each other when we saw each other. We were always around.

I knew it was something bad. I knew it was our brother Tim. I knew something bad must have happened to Tim.

Sirens.

One after the other. As I sat at the longest red light I had ever sat through in my entire life, I heard nothing but sirens—one more with a different pitch firing up just as another faded away. All of them were heading away from me…in the direction of my mother's house.

My brother Mike called me.

"Hello?"

"Hey, do you know what's going on?"

"No," I said, my voice raised to overcome the sirens. "Jon just called me, but he was screaming and I couldn't make out anything he was saying."

"I think Tim's dead."

A pause.

I said, "I don't know. I'm on my way now."

"Yeah, I am too."

"Okay."

"Okay."

The light turned green. I sped past the Unitarian Church, past Baker's Pond, and past the police station. I made a right turn toward my childhood home.

Fire engines. Police cruisers. Red and blue lights. A dozen random cars. Every neighbor in their front yard, looking toward our backyard.

Yellow police tape.

I parked in the road, got out of my car, and ran. A police-woman directing traffic yelled at me, just like in the movies.

"Hey, you can't go in there!"

"It's my mother's house!"

Bobby LaPlante walked out from the backyard and calmly put up his hand to the officer, telling her it was okay. He was calm, but his lips were pursed. Bobby was a young guy who owned his own landscaping company, but also worked as a part-time firefighter. A heavy tan-and-neon jacket was over his street clothes.

I held out my hands.

"What happened?"

"They didn't tell you?"

"No."

"He hung himself out back."

I turned away, placed my hands on my hips, and looked up to the early evening sky.

"I'm sorry, man."

I looked back to the earth, to the gravel in the driveway.

"Jesus Christ."

"I'm sorry, man. I know he was in trouble."

"Who found him?"

"I think your mom did."

"*Fuck.*"

"I know, man. I'm sorry."

I could hear my mother screaming from inside the house. I nodded toward the ground and said, "All right." I walked to-ward the porch, filling up with so much dread that I could barely move. Jon was on the floor in the fetal position, screaming and crying. Our cousin, a firefighter in the next town over, was consoling him. I walked past him, trance-like, into the kitchen.

My mother.

My mom.

Over the years, I had seen my mother upset. But this was something different. This was shock, and pain, and horror—the likes of which most people would never know. She was pacing back and forth among the paramedics, screaming and crying. Her face was beet-red, nearly blue.

She hugged me as soon as she saw me, as if my physical existence confirmed that at least one more of her five sons was still alive. She held on to me as if that was the only thing she had left.

"I'm sorry," she cried. "I'm sorry, Sean. I'm so sorry."

"For what?" I said helplessly. "You didn't do anything."

"I could've saved him," she said, between dry heaves. "I could have saved him! Oh my god! Oh my god!"

I took her by the hands and led her to a chair in the dining room. "Sit down," I said. "Just sit."

She did. A female paramedic, presumably the one I had spoken with on the phone, asked me to step outside. Jon was finally upright. He walked over and sat down in a chair next to my mom.

"I'll be right back," I told my mother.

She nodded, dry-heaved, and screamed.

Outside, the paramedic said to me, "I'm Jane. I live next door."

I looked over my shoulder to the house across the street and had a vague recollection that the woman next door worked for the town.

"Oh, right" I said. "Okay."

"Your mom needs to go to the hospital. Her blood pressure is dangerously high and she's very close to going into cardiac arrest."

"She has high blood pressure anyway," I told her.

"I know. She needs to come with us, but she doesn't want to leave the house."

I nodded curtly and said, "Okay."

We went back inside. Another paramedic, a young man, was kneeling down in front of my brother and my mother, telling them to inhale and exhale. I knelt down on the floor next to him and took my mother's hands in mine.

"Listen to me," I said. "You need to get in the ambulance and go to the hospital. I'm here. I'll take care of it."

All at once, it occurred to me that Tim was still hanging from a tree in the backyard.

My mother doubled over and screamed, "Oh my god, Timmy! Oh my god!"

"*Mom*," I said. "I know. Just get out of here. Just go. I'll take care of it."

We sat in stillness for a few long minutes. Everyone's attention was focused on my mother. She was bent over in the chair, cradling her stomach. Time passed in silence.

We waited.

She finally sat up and breathed. "Okay," she said weakly. "Okay. Where's my purse?"

"Right here, Doreen," Jane said, lifting my mother's purse off the kitchen counter and slinging it over her own shoulder. "Do you need anything else?"

"No," my mother said absently. "No. Just my purse."

"Okay," Jane said, helping my mother out of the chair by putting her arm over her other shoulder.

"I'll go with you, Mom," Jon said after finding his own composure.

The male paramedic said, "That's a good idea."

"Good," I said to everyone. "Okay."

We escorted my mother across the front lawn to the ambulance. Once on the stretcher, the paramedics swabbed her arm with cotton and fixed her vein with an IV of Ativan. "It's a sedative," Jane said, after my mother asked what it was. "It will help you relax." I looked at the bag of clear liquid, wishing I could be hooked to it as well. Jon took a seat and put his head in his hands. He continued to calm himself with long, deep breaths.

"What hospital are you going to?" I asked Jane.

"Norwood," she said, without looking at me. She was fastening a blood pressure cuff around my mother's left arm.

"Okay," I said to my mother. "You're all set. I'll come by the hospital later."

"Okay," my mother said, weakly. "Okay, Sean."

"Okay."

I climbed out of the ambulance and walked back to the house. The police chief had arrived. He was dressed in plain clothes, holding a black leather folder against his chest. A friendly guy with a moustache and a horseshoe of brown hair, he had been high school classmates with my mother back in the '70s.

"You're the oldest?" he asked me as he held out his hand.

"Yeah," I said, shaking his hand. "Sean."

"That's right. Sean. I'm so sorry."

"Thanks," I said. "Where exactly did he do it?"

"In the big tree out back."

I glanced to the dozens of big trees out back. Like most suburban yards, a large thicket of woods picked up where our green lawn left off. "What big tree?"

"It's a big oak tree behind the shed."

It still meant nothing to me. "I don't know," I said. "Okay. Should I go back there?"

The chief closed his eyes and shook his head. He said, "That's not necessary. What you're imagining is what it is."

What I was imagining was my brother Tim hanging from a tree by white rope. What I saw was a still body and his neck crooked to one side. What I could see was the look on his face right before he leapt—the same look he'd had as a kid when he jumped into a pool—excited, wild, yet determined. What I imagined was him dressed in black, which he so often was. I wondered whether he was wearing the baseball cap that almost never left his head.

I looked out to the woods where my brother was still hanging. The police had fastened a large pair of blue tarps across two trees like a makeshift theater curtain. The first officer on the scene came from behind the curtain with large eyes and a pale face. He was going through the motions, but looked as if he had no idea what planet he was on. For a small town cop, this was no ordinary day.

The chief, on the other hand, was totally composed. "I've been in this situation before," he said to me. "And I understand why people in the moment want to look, but I know from experience that it's not a good idea. If you're still interested in a few days after everything settles down, there will be photographs at the station."

"No," I said, thinking about the movies. "I just didn't know for identification or whatever."

The chief shook his head. "No. Totally not necessary."

I nodded and told him to get me if he needed anything. I walked out to the back deck. I looked out over our yard to the blue tarps where the officers and firefighters were coming and going without urgency. I could see how it all had unfolded. I could see how my mother had gotten home from work, seen Tim's truck in the driveway, and wondered where he was. I could hear her calling his name and, when there was no answer, walking out back. I could see how she looked into the shed where he kept his motorcycle, and when she saw he wasn't there, how she kept walking. I could see her take the corner.

And finally look up.

I didn't know why I was compelled to see Tim's body while it was still suspended in midair. Part of it was probably just morbid compulsion—the need to see the worst, the need to slow down and look at the car crash, or watch people jump from the Twin Towers. Part of it may have also been the need to spare my mother the burden of being the only one to have seen him. As it was told to me, Jon had come running out once he heard my mother screaming, but my mother, between screams and sobs, begged him not to look. As it was told to me, she crawled from the back-yard to the house because she couldn't walk. As it was told to me, she eventually dialed 911, but several calls had already been made.

My mother's screams were so loud and horrific, the neighbors thought someone was being murdered.

I walked back into the house and through the living room. There, above the television, were the five high school photographs of my brothers and me, all in sequential order, from oldest to youngest—Tim's friendly smile, second from the right.

Just as I went outside through the front door, Mike pulled up in his white Ford pickup. He got out and walked across the lawn. He was still in his work clothes and wearing dark sunglasses. He held out his hands exactly as I had.

"Did you hear?"

"No."

"He hung himself out back."

Mike's head snapped to one side as if he had just taken a punch. I put my hand on his shoulder, but he walked past me. He shook his head, as if his mind was refusing to accept the information it had just been given. He walked across the lawn, past the driveway, and into the adjacent yard. A group of friends, neighbors, and relatives had all started to gather.

The chief found me and told me that he needed to secure the area and search the house. He said, "You can stand over there at your neighbor's house. It might be a while before the coroner arrives, but the detective from the state police should be here fairly soon. He'll probably have some questions for you."

I said, "Okay," and joined Mike. Our neighbor, a woman named Tracy whom I had known since I was a kid but hadn't talked to in a while, came out of her house with a bottle of Poland Spring. "Here you go, Sean," she said, handing me the water. She gave me a hug, which I only half-reciprocated. "Are you okay?" she asked, pulling away and looking into my eyes with the most genuine concern.

I unscrewed the cap on the water bottle and said, "Yeah. Yeah, I'm okay right now."

She rubbed my left arm and said, "I'm sorry. You're handling this well, though. You're doing great."

I said, "Thanks," and took a sip of water.

Mike's wife came. My sister-in-law, Kristen, was four months pregnant. The two of them hugged and held each other. Eventually, Mike sat down on the edge of an empty trailer while Kristen stood and rubbed his back. Mike wrapped his arms around her pregnant waist and buried his head next to his unborn child—a niece Tim would now never know.

I needed to do something. After looking around and seeing the shock on a dozen faces, I decided to give the word. I took my phone out of my pocket and saw that Fraser had already texted me.

Is it true?

I typed back: *Yeah.*

He immediately wrote back: *Fuck. Anything I can do, let me know.*

He was working his part-time job at the liquor store and I texted him that I would definitely be by later for shots of whiskey.

Not a problem, he wrote back.

I stared at the blank message screen on my phone and prepared myself to tell people the worst possible news I could think of. *Tim is dead*, I wrote. *He hung himself in the backyard.* I paused before hitting the send button. I unexpectedly stared at the word *hung* and thought it should be *hanged*. I tried to remember some mnemonic device from high school English, but I couldn't. I almost changed it to *hanged*, but it didn't sound right and I didn't want people to think that, in the midst of mayhem, I was pretentiously thinking about grammar, but apparently, I was. After a few moments of contemplation, I finally just sent the message off as it was. I sent it to everyone closest to me—everyone who needed to know.

My grammatical contemplation gave me some momentary relief. I still had my wits. I was assured, even if just for a moment, that I might get through this.

I called my brother Joe and his girlfriend Kim, but neither of them answered and I didn't leave a message. Mike finally stood up from the trailer he was sitting on and walked over to me.

"What the fuck?" he said softly, so the neighbors wouldn't hear. "I can't believe he did that out back so Mom would find him. I mean, what if I had walked back there with Vin?"

I thought about my niece, Vincenza—the smiling Irish redhead with the most Italian name. I thought about how her innocent three-year-old world would have been destroyed if she had seen what my mother would now never unsee. I thought about how Vincenza would now wonder what had happened to her favorite uncle—the uncle who always dropped whatever he was doing to sit on the floor and play with her whenever she visited Nana's house.

Thinking about it briefly turned my shock to ire. Tim had been dead for only ninety minutes and I had already reached the

Anger Stage. I looked down at the ground and quietly said the first two words that were in my mind.

"Fucking asshole."

Mike said, "Were you able to get a hold of Joe?"

"No. I tried calling Kim too, but there was no answer."

Our brother Joe was camping in Maine with his girlfriend. He went every year. I had never been, but the campground they stayed at was always described as "in the middle of nowhere"—one of the few places on Earth still devoid of cell phone towers. Mike and I took out our phones and sent text messages he probably wouldn't receive. I suggested sending e-mails, thinking that the campsite they were at might at least have an office with Internet access.

Mike, typing on his phone, said, "That's a good idea."

The police searched the house for an hour. More emergency vehicles left. The air felt static. Things around me were moving, but it was like I was watching them through a hazy electrical charge where a lightning bolt had just struck. I stared off into nothingness and the people in the yard left me alone. The respite while the police searched the house gave me just enough time to contemplate everything, even through a lens of total shock.

My brothers.

The unwritten rules of writing decree that characters should never be introduced at the end of a book. And after the publication of my first memoir about my life in pro wrestling, some of my friends (especially Fraser) were quick to bust my balls about my four half-brothers (though I never referred to them as that) never being introduced at all. My reason for leaving them out weren't devious—I wasn't trying to paint anyone out of the portrait of my life. The reason for omitting my brothers, as I told everyone, was simply mechanical. When it came specifically to my unreal story in pro wrestling, my brothers were only brief players in the very beginning. I had started watching wrestling before any of them besides Mike were even born. I disliked books with too many characters that went off on too many tangents. My memoir was already getting long. So, in the interest of brevity and clarity, I took them out. I figured that there was no point in mentioning my brothers in Chapter One if they were going to just disappear and never be mentioned again by Chapter Forty-Four. At first, I actually did write about my brothers, but as I wrote on, I imagined one of my old writing professors looking over my shoulder and saying, "Might as well just take them out. Keep it simple." As I told everyone after the book was published, "I never said that I had brothers, but I never said that I *didn't* have brothers either." I sounded like a lawyer, but it was true.

Plus, none of my brothers really gave a shit about not being in the book anyway.

But in the story of my real life, I was the oldest of five boys. Mike was born when I was seven, shortly after my mother married my stepfather. He was followed by Joe, Tim, and Jon. As a kid, I met my new role as an older brother with reluctance, especially since my grandparents and uncles used to pour heaping ladles of attention over me when I was an only child. Like most older siblings, I was cruel to Mike when he was a toddler—always hurting him in the living room during wrestling matches, mostly unintentionally, but, embarrassingly in hindsight, intentionally sometimes as well. Over time, though I came to not only embrace him, but genuinely like him. We played together and watched TV together, and I took him to his first concert when he was fourteen (the Insane Clown Posse at the Worcester Palladium).

When I left home, my brothers were kids. When I came back, they were adults. I was gone from home—both in the flesh and in the mind—for about ten years. I wasn't always there for the hard times when my mother divorced my stepfather, which, after seeing how much it had affected my brothers back home in Medfield, gave me a large sense of survivor's guilt. It was a helpless feeling, knowing that while I was living comfortably in Boston, they were living in a war zone. I spent more time with my brothers as adults when I moved back to the suburbs just before my thirtieth birthday (city life had run its course for me). Mike had become a truck driver, a husband, and a good father. Joe had become a heavy equipment operator—quiet, hardworking, and no-nonsense. Jon had become a laid-back diesel mechanic and an all-around good guy.

But Tim.

Tim had been in trouble. Tim had *always* been in trouble, but by the time he was twenty-six, he was in serious trouble. That day, Thursday, was the day he was going to go to the police and turn himself in. With just twenty-one days left on his probation, Tim had failed a random breathalyzer test at the parole office. After his parole officer told him to go wait out in the hall, Tim took off, to St. Louis, apparently. He had been, as Mike and I put it, "on the lam" for just under a week. "Yeah," Tim had told me just two days earlier, "I rode the Harley out to that arch thing. I bought some fireworks." Fraser and I had run into him outside of the liquor store Fraser worked at on Tuesday night. It was the first time I had seen him since he'd fled the state.

"Oh!" I exclaimed as he walked up to us. "Look who it is. Where have you been?"

"What?" Tim said sarcastically. "Is something going on?"

We laughed, and Tim recounted the story, or his version of it anyway. Tim never lied, but as Mike once said, "With Tim, it's like you're only getting about 40 percent of the truth."

As Tim told it, he had been stone-cold sober. After blowing a positive into the breathalyzer, Tim said to the parole officer, "It can't be. I haven't had a drop all day. I literally just came from work." The officer told him to blow into it again, and the second time, it came up negative. "See?" Tim said. "That thing is fucked up." At this point, as Tim told it, he handed the breathalyzer to the parole officer and said, "Here. You blow into it."

So he did and it came up positive.

Outside the liquor store, Tim said, "So I said, 'See what I mean? Have *you* been drinking on the job?'"

I smiled a little, thinking the story sounded both somewhat believable and somewhat unbelievable. Then Tim told us about how the parole officer told him to wait out in the lobby, but after sitting there for more than an hour and asking repeatedly what was going on, to no avail, he decided to just walk out the door. Like Mike said, there seemed to be some kernel of truth to his story, but I just couldn't help but wonder whether there was something else to it—something I would never know.

"So I left," Tim said with a smile. "Fuck it."

"Well," I told him, "if that happened in the parole office, then it must be on video. I mean, any decent lawyer should be able to get you out of that."

"Yeah, I guess," he said. "I dunno. I guess I'll have to face the music on Thursday."

After talking in front of the liquor store for a while, the three of us went to the bar at the sushi place next door, where I had the last round of drinks that I would ever have with my brother Tim. We laughed and told stories just like always. We joked about being the black sheep of the family. We hung out for only a couple hours. Since it was a weekday, Fraser went home after just one beer. I stayed for two more, then decided to call it night. Tim said he was going to stay for a few more. I stood up and said, "If you need anything, let me know." Tim nodded and thanked me.

Before I left, he insisted on paying my tab.

Apparently, what Tim had meant by "face the music on Thursday" was something altogether different from what I'd imagined when I walked out of the bar that night.

There had always been a joke in our family as to who in adolescence had caused my mother the most headaches. Tim and I were neck and neck for a while, but Tim's troubles with the law went past adolescence and into adulthood and became less funny. As a friend of the family once said to me, "You're wild, but Tim is reckless."

I knew exactly what she meant. Tim and I were so alike in so many ways. We were natural born hell-raisers and, even though only half-blood in body, in some family photos we legitimately looked like twins. We both liked heavy metal and we both liked to get drunk and get loud. We both tried to make every occasion an occasion to remember.

But Tim would always have *that* drink—that last vodka that would take him across the threshold from drunk to obliterated. That one drink everyone else declined, Tim would have, turning himself into another person entirely. I noticed, as the years went on, that when Tim got drunk, he became vacant, almost zombielike. He would stop talking and start swaying. Though still upright, his eyelids would sink, then open slowly, revealing a gaze into nothing. When someone would finally say, "Hey, are you all right?" he would take a long drag from his cigarette, and say, "Yeah...Yeah, I'm fine."

That wasn't me. While I could get as drunk and crazy as anyone, my eyes were always open and my mind was always conscious. I functioned in controlled chaos, not literal mayhem. I rarely did anything on Saturday night that I regretted on Sunday morning. I had never crashed a car.

Tim had crashed three.

If Tim was a wildfire, he eventually met the gasoline that would make him explode. It was a girl. It was a girl with the reputation. It was a girl none of my brothers liked and all repeatedly warned him about. She and Tim went through the typical pattern of romantic dysfunction: drink, fight, break up, get back together, and do it all over again. After Tim got out of jail the first time, I had a heart-to-heart with him one day in my mother's living room. I told him that he should see a therapist. "If Tony

Soprano did it, so can you," I said. I also told him that an ex-girlfriend wasn't worth fucking his life up for.

But like the drinks and the drugs, the girl became just one more thing that Tim couldn't quit. His real trouble with the law came one night after the two of them had a blowout that resulted in the cops being called. As Tim told it, his girlfriend wound up sitting on his chest, pummeling his face with her fists. "I was actually letting her do it," he told me, "but eventually I just grabbed her and threw her off me."

Although I had come to take all of Tim's stories with a grain of salt, I believed this one. Mostly because he let me see the police report after my mom bailed him out of jail. We were in my mother's kitchen after his release and I said, "Do you mind if I take a look at this?" Without hesitation, Tim said, "Go ahead." I opened the manila folder, looked at the pictures of his girlfriend without a scratch on her, and then I looked at Tim's battered face.

I said, "And they arrested *you*?"

Tim shrugged his shoulders and shook his head. "You know how it goes," he said. "They always arrest the guy."

It wasn't the first time I had heard that sentiment from someone.

While the impetus for Tim's first arrest may not have been his own doing, the next one was. He violated his no-contact order within minutes of being released from jail: He sent his girlfriend a text message, literally, from the parking lot of the police station.

That's when he went in for a month.

That's when he went to the county jail in Dedham.

That's when it was no fucking joke.

By this time, my brothers and I had had it. We had always supported Tim and had all tried talking sense into him, but the well of our sympathies ran dry when his plights became so easily avoidable and so blatantly self-inflicted. Tim certainly had his fair share of bad luck, but as Mike once said, "Tim can never seem to catch a break, but he can't seem to give himself one either." When my mother told my brothers and me that Tim was in jail again, the four of us were angrily indifferent. My mother looked at us, waiting for some show of empathy, but was met with only silence, apathetic sniffs, and unconcerned shoulder shrugs. After a few moments of quiet, I finally said, "I guess he wants to do things the hard way."

And that was the end of it.

My mother never lost hope, though.

Tim kept repeating the same self-destructive patterns over and over, but she never lost faith that he would finally be okay and do the right thing. My mother loved him unconditionally until the very end.

My mother.

The one he had just hurt the most.

A man wearing a white shirt and khakis came out of the house and started looking around. An officer pointed to where I was standing. I walked back over to my mother's house and met him in the driveway. He was tall with a square jaw and well-styled black hair. He looked like the Hollywood version of a cop. He held out his hand and I shook it.

"I'm Detective Levasseur," he said. "I'm sorry about your brother."

"Thank you."

"So it looks like everything here is what it appears to be. By that I mean I don't think there was any foul play or anything like that."

"Right."

I looked over his shoulder and saw a white van slowly pulling out from behind the house. It was rolling over the lawn and Bobby was directing it to the road. The side of the van read, "Office of the Chief Medical Examiner." I watched it come down the front lawn, slowly turn, and drive away down the road.

Tim was dead.

In that moment, everything ceased to be dreamlike. Knowing Tim's dead body was inside that van hardened the reality that I would never see him again. I would never have a beer with him, or break someone's balls with him, or laugh with him about everything. I would never hear his motorcycle engine, his voice, or his laugh, which was heard quite often. I would never sit across from him at the dinner table during the holidays. In that moment, I wanted so much for him to be alive.

I blinked away my thoughts, but instead of looking at the detective, I looked at the ground.

"So we didn't find a note or anything," he said. "Do you think he may have left a note?"

"Hell no."

The detective let out a slight laugh and said, "No, huh?"

I looked up from the ground and said, "No. I mean, no. That just wouldn't be his style."

"Okay." The detective went over his notes and said, "The only thing in his pockets was four dollars and fifty-five cents and a receipt from the hardware store where he bought the rope. That was at noon today."

I said, "Okay." I could see Tim at Wills Hardware buying the rope to end his own life. I knew exactly what aisle he was in.

"That's about it. Do you have any questions?"

"Did he tie his hands?" I asked.

"What for?"

"You know," I said, "so he wouldn't be able to get himself free. Don't people who hang themselves do that?"

The detective smiled. "I've never seen anyone do that, and I've been doing this for a while." He said, "It sounds like you watch a lot of movies."

I looked down at the gravel driveway again. "Yeah," I said. "Yeah, I watch a lot of movies."

The detective handed me his card and told me to call him if I had any questions. We shook hands again and I thanked him. I turned back toward the neighbor's house. Colin was there.

Colin and I had known each other since high school, when he was a freshman and I was a senior. Like my brothers and me, we had spent more time together as adults when I moved back from the city. Colin was an electrician and I saw his white box truck parked on the corner down the road. He had been in the area and come as soon as he heard.

"Hey."

"Hey."

We grabbed hands, pulled in, and hugged.

"Are you all right?"

"I guess so. Fuckin' Christ."

"I know."

Mike and Kristen came up to us and Mike told me that they were going to the hospital to see Mom. Mike asked me if I needed anything. I told him no and said I would finish up and come to the hospital later. We said solemn goodbyes and Colin and I walked back to the house. Bobby and a few other cops were still there. The sun had set. It was dusk, but still light enough to see. A few night peepers had started their small chorus from the backyard. My mother's house had always been home, but it now felt eerie and unwelcoming. Bobby looked at Colin and me and shook his head.

"Unbelievable," he said. "I'm sorry again."

"Thanks."

Colin said, "Hey, what about that tree?"

Bobby looked to the backyard and then back to us. "I'll take care of it," he said.

"Oh, yeah," I said. "That's a good idea."

"It'll be gone by tomorrow," Bobby said.

"Whenever," I said. "Just before my mom comes home, anyway."

Bobby said, "No, I'll be here first thing in the morning with my guys. This one's on the house."

I typically would have protested, but I just said, "Thanks."

"No problem."

I pointed to the last two police officers in the yard and said, "Is there someone that can take me through it? I just want to know what happened."

Bobby said, "Yeah, all right. Are you sure?"

"Yeah," I said. "I actually still don't know what tree it was."

"Oh, okay," Bobby said. "One sec."

He walked over to one of the officers. I couldn't hear everything being said, but I overheard Bobby say, "Yeah, he's okay." An officer with silver hair still rusted with red stepped forward and came over to Colin and me. I didn't know his name, but I recognized him from doing traffic details around town. We shook his hand.

Colin said, "I used to live at Wilkins Glen. You came to my house a lot."

The cop said, "Oh, I remember."

"Really?" Colin said. "That was, like, twenty years ago."

The officer nodded and said, "Oh, believe me, I remember."

Colin let out a slight laugh and said, "Ah, okay."

I didn't know what they were talking about, but assumed it was something from our teenage years when all of us were suburban hellions. All things considered, we had all turned out fine.

The officer motioned with his arm. "Okay," he said, "let me take you through it." He walked at a quick pace while Colin and I lagged behind. I looked around the yard to things I had known since childhood—the small pond, the tall trees, the flagpole topped with an American flag. I looked at them now as if I had never set eyes on them. I walked Tim's final walk, taking in everything he would have seen just before he died.

We went far into the backyard and past the shed. Tim's Harley was parked inside. Its chrome was still shining in the darkness.

Once we were behind the shed and into the woods, the officer stopped in front of a large tree.

"Okay," he said. "It was this tree here."

Colin and I looked up.

It was a tall oak. The cop pointed to the first sturdy limb. "He tied the rope to that branch there. So, pretty high up."

Colin and I held our gaze. The officer stepped directly in front of me and put his hand in front of my eyes.

"His feet were right about here. So, about six feet from the ground."

There was a pause.

From behind my shoulder, Colin said, "He wasn't fucking around."

The cop turned to Colin and said, "No. He wasn't fucking around."

I stepped back to get a different view. The officer looked at me and said, "What that means is that it wasn't strangulation. His neck broke as soon as he hit. So, he probably didn't suffer much."

I didn't say anything.

"If at all," the officer said.

"Okay."

"So, that's about it."

Colin and I nodded with our arms folded across our chests and we walked back toward the house. The officer told me to contact the police station if I needed anything. I thanked him and he got in his cruiser and left. Colin and I were the only ones left in the yard. It was finally dark enough to be called night.

I said to Colin, "I'm going to mark that tree just to make sure Bobby cuts down the right one."

"Good idea."

We went into the house through the basement door. I flicked on a light and grabbed the first can of spray paint I saw. We walked back to the tree, quicker this time. Without looking up at the limb, I uncapped the paint and colored a red X on the bark. I mindlessly sprayed back and forth, over and over again, until the fresh paint glistened in the moonlight. Colin, standing behind me, laughed a little. He finally said, "Ah, yeah, I think that'll do it. I think he'll see that." I stopped spraying and stepped back to where he was standing. The X was huge, dripping at every angle. It would probably just be a large red blot in the morning. I smiled a little and put the cap back on.

"All right then," I said.

"All right."

We went into the house, where I put the can of spray paint back and turned off all the lights. The night peepers and frogs were now in full chorus. Outside, Colin and I hugged again, the two of us throwing hard slaps into each other's backs. Colin said, "I'll see you tomorrow."

I didn't know where, but I knew we would see each other. Tomorrow was Friday. I knew I would see everyone tomorrow. I knew we would drink. I knew we would laugh. I knew we would cry. I knew for now that my mother needed me, but not before I did those shots with Fraser. I looked up and saw the same swath of twilight I had seen as a child. I got in my car and left. The entire world had changed around me. I drove down roads I had known forever into a different kind of place. I hoped for sleep I knew would never come.

The severe summer heat had one last go in the days that followed Tim's death. It was humid and in the low 90s.

I walked.

I walked in circles for miles.

I simulated moving on.

Earbuds deep in my canals, I walked until I was covered in sweat and the sunscreen streaking down my face turned the whites of my eyes a blistery red. I blasted Metallica into my skull—songs about anger, death, and suicide. I knew every word and every note. For the most part, I avoided the main roads in Medfield so I could be left alone. Anytime I was forced to march along Main Street, however, someone I hadn't spoken to in years would come up to me.

A retired cop directing traffic stopped directing traffic and walked over to the sidewalk and told me how sorry he was. The UPS driver stopped his brown truck and asked me whether that was my brother he had heard about. I told him it was. He said, "Jesus Christ, that's terrible." A guy I used to work with at the Highway Department stopped digging a ditch and told me how your twenties can be a tough time. "I was real fucked up on coke in my twenties," he said, thumbing his nose.

I ran into my stepfather—a character from the story of my life that had been notably absent in the past twenty years. I had put him aside when I was younger, just as I'd intended to. But like most children, I couldn't totally put a parent aside forever, and now he was here. We saw each other in the parking lot of a bank while I was walking. We approached each other slowly, almost cautiously. We neither hugged nor shook hands, not that we would have, or ever did. Rather, we just found our respective ground and stood it, me folding my arms across my chest, him hooking the pockets of his jeans with his thumbs. When we spoke, the two of us hardly looked at each another, choosing instead to stare down at the asphalt, or off into the quiet distance of Medfield center.

I could tell that beneath his surface he was sad and shaken, but like me, he held a sturdy composure. No stranger passing by would have known the loss we had just suffered by only looking at us. He had been a marine in another life and had often applied his military training to my child-rearing. It had never quite prepared me for life, but it had prepared me for war. It had prepared me for the chaos of Tim's death, especially during the night it happened. It had prepared me for the very moment I was standing in. In an odd twist of emotion, I was suddenly grateful to him, something I had rarely ever been as a child, even less so as an adult.

Our relationship had always been a cliché—the same complicated and horrible stepfather-stepson relationship you could read about in any bad memoir, or see in any weepy TV movie. As a result, my adolescence had been spent with my stepfather and me just silently staring at each other, waiting for the clock to turn eighteen. When I finally left my parents' house, I left for good and never came back. And ever since that time, especially after my mother divorced him, our connection to each other was nothing more than short pleasantries and catch-up conversations in the infrequent moments when he and I ran into each other on the street, or at the store.

He was ten years older than my mother, now looking gray, leathered, and faded. He had lived in Medfield his whole life and still occupied a place in its history that no longer existed—a time when Medfield was a rural, working-class town—more farms and fields than SUVS and McMansions. When I was a child, my stepfather's parenting was what would have then bordered on abusive and what now would have bordered on criminal. I knew the times had changed and I knew he would have disagreed with my take on things. In his mind, I had had it easy. In his mind, I was an ungrateful complainer because he'd had it worse. In his mind—a mind that never saw books or television or anything else from the outside world that might have placed him in the present—his parenting was normal and probably just like his own had been. As a teenager, I was fully aware that I was being raised like a farm boy in the mid-1950s.

It had done me no good.

There was so much I could have said to him—melodramatic declarations that always went unsaid. That he had done my mother wrong. That he had put me behind the eight ball before the game even started. That his blood was not in mine, but sometimes it felt like it was. That he had blighted the seeds of my crops. That he had poisoned the wells of my brothers. That I was thankful to him for making me tough and being the role model for the man I never wanted to be.

But I didn't.

If there was ever a day for those words to be spoken, this was not the day.

Instead, I just let him speak.

My stepfather told me about being in contact with Tim while he made his final motorcycle ride out to St. Louis. Tim was apparently calling him from random rest stops on his way home. "He was really afraid," my stepfather said to me. "I could hear it in his voice whenever he'd call. Somewhere in Ohio he finally said to me, 'Dad, I'm really scared to come home.'"

The two of us paused in silence. We were stoic. Our feelings were locked away. The only emotion either of us was showing was the emotion in our eyes. Finally my stepfather said, "I told him to just tell me what to do. I said, 'Tim, just tell me where to go and I'll meet you out there with the trailer and the truck.' My stepfather made a brush-off gesture with his hand. "'No, no, Dad, I'll be all right,' he said." There was another pause. "And then Tim just changed the subject. He said, 'I can't believe how fucking long the state of Ohio is.'" And with that, my stepfather and I laughed, but briefly, the two of us looking down and shaking our heads in unison.

My stepfather did most of the talking. I looked at him when he wasn't looking at me. I noticed how much taller I was than him now. I remembered a time when I was either twelve or thirteen when he was yelling at me and he grabbed my arms and shook me. It was the first time I noticed that my eyes could see over the top of his head. While he hollered in my face, I looked out the window to the road outside, almost peacefully. I was now a full foot taller than him. And although my stepfather was no longer as oxen-strong as he once had been, he was still solid for a man pushing seventy. The white tank top he wore showed the hard, wiry arm muscles beneath his wilting, sun-beaten skin. His hands were the same gnarled tree branches they had always been—dirty and crooked from a lifetime of physical labor.

"Yeah," my stepfather said, "I just don't think he could have gone back to that jail."

"Dedham is no joke," I said.

"No, no. Not at all."

We noticed a passing car. It was an old neighbor of ours from a life that now felt like a lifetime ago. My stepfather and I both raised our arms in a solemn wave. The woman inside smiled and waved back. I figured she didn't know. Even in a small town, not everyone hears about everything, at least not right away.

"Yeah," my stepfather repeated, "he just couldn't go back to that jail. I remember when I picked him up after he got out, he just sat down in my truck and said, 'Dad, I am never going back there.'" We looked at each other for what seemed like the first time. My stepfather said, "I could see in his face that something had changed."

I looked away again, as did he. From the roof of the bank, a murder of crows took to the sky. More silence. Again, my stepfather went on. "I ran into Billy Sullivan yesterday. I guess he saw Timmy the day he died. He said, 'Yeah, I saw him going like hell on his motorcycle down 27. And I gave him a wave, but he didn't wave back. I thought that was strange,' he said. Billy said, 'You know, anytime Timmy would see me on his bike, that long arm of his would always shoot up in a big, friendly wave, but not that day.' Billy said, 'Naw, that day he wasn't even there.'"

I just nodded and kept my eyes on the ground. I didn't want to hear any more. And I didn't want to hear anything else from my stepfather. There was too much history that I didn't want to deal with—that I *couldn't* deal with. I had the present to deal with. I needed to keep moving. Life wasn't always like a movie, at least not a sappy one where everything was neatly tied up at the end. Stones between my stepfather and I would remain unturned. Issues would remain unresolved. I put one of my earbuds back into my ear and told my stepfather I needed to go check on Mom. He just nodded and said, "Yup. Okay, Sean. When is the wake and everything?" I told him I didn't know yet and said that I would have Joe let him know. He said, "Okay," and I said, "Okay," and we both said, "See you later."

I kept moving and walked farther than I had planned.

Everyone I ran into asked how my mom was doing and I could only reply, "As good as can be," which was true. After being released from the hospital, she spent the following week at my great-aunt's house where the doorbell rang throughout the day and the telephone rang throughout the night. She watched daytime television and cried when company visited. The house was filled with food and flowers. She ate small bites of baked ziti and cold cuts. Despite being surround by food, we were all losing weight.

Mike and I arranged Tim's wake and funeral and suddenly we were the adults. We picked out a black-and-chrome casket because it looked like Tim's motorcycle. The local florist arranged a bouquet for the top of it. She laid out red, white, and yellow roses that matched the flames on Tim's gas tank. When the funeral director asked us what Tim was like, Mike and I looked down and smiled. "The life of the party," we both said, almost simultaneously. The funeral director, a frail man with a serene voice who looked about eighty, took off his glasses and put down his pen.

"You know," he said, "it might seem strange that someone who seemed so happy was suffering so miserably. But oftentimes, those are the very people who have severe depression. The laughter and happiness they're projecting is a cover-up for what they're actually feeling inside. Think about Robin Williams."

Mike and I nodded in quiet contemplation. Something sank in. It wasn't a profound statement, or anything I hadn't heard before, but it was the first time since Tim's suicide that some sense of it was being made.

Making sense was something I was trying to do during my long walks through the thick summer heat. Metallica had always been the soundtrack to my life—getting me through both good times and bad—but their music could only drown out my thoughts for so long. My brain was revving in high gear about everything all the time.

As I walked, I saw my life as a movie, now more so than ever. For as long as I could remember, I had always viewed my reality through the lens of an imaginary camera. I often wondered if I was the only person who did this: saw their life as a movie with themselves as the main character. Whenever I rewound my consciousness back to its earliest memories, I always pictured myself, as a child, sitting in front of a television, or looking up at a movie screen. So many of my formative years were spent watching stories unfold in a three-act structure. Unreality had molded the way I saw reality. Even though I knew that real life didn't always play out like a movie plot, I still organized it like one in my mind.

Tim's death was my second act.

What was happening didn't happen in real life, it only happened in the movies. As unoriginal as that thought was, it was impossible not to think it. I had always seen my life as a linear picture, each day happening frame by frame until my entire life would become one long reel of film. Imagining that life rolled up in an old film canister made me remember something I had once read in a philosophy book about eternal recurrence—the idea of time being circular, rather than linear. In that way, everything was occurring and recurring endlessly and simultaneously. In that way, Tim's suicide was happening over and over again, which it certainly felt like it was. In that way, Tim's suicide was also happening at the same time I held my newborn niece for the first time, or was driving my old Chevelle in high school. Tim had died when I was just a little boy watching my grandmother snap green beans, just as my mom was holding my small hand at the grocery store, just as I was having my first kiss with my first crush, just as I was looking out to a thousand wrestling fans screaming my name, just as I was laying my eyes upon the Eiffel Tower, the Roman Colosseum, or the pyramids of Egypt, and just as Fraser and I were laughing with our friends at our local bar. Thinking about this circular time brought some momentary comfort. It reminded me of all the good things my life had been. It brought the whole picture into focus.

I was thinking myself crazy, but I decided to just go with it. I had energy that needed to burn.

I thought about how Tim's death had changed the entire tone of my life. It suddenly felt like all my past tribulations were nothing more than trivial first-world inconveniences—teen angst, heartaches, and never enough money for fun, yet always plenty to live. As a young man, everything was dramatic and overwhelming. It was all yelling, and crying, and bad poetry. I had spent thirty-eight years on the planet thinking I had been through some shit, only to realize I had been through nothing. Tim's suicide brought me all the way back to being sixteen years old. All my insecurities from that time returned. I didn't know what to do or how to handle it. Once more, I felt like little else but a high school misfit trying to navigate myself through the vast Nowhereland of twenty-first-century America.

At the end of my walks, when I was flushed red and dripping with sweat, I could actually slow myself down and think like an adult. In brief mental calm, I could think of Tim's death like Hurricane Katrina—shocking and horrific, but not unexpected. In the past few years, I had spent a fair amount of time talking with friends about how Tim was going kill himself, but I was certain it would be by the hands of recklessness, not literally his own hands. In that way, Tim's death didn't come out of the blue, only the light blue.

The thought that he might commit suicide had crossed my mind, but that thought was fleeting and without enough merit to sound an alarm. I could remember thinking that it seemed so strange that someone could be in so much trouble and not seemingly care. A few times, I wondered whether he might end it all to finally avoid it all. There were brief moments when I considered the possibility that Tim was hiding the deep psychological pain the funeral director suggested he had been.

But Tim had never attempted suicide. Nor had he ever talked about it.

Never.

Not even once.

In that way, there wasn't a single warning sign. In that way, Tim defied all the psychology textbooks and refuted all the notions that suicides can be prevented. In that way, his death came out of the dark blue.

In the days after Tim's death, I talked a lot on the phone with Danielle, my ex-girlfriend from college who ditched an acting degree for a degree in social work. She had settled back into her hometown in New Jersey. Each time I called, Danielle picked up after one ring, no matter what time of day it was, even in the darkest hours. Hers was a comforting voice from the past, in my present.

Danielle made me aware of things I had never given much thought to. When she explained depression, I thought about Tim and said, "Honestly, that doesn't really sound like him."

"Okay," she said, "so he never seemed depressed to you?"

"I guess he was," I said. "Obviously. But he never really showed it. He could be a moody prick, but I would never really categorize it as 'depression.' For the most part, he was pretty happy-go-lucky. He was really funny."

Danielle explained bipolar disorder, which described Tim somewhat better. Tim was always going through these patterns of royally fucking up and then rebounding admirably. He would fight with his girlfriend, break up, go on benders, and lose his job…only to shake it off, find a better job, live a better life, and then repeat the process all over again.

"I guess I never saw the depressive side," I told Danielle.

"It sounds like the depressive side was masked with drugs and alcohol."

"Yeah," I said. "Yeah, I guess that makes sense."

I didn't like psychological pigeonholing (I thought people were too complex to just be whittled down to a bunch of terms and acronyms), but the more Danielle spoke, the more I realized that Tim was probably like the millions of other people who suffer from their own minds. When death comes in America, some walk toward the pews of a church and some walk toward the couch of a shrink. Talking to Danielle made me realize that both paths led to the same fundamental place.

One thing I desperately needed to know from Danielle was why he'd killed himself in the backyard, knowing full well that my mother would find him. It was the one thing that still turned my shock and sadness into clear, focused anger.

"I mean, seriously," I said to Danielle, "what the fuck is that?"

"Okay," Danielle said calmly. I could tell that she had been expecting the question, but she still took a moment before answering it. "Here's the thing—it was his home. It was a safe place. People with cancer go home to die."

"Okay," I said. "But he didn't know my mother was going to find him? He killed himself an hour before she got home from work."

"I understand why you're angry—"

"Bullshit. Just give it to me straight."

"Okay," Danielle said firmly. "The other thing you have to remember is, someone who is about to commit suicide is not in their right state of mind."

"I believe that," I said. "But here's the thing—he was coherent enough to go to the hardware store and buy rope. He was coherent enough to Google how to tie a noose. And he was coherent enough to text his skank ex-girlfriend before he killed himself. But he wasn't coherent enough to know that my mother was going to find him? I'm sorry, but I just don't buy that."

Danielle said, "It might not be something you'll ever understand."

I calmed myself and apologized. She said it was okay. I thanked her for her help. "But," I said, "there are some times when I just part ways with psychology. You know how some psychologists will say that suicide isn't a selfish act? Well, whoever said that has never had to clean up the mess after someone commits one. I'm sorry, but you'll have to sell that bullshit to someone else."

Danielle knew me well enough to just let me vent. She listened silently and we eventually moved on.

I tried to stay as clearheaded as possible in the short days between Tim's suicide and his funeral. I went out to the bar only once. I drank with my brothers and our friends, but as the night wore on I noticed that I wasn't getting drunk. My brain was racing so fast that not even alcohol could slow it down. The only thing drinking did was make my hyper-focus a bit cloudy. It never shut me down completely, which was what I wanted, so I decided to just stop altogether.

My family gathered every night at my great-aunt's house. The nights were warm and we ate pizza and drank beer on her deck. There was loud laughter and a lot of smiles, but everyone's smile had a veiled hysteria. One night while watching everyone carry on, for some reason, I thought about the parties that were thrown in Hitler's bunker during the last days of World War II. Unlike the Nazis, my family had not committed any war crimes or atrocities. But I imagined we were all engaged in the same odd social panic as the partygoers in the bunker: *This is totally insane, but we're fucked and we don't know what else to do.*

Tim would never know.

Tim would never know that more than five hundred people came to his wake—a wake that was a dreamlike version of my own death, where my entire life flashed before my eyes. For three straight hours, I shook hands with a line of people from every part of my thirty-eight-year story. There were co-workers and former co-workers, neighbors, relatives, high school teachers, and close friends from the past and the present. There were people I hadn't seen in thirty years and some I had seen thirty minutes before. Brown even came out of seclusion. Olivia smiled sadly and hugged me warmly. And I saw some of the toughest men I had ever known openly cry.

Tim would never know that news of his death went everywhere and sympathy came from even farther. Facebook was flooded with sympathies from California and New Jersey, and people attended the funeral from as far away as Florida and New York. Tim would never see how a small town kid who had never left home was loved by so many people all over the country. A truck driver Tim worked with stopped in front of me at the wake with tears in his eyes. He pointed to the never-ending line behind him and said, "If only he could have seen all this."

Tim would never know that several mothers had to explain to their young children why he was dead. He would never see the children cry, or see the look on their faces as they tried to understand. Tim would never know that some of his friends went to the cemetery and screamed at his grave.

Tim would never know how badly he devastated our mother—a woman who had already endured no small amount of tragedy in her own life. A woman who had already buried both her relatively young parents from cancer. A woman who had already had to bury each one of her three brothers—two from cancer and another from a fatal car crash. A woman who, as she once told me, had wanted nothing else in life except to be a mom.

I remembered our last Christmas together. That December, Tim and I were eating lunch one day in our mother's dining room while she was out running errands. "Yeah," he said, "I'm gonna get mom something nice this year. You know, for all the shit I put her through. I put in an order for a nice necklace."

I told him that was a good idea.

Danielle was right. I would never understand why he would hurt my mother so badly. Though he might have put her through hell, he never once expressed anything but love for her. I figured that maybe the reason he always crashed, burned, and fell to Earth was because he knew she would always be there to catch him.

As time went on, I wore myself out thinking about everything. Sleep eventually came back. And we all came back to our mother's house. For a while, it felt strange to sit on the back deck drinking beers while having to look out to the place where Tim had hung himself. But the tree was gone, and though it took some time, I finally saw our backyard as the same backyard it had always been. There had been more good days there than bad and, more comforting almost, more boring days than anything—lazy days when nothing happened and things were quiet. It was just our backyard and it was just starting to feel normal again.

We all returned to work. Tim may have been dead, but there were trucks to be driven and engines to be fixed. All of us used our anxious energy to do different things. Jon fixed the driveshaft in his pickup. Joe paved my mother's driveway. Mike literally built a stone wall.

I spent time walking, lifting weights, and sending thank-you e-mails. I drank beers with friends at either my house or theirs. For a while, I avoided the bars where Tim and I used to hang out. I didn't want to hear some drunk kid I didn't really know slobbering on about my brother. I had heard enough. At my house, sometimes we talked about Tim and sometimes we didn't. Eventually, I found myself repeating the same things over and over and it became obvious that I had exhausted my words and emotions. There were only so many consonants and vowels and only so many ways to express grief and anger. It became a classic case of nothing more to say.

The only thing I remained silent about was my guilt, but not the guilt of wondering whether I could have done more for Tim. The heart-to-heart I had had with him in my mother's living room eased that particular guilt. For my own sake, I was glad

I'd told Tim the right things to do that day. Because I shuddered to think what I might have felt if I hadn't.

Rather, the guilt I was feeling came with seeing that I was coping with things much faster and better than my brothers and my mother. About a week after Tim's funeral, I was driving with the windows down on a sunny afternoon and I found myself singing along to an old Aerosmith tune. I was singing and humming and tapping on the steering wheel with my thumbs when I abruptly stopped, suddenly realizing what I was doing, and suddenly racked with guilt that I was doing it. Tim had hung himself in my mother's backyard and was lying under six feet of earth and I was merrily singing along to "Same Old Song and Dance." For a moment, I completely hated myself. I hated myself in the same way I had hated myself just days after his death, when I was dusting my living room. I remembered it felt so strange to be doing such a mundane task after the whole world had come to an end.

But my coffee table needed to be dusted. That was the reality of it. When an Aerosmith song came on the radio, I sang along to it. Tim was dead, but I was alive. That was the reality of it all.

I felt completely isolated with my guilt. No one else could relate, so I sat alone with it. I wondered if people saw me as a selfish, uncaring asshole. If they did, I would have told them that I had unconsciously prepared myself for Tim's death. After years of watching him unravel, I eventually readied myself for the very real possibility that he was going to die. It had hardened my senses and softened the blow. Thinking Tim might die young wasn't an all-consuming thought, but enough of a thought that when his death finally came, I was ready. When Mike called me the night it happened and said, "I think Tim's dead," I could remember thinking, *This is it.*

One night, after our twentieth round of beers, Fraser looked at me and said, "Man, I've gotta tell ya, you're handling this really well."

I probably was, but there was no solace for the guilt I was feeling—no support group or self-help book to see me through it. I could have found a thousand articles about how to handle the anguish of a suicide, but could never have found a book titled *How to Cope When You're Coping Better.*

Except I wasn't coping entirely well. Tim would also never know about the migraine headaches I started suffering from after his death—an ailment that had never once in my life plagued me. Headaches were so foreign to me that the first day one of them settled into the left side of my skull, I couldn't make any sense of it. I didn't understand why I had a headache if I wasn't hungover. I considered every possible thing that it might be: food poisoning, caffeine, a tumor. It wasn't until my third migraine that I finally understood what was happening. And once I did, I sat alone in a quiet, dark room, visiting my old friend, the Anger Stage.

One day as I sat home with a headache, I went outside and opened my mailbox and found a package from Colin: It was a copy of Cicero's *Tusculanae Disputations*. Colin sent it to me because, besides being an electrician, he was also the world's foremost authority on Thomas Jefferson. Cicero wrote *Tusculanae Disputations* after the death of his daughter. Jefferson read it after the death of his father and the death of his wife. He noted in his diaries how much it helped him with his grief. I read some parts of it and embraced Cicero's stoicism. I read it along with my own copy of Marcus Aurelius's *Meditations*. I liked hearing people from thousands of years ago tell me that death, no matter how tragic, was part of life. I liked how calm they were about it. It was reassuring to know that the ancient Romans had their own translation for *shit happens*. Their words nestled softly into my gray matter, reaffirming what I already knew—that life was unbearable if you only expected its soft plateaus and its highest peaks, and never its lowest valleys.

The day I went to my bookshelf to get *Meditations*, *The Letters of Mark Twain* caught my eye, as if it was flickering like a lighthouse on the shore. I had some vague recollection of Twain writing something about the death of his younger brother Henry after Henry was killed in a riverboat accident. I took *The Letters of Mark Twain* off the shelf and flipped through the pages until I found the passage. I sat alone in my office and read the words through blurry, welled-up eyes: *But have mercy, mercy, mercy upon that unoffending boy. The horrors of three days have swept over me— they have blasted my youth and left me an old man before my time.*

And as I put the book down and wiped tears from my eyes I saw another way that Tim and I were different. *That unoffending boy.* In so many ways, he was. While Tim and I both found ourselves in trouble throughout our lives, there was something eternally benevolent about Tim. I couldn't always say the same for myself. I could be a dark and vicious thing, especially with my tongue. That wasn't Tim. He was gentle and selfless. I had always known in the deep interior of my heart that Timothy Gorman was a much kinder and generous man than I would ever be. Tim letting his girlfriend pummel him with her fists was beyond an allegory. He never hurt anyone but himself. He took all the shots. He took it all in.

That wasn't me. At some point—for better or worse—I withdrew and started firing the shots back. It had often done me no good. It had oftentimes turned me into a walled-off, hateful, wretch, but it had probably saved my life. I wished I could have told Tim that it wasn't his fault. I wished I could have helped him steer his anger. I wished I could have been a better brother.

I wished I could have been a better friend.

I also dove headlong into psychology books, which I hadn't done since college. I learned that 80 to 90 percent of people with depression are treated successfully. And the more I read about suicide, the more I could see that Tim fell right into all of its conventional trappings. He was a white male in his twenties. He had substance abuse problems and, most likely, an undiagnosed mental condition. He had unstable romantic relationships and had been in jail and was going back. He had chosen the second-most-popular form of suicide. The hard clinical facts were also strangely comforting.

Tim would never know that he was far from alone and could have been saved. Apart from all my armchair psychology, the DPW guy who stopped me on the street and told me about his coke habit had actually imparted a small amount of wisdom when he told me how your twenties can be a tough time. He was right. I thought about my own life—how some events in my twenties had seemed so catastrophic because I'd had no perspective. One of the sad clichés of growing older is realizing that life teaches you how to live it.

The more psychology I read, the more I could see how bottled up Tim really was. While his behavior clearly indicated a silent inferno in his mind, his words never did. His laughter was real, but it hid a wounded soul. He duped everyone. On the one hand, this showed how fucked up he really was, but on the other hand, it showed a tremendous amount of strength and compassion. Just as he had expressed that Christmas, he hated the idea of burdening anyone, especially my mother.

The last thing I read on suicide was about the mechanics of hanging. Just as I had felt the need to see the worst by wanting to see Tim's dead body, I felt the need to imagine the worst by learning how he died. The officer at the house had been right— Tim didn't die by strangulation; he died by cervical trauma. Apparently, this was called "drop hanging." I read some accounts of people who had attempted hanging themselves but survived. Many of them reported seeing flashing lights and hearing a ringing in their ears.

Reading the particulars of Tim's death didn't disturb me. Part of that may have been my prior reading by the Stoics, but part of it may have also been knowing that he hadn't suffered. And as mad at him as I was, reading about how he'd died put me even closer to some ultimate peace with my brother. I thought of Tim in his final seconds here. I thought of him being so trapped inside his own mind that he couldn't escape. Just like everyone, I wished I had been there to stop him. I wondered what might have happened if I had stopped by the house that day.

But I hadn't.

"He wasn't fucking around."

There was no point in circling hypotheticals. Tim was gone. We all wished he was still alive, but he wasn't. He wasn't coming back. Tim's high school picture had frozen him in time. He would never grow old. He left his young self to our history. The only thing we could do was move on into the history that followed. As angry as I was at him, I finally relented. I thought about his last moments here. And I hoped that when the ringing in his ears finally stopped—in that small moment between this life and the death boundary—that Tim found the silence his mind so desperately needed.

Fraser and I found ourselves in New Orleans that October. Autumn was a welcomed season back home—the turn from hot, humid sunshine to cool days and colorful leaves made Tim's suicide feel like it was further in the past than it actually was. Things were changing. Time was moving forward. And although the weather in New Orleans brought us back to summer again, literally being away from home made it feel that much further.

We had planned the trip months before Tim's death. After everything happened, there was never a thought in my mind that I wouldn't go, but the date came up on my calendar unexpectedly; I had forgotten about it entirely. Fraser and I usually traveled in the fall, and the only difference with this trip was that I helped plan nothing. Fraser, seeing that my time and mind were rightly occupied, had taken care of everything. On a Wednesday night, I just packed my things, and I got on a plane early the next morning. Unlike all my other trips, I had done no research on New Orleans. Beyond Bourbon Street and the bayou, I knew almost nothing about where we were headed.

But I fell in love with the city as soon as my feet hit the ground. People said "Mornin'" as we walked down the street. Homes had beautiful front porches and the French architecture reminded me of my time in Paris the year before. Dive bars were everywhere—places with cheap beer and kitsch behind the whiskey bottles—stuffed bobcats and *Star Wars* action figures. Jazz could really be heard just about everywhere.

We spent the first few days taking in everything we could: Cajun restaurants that the locals recommended, and an obligatory airboat ride through the bayou navigated by an old man named Captain Ernie, who knew more about swampland than I probably knew about anything. We spent a total of forty minutes on Bourbon Street. The only interesting thing there was a young homeless hipster with swollen eyes. He was holding a cardboard sign that read: "Punch Me in the Face. $20." I promptly took out my wallet, but then figured it might be more trouble than it was worth.

We moved on.

One night, the two of us went to the outskirts of the city to a joint called Bullet's. Fraser had heard that some relatively famous saxophonist was playing there. At first, we had no idea we were in the right place. There was no sign out front indicating it was a bar. The building just looked like the first floor of someone's house sitting on the corner in a residential neighborhood. We got out of the cab and stood there for a minute, wondering what to do. Finally an old black man with a thick Creole accent came out and saw our confusion. He shook our hands. "Go'n inside," he said with a laugh. "You at the right place."

We took seats at the bar and ordered the local beer. The bartender, a young black girl with a perpetual smile, called us "bay-bee" each time she spoke to us. Fraser and I were instantly smitten. We were the only white people in the place. No one paid us any mind until a wiry black man wearing a leather vest patched with the name of a motorcycle gang came up to me and said, "Where're you from, my man?"

"Massachusetts," I told him.

"Massachusetts? Do they even have black people in Massachusetts?"

"No," I said. "You're the first one I've ever met."

The man reeled back with laughter and held out his hand, which I took in mine and to my utter surprise, I successfully followed his intricate handshake.

"Right on," he said, before rejoining his fellow bikers.

The saxophonist never showed up. Instead, the owner called four local jazz musicians who walked in from the street one by one with their instruments in hand, ready to go. Even though the four guys had never played together before, by the end of the night they were in total sync, jamming and scatting and improvising. Musically, it was some of the realest shit I had ever heard or seen.

While the band played, we got drunk with the locals and ate fried catfish sandwiches. Two a.m. approached, which would have been last call back home. Fraser and I were exhausted, but

Bullet's showed no signs of letting up. We decided to call it a night, and when we told the bartender we had no idea where we were, she said, "Oh, let me call y'all a cab. You folks don't wanna be walkin' 'round here."

We stumbled outside, where the crowded sidewalk was just as lively as the bar. We said goodbye to everyone and plopped ourselves in the back of a yellow taxi, nothing but smiles and laughter.

Morning came hard. We woke up in a silent room with red-rimmed eyes, groaning and hungover. Fraser, lying in bed, switched on his iPad and started scrolling. For several minutes, the two of us lay in late morning silence. Looking at his iPad, Fraser finally said, "You know that place we were at last night?"

"Yeah," I said, staring at the ceiling.

"Apparently it's in the Seventh Ward, and the crime rate is about 80 percent higher than the national average. You have a one-in-eighteen chance of being a victim there."

I sat up, rubbed my eyes with the palms of my hands, and said, "Well, fuck it. We survived."

We had survived.

Because Medfield could have killed us.

It wasn't hyperbole.

I thought about this as I got out of bed, gathered my toiletries, and made my way to the shower. I recalled all the kids Fraser and I had known who had taken their own life. It seemed like a lot. Four names easily came to mind. One of them—a guy in our class named, Justin—hung himself in his parent's backyard the year after we graduated (a little girl walking down the street found him). I remembered him from my creative writing class, where he once confessed an odd fear that he was going to be kidnapped while he had a sinus infection and would die from suffocation if the kidnappers taped his mouth shut. When Justin finished speaking, I said, "I've totally had that same thought." He looked at me and said, "Really? I thought I was just crazy."

When I found out Justin had killed himself, I was surprised at first, but then not. Even though he was a laid-back guy who liked to get stoned and listen to the Grateful Dead, he was one of those people who just seemed to have an underlying sadness about them. Justin was quiet, but sometimes he was too quiet—the complete opposite of Tim.

A friend of mine from Medfield once asked me, point-blank, "Why do people keep dying here?" In one of the many e-mails I received after Tim's death, another one of my classmates wrote, *We have known far too many folks from Medfield who committed suicide.* I didn't know if he was entirely right—if it was a small town epidemic—or it just felt that way because Medfield was a small place where everyone knew each other.

The more common thing that killed off the kids in Medfield was drugs. My mother kept four yearbooks from the '70s on her bookshelf and the first page of nearly every one began with a dedication showing a black-and-white photograph of some smiling, fresh-faced teenager who had died from either a drug overdose or a drunk driving accident. Decades later, I found out from my brother Mike that heroin had made its way into the high school. A few kids from his class had either overdosed or died, always after graduation. It seemed like the kids in Medfield who died young could maintain right up until the point when they donned their cap and gown. After that, their worlds came undone.

Medfield was a uniquely un-unique place. It wasn't a town where you had to worry about being mugged or shot. You could leave your car unlocked at night, but if you grew up there, there was a chance you wouldn't make it out alive. Young death in Medfield never came at the hands of another. The conflict was internal and cerebral. Some kids just couldn't handle the pressure of the parents, or the sports, or the grades. Others just couldn't deal with the money or the lack thereof—the insular class struggle between the haves and the have-it-alls. Fraser and I had seen our fair share of adolescent collapse, yet somehow we had always known that the only way out was through. We had survived as teenagers by always seeing Medfield as a bit of a joke—making fun of everyone and thinking everything was funny. In some ways, we had survived our hometown by being its court jesters. And we had also ventured out of Medfield enough through the years to put the place in its proper context. The two of us never felt trapped inside it, as so many others clearly did. I sometimes wondered what might have become of me if I didn't have Fraser and Brown standing beside me as we grew up in Medfield. Thinking about not having them brought me down a dark corridor in my mind. When I thought about having to navigate my adolescence alone, it was hard to not see myself in jail, or likely even worse.

It wasn't hyperbole.

For the most part, Medfield was a good town with good people, and I wouldn't have traded my childhood there for anything. But I knew that behind the symmetrical McMansions, the tail-wagging golden retrievers, and the chemically green lawns, there were children inside their bedrooms who were quietly suffering—children whose cries went unseen and whose screams went unheard. I had known them my whole life. I knew for certain they were there. And in that way, there was a price to be paid for small-town perfection.

For the rest of our trip, I thought about Tim, but not overwhelmingly. I was away from home, in an unfamiliar place, and very much in the present tense. I was having fun, which I no longer felt guilty about. The only time I ever spoke about Tim was one night in front of the hostel we were staying at. The sun was setting behind the Victorian homes across the street. Fraser and I were sitting on the front steps, him smoking a cigarette, me watching the traffic. It was a familiar pose for us—a pose we had first struck more than twenty years earlier, back home at Baker's Pond.

I had always sought Fraser's counsel, and I needed it now more than ever. I had never known anyone in my life who never put any thought or effort into simply being *them*. There was no one more straight, honest, and authentic. Next to Fraser, I had always felt humanly inadequate. Though I tried to be just as straight, honest, and authentic, I could sometimes be a total imposter, depending on where we were or who was around—a *poseur du jour*. I had to act cool. Fraser just was. I could be an asshole of the grandest kind and Fraser was anything but. We had met when we were four and now we were both pushing forty. Discussions about heavy metal were now interwoven with discussions about vasectomies. We now had more yesterdays than tomorrows. And after so many years, Fraser's positive influence had settled firmly in my being. Anytime I did something kind and generous, it was Fraser. Anytime I did something selfish and stupid, it was me. After so many ages of friendship, we were two variations of the same one. Wherever I ended, Fraser began.

"I don't know," I finally said on the steps, interrupting what was—and maybe should have been—a peaceful silence. "Some people have nothing, you know? They're homeless. They have no friends, no family, no money. They live in a ghetto, or some fucked up place like we were last night. Tim had everything— a lot more than most. I mean, he had so many people looking out for him and telling him the right things to do, but he just wouldn't listen. I feel bad, but I'm sort of done with it. It's not like I'm going around saying, 'I could have done more.' Christ, the whole town was looking out for him."

"Yeah, I hear ya," Fraser said. "And, you know, I remember he came into the liquor store one night I was working. He had just gotten out of jail, or rehab, or whatever. I know he had quit drinking and he brought up a couple of Red Bulls and vodka and I said, 'Are you sure you wanna do this?' And I remember he thought about it for a second and finally said, 'Yeah...Yeah. I'm all set.' I mean, I work at a packie. I sell booze. What am I going to do? I said my piece to him."

"We all did."

"It sucks, but what can you do?"

"Nothing," I said. "There was no stopping that kid. There just wasn't. Honestly, I think I just sort of mentally prepared myself for the fact that he was going to die young. Like, when I was up there giving that eulogy, I had actually imagined that scene in my head before he died."

"Really?"

"Yeah. I mean, how many cars did he crash drunk driving? Three? When he finally wiped out on his motorcycle in front of my mother's house this summer, I think I finally said, 'This kid is going to kill himself.' I just didn't know he was going to literally do it from a tree in the backyard...Well, you know what I mean."

Fraser took a drag from his cigarette and said, "Yeah, I know what you mean. He was out of control, but like, not in a good way."

"So, yeah, I guess I've had an easier time dealing with it than my brothers and, obviously, my mother."

"Right."

"Actually," I said, "you wanna know the truth? I've actually had an easier time dealing with this than I've had dealing with some breakups with girlfriends."

"I can see that."

"I mean, death is death. There's literally nothing you can do about it. Breakups fucking suck, though. Like, you know the person is still out there in the world and moving on with their life. Grieving over the loss of someone who is still alive can be worse. And you think you can fix it, so it becomes this long, miserable, drawn-out thing. I don't know. I feel bad about it, but even though this was like a nuclear fucking blast, once it was over, it was over. There was no fixing it. Breakups can be prolonged torture."

"Yeah, no, that makes sense."

"I don't know," I finally said. "Maybe I'm just a narcissistic asshole."

"Oh," Fraser said, "you're definitely a narcissistic asshole. I mean, that's never been in dispute."

We laughed. Fraser checked the time on his phone, inhaled his cigarette, and put his phone back into his pocket. I looked across the street and watched people getting on and off the trolley car. The woman in the driver's seat greeted everyone, whether a tourist or a local, like she had known them for years. It was so different than Boston. I didn't want to dwell on Tim much longer, mostly because I felt like I was just repeating things I had already said. And although I knew Fraser would listen no matter what, I didn't want to burden him with morbid bullshit, especially since we seemed so far away from it. I knew there would be other times to talk about Tim. And I knew that I would think about my brother every day for the rest of my life. Not wanting to talk about him all the time didn't diminish the fact that I would always love him, and miss him, and wish he was still with us. But before Fraser and I made our plans for the evening, I couldn't help but say one last thing.

"I don't know. I also feel guilty because whatever he had, I just don't have it. Depression, I guess. Like, we're sitting here in New Orleans. We're driving up to Memphis in a few days. We're having a great fucking time. I mean, Tim's never gonna do shit like this, you know? Why would you end it?"

Fraser crushed out his cigarette on the concrete steps. "It's nothing to feel guilty about. The kid had problems. There's just nothing you can do about it."

I gazed up at the Spanish moss growing downward from the live oaks that lined Canal Street. I liked the way it looked and wished it could grow on the trees back home. The sun had finally set behind the Victorian homes on the other side of the road, which turned the southern sky into an orange swirl of steamy, golden clouds. An old black man in a white T-shirt walked past us. He had a bag of something slung over his shoulder. It looked like laundry. He smiled and nodded and Fraser and I did the same.

"Yeah," Fraser said as he stood up from the stoop. "When you're dead, you're fucked. And you don't get to do cool shit anymore."

I nodded and stood up. I was hungry and looking forward to the Cajun place the cute girl sitting at the front desk had recommended so highly.

"So we're going to that place tonight?" I said.

"Yeah," Fraser said. "Is that cool? Everyone has been raving about it."

I took one last look at the early evening sky.

"It should be good."

88358051R00211

Made in the USA
Lexington, KY
10 May 2018